Otherland

MARIA TUMARKIN

Otherland

A journey with
my daughter

VINTAGE BOOKS
Australia

A Vintage book
Published by Random House Australia Pty Ltd
Level 3, 100 Pacific Highway, North Sydney NSW 2060
www.randomhouse.com.au

First published by Vintage in 2010

Addresses for companies within the Random House Group can be found at
www.randomhouse.com.au/offices

National Library of Australia
Cataloguing-in-Publication Entry

Tumarkin, Maria.
Otherland / Maria Tumarkin.

ISBN: 978 1 74166 679 3 (pbk.)

Tumarkin, Maria.
Tumarkin, Svetlana.
Tumarkin, Billie.
Russians – Australia – Biography.
Russian Australians – Biography.
Immigrants – Australia –Biography.
Mothers and daughters – Australia – Biography.
Vacations – Russia – Biography.

Cover design by Christabella Designs
Internal design and typesetting by Post Pre-press Group
Printed and bound in Australia by Griffin Press, South Australia,
an accredited ISO AS/NZS 14001:2004 Environmental Management System printer

10 9 8 7 6 5 4 3 2 1

This project has been assisted by the Australian Government through the Australia Council, its arts funding and advisory board.

The paper this book is printed on is certified by the © 1996 Forest Stewardship Council A.C. (FSC). Griffin Press holds FSC chain of custody SGS-COC-005088. FSC promotes environmentally responsible, socially beneficial and economically viable management of the world's forests.

Mixed Sources
Product group from well-managed forests and other controlled sources
Cert no. SGS-COC-005088
www.fsc.org
© 1996 Forest Stewardship Council

CONTENTS

PROLOGUE

IT IS ON THE train from Russia to Ukraine that the moment I have been waiting for finally comes, and Billie refuses to use the toilet, point-blank. She will hold on, she says: she was not born a woman for nothing. The problem, I discover, is not the soggy brown rug thrown over a hole in the toilet's floor, but something that inhabits a hole in the toilet's wall – something my daughter, with the full force of her adolescent pessimism, has immediately classified as a used sanitary pad. And so she goes on strike, inconsolable in her revulsion.

'You have not travelled,' I tell Billie, 'unless you have seriously considered just how far you are prepared to go to keep your bladder from bursting. This is the real journey every semi-decent traveller must take.' We are going from my favourite city in the world, St Petersburg, the 'Venice of the North', to my mother's hometown, Kiev, or the 'Jewel of the East', as those shameless, pimping guidebooks would tell you.

And the toilets are a trade-off for the way simple black tea tastes on the overnight trains, for the stories that fall out of people at this meeting place of intimacy and total anonymity; and for the special kind of sleep, not found anywhere else, when your body is floating, weightless, in the thick of the train's forward movement. As one habituated insomniac to another, I show Billie that special flavour of train sleep as if it were one of the Seven Wonders of the World.

I would gladly claim as my own country the weary trees, the tightly stretched sky, the numbered light poles outside our window, except that in my years of absence this place has undergone an extreme make-over. It has divided like some monstrous parent cell into a myriad daughter cells, each with its own currency, its own petty tsar swaying an iron fist, its own intractable visa entry requirements. 'This is where your family comes from,' I tell Billie, swallowing countless disclaimers and footnotes. I make it sound plain as plain, desperate not to overdo it, to keep the theatre out of the moment. 'This is it, Billie, the Point A, the mother of all destinations.'

I try to imagine what she sees and whether her eyes get fogged up by all the slimy grey colours, the piles of rubbish, the ribs sticking out from the surprisingly sprightly cows and horses we pass by – that first all-deceiving layer that in any unkempt place makes you feel like you know exactly where you are yet tells you absolutely nothing. 'So you are going to write about how everything is dirty and falling apart,' my second cousin in Dnepropetrovsk says a few weeks later. There is sadness in her eyes, not contempt. 'Look at our roads,' she says, 'our public transport, our buildings, our women in their war paint and impossible heels. God, I can only imagine what you must be thinking.' But I am not thinking what you think I am thinking, my dear cousin. I am not here to write a coy, sympathetic account of the freak show that was once my home. Frankly, I don't think the world needs another book about how everything is *dirty and falling apart* somewhere else; or even another book about the sort of somewhere else where everything is idyllic.

Dubravka Ugrešić, a Croatian-born writer I admire greatly for the way she can unpick the stupidity and spin of hyper-nationalism, says that after the Berlin Wall came down the Western literary market was flooded with all kinds of books in which the writers regaled readers with clichéd images of post-Communist Eastern Europe: pre-Industrial-era public toilets; waiters dripping with contempt for their customers; crumbling exteriors and inebriated masses; the triumph of jingoism; oh, and not forgetting, locals 'who ate dog food instead of steak'. 'The authors of these works managed to find the pressure points in the imagination of the Western reader,' Ugrešić says.

So, no, although this book begins in a rather disgraceful Russian toilet it is, I sincerely hope, not one of *those* books. It is certainly not an exercise in revealing and revelling in the former Empire's underbelly – I am no expat on a mission. My motives are altogether different if not entirely clear, even to myself. There is, first and foremost, the urge Billie and I share to connect her viscerally to her family's history, to set that history going again – to get its blood pumping and its joints moving, make its connective tissues elastic but firm. There is also my own self-serving desire to come back to people and

3

places still powerfully alive that speak to me daily despite (or perhaps because of) the years and kilometres separating us.

Last but not least, if I call myself a writer, then this book seems to me a literary bridge that I must inevitably cross. The journey home is, of course, an archetypal narrative, and I am sure you know that it has been done to death. Me too: I spent months being scared of making this trip and, at the end of it, having nothing of any value or originality to say. But one thing you learn from travelling is that it is far scarier to think about than to do. In the end, it can only make sense if you give up the worry and throw yourself in at the deep end, not necessarily with gay abandon, but with something perhaps more akin to fatalistic wonderment – how else do you get anywhere, really?

On this train taking us from Russia to Ukraine across a border that did not exist when my parents and I still lived here, and that feels, perhaps ominously, like a plaything to me, like one of those little bridges that go over the railway tracks in a model train set, we throw ourselves into our diaries. Billie's diary is a hard, green notebook with a floating love heart and a few leaves stuck midair on its cover. Mine is a soft, yellow Spirax with four note pockets and no visible adornments. Billie starts her every entry with the conventional 'Dear Diary'. I only note a day and a place, addressing no one. My sentences are incomplete, cryptic and dry. Hers are winding, lyrical, thickly coated in drama and sarcasm:

Dear Diary,
In Pavlovsk outside of St Petersburg we attempted to feed the squirrels but no squirrels came to us and I was so disappointed but I guess the five American tour buses had already been there.

In some ways, I am probably the person least qualified to speak about Billie. For years I had not even noticed she had a lisp until an incredulous orthodontist picked it up at a pre-braces appointment a few months before our trip. Of course, he said, you had known about the lisp for some time. Far from it, did not have a clue. Who knows what other attributes and mild impairments, staring straight at me, I have managed to over-look. Certain things are, of course, impossible to miss. When Billie walks, her every step is drilled into the floor (I call them 'elephant steps'); much of her movement is accompanied by the sounds of doors slamming, kitchen utensils ringing and objects vibrating off shelves. The elephant in the room, the bull in the china shop, the three-year-old at a chamber music recital – with Billie I repeat 'Shhhh' as an incantation, more often than any other sound I make. Yet my daughter is by no means an elephant. She was born already feminine, a perfectly defined little girl. Before my first gender-appropriate haircut at the age of twelve, I was often mistaken for a boy. No one would ever make such an error with Billie. *Oh those eyes*, people say, *so blue, so big, so penetrating. Oh that hair, so long, so thick, so curly.* So it is not so much my daughter's difficulty in inhabiting her own body, but her need to impose herself on her environment – to hold fort, so to speak – that makes our house shake.

I must add that this wall of sound that surrounds my twelve-year-old (unless she is exhausted and, thus, uncharacteristically quiet) is made up not simply of random clatter and commotion. A lot of it is the joyful, self-aware deployment of language. Billie, I have come to realise in the last few years, is defined by her relationship with language, even more so than by her temperament, her paper-thin skin or the fact of being raised without a father. She may not be able to control the emotions constantly accelerating within her, but she sure can channel them into words. The English language is Billie's true home. She floats in it as in a warm bath of sea salts, resting, ridding herself of aches and pains, almost visibly regrouping.

Billie loves adverbs more than adjectives, because they marry action with emotional intensity. She has her favourites too – *enthusiastically*, *dramatically*, *overwhelmingly* and *massively*. She stuffs even the most mundane, fleeting conversations with metaphors – pure, mixed, triple-deckers. She loves words that hit you over the head – *misery* and *despair* have been her staples ever since she was eight. In no small measure because Billie views language as the natural domain of meritocracy, rather than of an autocratic pecking order, she is often a nuisance at school. She speaks to 'authority' figures in her abundant, uncensored and overflowing English. She talks back and she talks forward, and only rarely does she show any evidence of self-restraint or pragmatic compliance. A primary school teacher with whom Billie developed a fully reciprocated animosity said to me more than once that his class functioned much better on those days when my daughter was away. Make of that what you will.

Billie's relationship with words is emblematic of her relationship with the world. There is nothing half-hearted about her. To my absolute delight, she cries a lot over books and movies. Neither overly rational nor stingy with her emotions, she refuses to draw a sharp distinction between the real and the imaginary. Instead of saying, 'This is not real, so why should I bother?' Billie says, 'How come this feels so real? How come this hurts so much?' 'These damn writers,' she mutters, weeping over the last chapter of yet another book, 'they just get to you. Why do they torture us, Mum?' But it is singing, not reading, that, for years, has been Billie's consuming passion. And she is so good that of late I have started claiming retrospectively some uncanny powers of foresight. Calling my daughter Billie after Billie Holiday, I insist, has been a self-fulfilling prophecy. I knew, I say, I always knew that my little daughter would sing one day. (You understand, of course, that just as with the lisp, I never actually had a clue.) When Billie sings, she closes her eyes, shutting off any possible distractions. Her way of devoting herself fully to the song is what people in 'the industry' call a 'committed performance'. I would call it a form of profound humility, an act of conscious surrender to the largeness of music.

When I was a teenager, a well-meaning friend of my parents described me as a natural calamity. It must run in the family. In both my case and Billie's, we did not gradually and gently shed our prepubescent skins still retaining some of that baby softness; we ripped them off ourselves. Or maybe they were ripped off us – by emigration in my case (I was fifteen when my family left the former Soviet Union); in Billie's by her mother's failed attempts to make a nuclear family. Because she has never met her biological father, she has already learned the rudiments of emotional self-defence – bravado, deflection, improvisation, acute storytelling. I have heard her matter-of-factly describe the father of her little brother, Miguel, as *my second ex-stepfather*, a title which sums up both the rather high turnover of male figures in her life and Billie's refusal to keep quiet and ashamed about her family's unorthodox ways. Sometimes I think Billie has been an adolescent all her childhood days. Because of her instinctive early recognition of the power of language, her innate stubbornness and her preoccupation with justice as she sees it, she knew and practised defiance well before her peer group was scheduled to encounter it on the 'rocky road to adulthood'.

We write, chewing on boiled eggs and biscuits, until the train attendant comes to check our papers. We are the holders of Australian passports; in the leaking, smelly, creaking carriage she presides over, as exotic as they come. Our attendant does not have a throng of golden teeth like the woman who checked our tickets and documents on the last train we took, and whose accidental smile made Billie jump with amazement. This one wears no jewellery, outside or inside her mouth. She is what they call unassuming – a middle-aged Ukrainian woman from a small town, who knocks on doors softly, speaks to passengers quietly and, all in all, runs her section of the train as a provincial bed and breakfast, not a battle-ready nuclear submarine.

The attendant keeps looking through our passports, searching for something. At first I imagine that she is simply lost in the unfamiliar travel documents, distracted by the frivolous kangaroo on the cover.

'Can't find your Belarusian visas,' she finally says.

'But we are not going to Belarus, God forbid. This train is going to Ukraine,' I say, by now completely confused.

'No, girls, on the way to Ukraine this train is passing through Belarusian territory, and all foreign citizens need to have Belarusian transit visas. I can go and ask my boss but chances are you will be taken off the train. Those Belarusian border-control guys are notorious and you cannot argue with them and you cannot even try to give them money or things. Maybe you should try to get off while we are still in Russia.'

She leaves to speak with her boss. 'It should be OK,' I say to Billie, who is struggling to hold back her tears. 'We had no idea,' I add emphatically. 'There is no information about this train going through Belarus anywhere, how were we supposed to know? No one told us when we bought the tickets. There is nothing on the web. Nothing on the ticket. Our St Petersburg friends did not have a clue. We will be fine. There was no way we could have known. We are not breaking any law.' For a brief moment Billie looks relieved. 'Exactly,' she proclaims, 'it is not our fault. No one has told us anything. How were we supposed to know?' Then the train attendant comes back.

'The boss said that it is not looking good. They will ask for visas. These guys are like the Fascists.' The weight of our train attendant's concern pushes her down onto Billie's already made-up bed. She knows that she should not be sitting around talking. She has teas to make for the quiet ones like us getting ready to be rocked to sleep and for the unruly ones who will use glasses of tea to pace their vodka shots. But she is visibly worried. 'There was an eighty-six-year-old man on this train not so long ago and they showed him no mercy.'

She comes in the middle of the night to give us one more chance to get off the train before we enter Belarus and seal our fate. We politely refuse. I have injured my back a week or so before, and I find distinctly unappealing the prospect of being stranded in some godforsaken Russian town in the middle of the night with our suitcase, sitting at some freezing railway station for hours and then having to zigzag across the country, to say nothing of spending whatever little money we have left on brand-new train tickets – all of this only to avoid going through Belarus. Why the hell should we? We are not guilty of anything. We are not scared. 'We'll take our chances,' I tell our attendant. 'We'll stay on the train.' All I want is to go back to sleep and not to have to think about visas and what the big, bad Belarusian border-control guys may or may not do to us tomorrow. All I want is just some more of my train-sleep brew.

Dear Diary,

When the caring and kind train attendant warned us about the Belarusian Border Control, she said, 'They were like the Nazis.' Fascists, she called them. Well, can I add a few words to that analogy – words like heartless and inhumane. The guy, Ivan Petrovich Sidorov, who kicked us off the train had an immense case of Inhumanity.

Billie is big on allusions to Fascists, especially after the *Secret Life of Adolf Hitler* documentary, which I let her watch in its entirety except for the bit about Hitler's predilection for S&M, although I cannot quite tell you why being peed on by one's niece is somehow more worthy of an MA rating than masterminding our people's genocide.

Ivan Petrovich Sidorov (not his real name), precisely the type of dedicated border-control professional our train attendant warned us about, is a study in breviloquence. 'It looks like we are going nowhere,' he says after a brief skim of our passports. The use of 'we' instead of 'you' is a calculated insult. Ivan Petrovich is not going anywhere because he works here, at

Teryuha railway border crossing. We are not going anywhere because he is about to throw us off the train.

I have to talk really fast now. I have the smallest window of opportunity imaginable to convince this guy that we are not some malicious transit-visa cheats but good girls from the far-away land of Australia (yes, it does exist), who simply were not informed by the relevant authorities and are, therefore, plainly not guilty as charged. I try to sound both confident and unambiguously respectful, but no matter. With this guy we do not stand a chance. 'And yet,' he replies mockingly to my tirade about how mere mortals like ourselves (mere *foreign* mortals, to boot) could not have possibly known. Sidorov quickly tires of my attempts to reason. 'Your luggage to the door,' he pronounces in a voice that says the conversation is closed. From now on we are in a no-man's-land of monologues and unilateral actions. 'Young man,' I shout, 'Comrade, Mister Mayor.' 'And nonetheless,' Sidorov barks back, walking away with our dark-blue passports in his hand.

We will meet Sidorov again, of course: after all, he has marched away with our lives in his hands. But first, dear discombobulated reader, I should probably take you back to the beginning, which is to say, Ukraine circa 1989.

I

1989

In our day Europeans have been hurled out of their biographies, like balls from the pockets of billiard tables.

Osip Mandelstam, writing in the 1920s

How DO YOU LEAVE if you are too grown-up to be cargo but not grown-up enough to cast a real vote? I am fifteen and have never once been out of the Soviet Union; now, together with my parents and my older sister, I am preparing to leave for good. So I sit like Alice in a pool of tears trying not to drown and muttering to myself, 'I never was so small as this before, never!' I sit and force myself to think packing thoughts, all of which boil down to one simple question: which bits of my life will make the cut? Books, letters, clothing, linen — every gram matters. It is like Olympic swimming, where male competitors shave off their body hair to make themselves a tenth of a second more aerodynamic. Migration, I have learned, has its own economies of scale. You are forced to think very big (America?

Australia? Israel?) and, simultaneously, very small (towels or another blanket? A sandwich-sized volume of Akhmatova or Borges?). The very big is, of course, something even my parents lack the processing apparatus for, because nothing they have ever known has been this final or mind-numbingly irreversible. We are burning our bridges and then smearing ourselves in the ash.

It is 1989, and I am about to embark on a journey that feels like part wild adventure and part deportation, and so I leave in a daze, one foot kicking and the other hurrying to the door. I leave thinking that it cannot be true. Are you telling me I might never see my best friend again, the one who feels closer than skin? Bullshit. Does it really mean that I will close my eyes and when I open them, everything will be gone – this light-blue balcony; this fold-out couch in the lounge room, on which I sleep with my back turned to the room when films not for my eyes are shown on the television; and this five-storey Stalin-era building in which we live? (Stalin-era, please note, here refers to the coveted architecture of high ceilings, as opposed to the measly proportions of Khrushchev's infamous 'shoeboxes'.) And gone too this corner near my home in Kharkov where two streets named after nineteenth-century authors with diametrically opposed fates run into each other – one honouring the proto-revolutionary Nikolay Chernyshevsky, whom Lenin counted among his defining influences, and the other, much shorter street, named for Vsevolod Garshin, a writer more famous for following in his father's suicidal footsteps than for the short stories he produced. How such a street name survived in a country where suicide was as entirely non-existent as homosexuality in Iran is a mystery; but there it is, about to stop being our address, about to become the hollowest of holograms.

My sister, Inna, eight years my senior, seems to be coping much better than I – than all of us, in fact. She is decisive and determined and insists on being practical: we need money; we need things to wear (we are not going to the West in these clothes); we need to get seriously and quickly organised (no second chances for us).

Inna does not let herself waver, at least I cannot see in her any traces of doubt or fear. I am too self-absorbed, and perhaps too young as well, to recognise the value of her fearlessness and composure. My sister does not lose her nerve in the face of what our family is about to plunge into. If anything, she seems fully mobilised, taut as a bowstring.

It is 1989, the year countless journalists and historians will dub the most momentous since World War II. My family is leaving a month after the Berlin Wall comes down, right at the beginning of the end of the Cold War. We are leaving soon after a national security briefing from the US State Department has spoken of America moving 'beyond containment' in its dealings with the Soviet Union, anticipating the end of the bipolar world and the ascent of the United States as the last superpower.

In the wake of the Soviet invasion of Afghanistan in 1979, and the international opprobrium that followed, the Soviet government had effectively banned emigration. Under Mikhail Gorbachev's presidency, the ban was lifted, but this does not make leaving feel easier, feel any less like passing through the eye of a needle; perhaps the opposite. In the final months of 1989, we find ourselves in a permanent state of preternatural suspense and suspension: Will we be granted visas? Will we be able to buy tickets? (In June 1989 only tickets for travel in the following year could be purchased.) Will we be able to surrender our apartment to the State? (If not, we are not free to leave.) And, if we finally make it to the airport, will the customs control there 'liberate' us from most of the things we care about? Most crucially, my mum's security clearance, through her job as an electrical engineer for a company with close ties to the country's defence industry, means that she has access to classified information and is therefore not allowed any contact with foreigners. Citizens in her position are often banned from leaving the country, so will they stop us from going? We hold our collective breath waiting for some terrible last-minute hitch, but borders are already blowing in the wind and Gorbachev is talking about nations' rights to self-determination. His words make millions across the Eastern bloc pinch themselves in disbelief.

Under Gorbachev, the Soviet Union effectively takes a step back and lets the whole Eastern bloc go. And, boy, does it go with a bang, most of its Communist governments ousted swiftly – first in Poland, then in Hungary, Eastern Germany, Czechoslovakia, Bulgaria and, finally, Romania, the only country where the 1989 revolution turns violent. There, in the last days of that year, President Nicolae Ceauşescu and his wife, Elena, are summarily executed after a two-hour hearing of an Extraordinary Military Tribunal eerily reminiscent of Stalin's show trials. Eastern Europe is freeing itself and there are no Soviet tanks rolling through the streets of Warsaw, Prague or Budapest: how is this possible? Surely, just as in 1956 and 1968, all of these uprisings are about to be quashed. But nothing happens, and in a blink of an eye most of the former Iron Curtain countries find themselves entering the pearly gates of post-Communism.

The Soviet Union itself is the last domino to fall. Our 'unbreakable union of free republics' still has a year and a half of violent and torturous breaking up ahead of it when my family departs. Don't believe anyone who tells you today that they knew then that the final curtain was about to come down on the Soviet chapter. No one could have predicted the speed of the unravelling, the acceleration, the whole spectacle of entropy. *Glasnost, perestroika* (there was a time, I must remind myself, when these words were not limp historical apparitions but bursts of energy and meaning), unprecedented media and electoral freedoms, the publication of banned literature, the opening up of secret archives, the last Soviet troops withdrawn from Afghanistan – all of these in a handful of years, with 1989 as the crescendo.

The irresistible idea that Communism's self-destruction was a massive jolt produced by a system correcting itself led a host of historians and commentators in the West (not all of them card-carrying anti-Communists, either) to declare 1989 the year that ended the twentieth century and even history itself. They got one thing right: 1989 was completely off the scale. *Ogonyok*, an independent Soviet journal, declared that even four years earlier the possibility of a UFO landing in the middle of Moscow would have seemed far more realistic than the thought that Pink Floyd, the British music group banned for decades by the Soviet leadership, would ever play the Soviet capital. But in 1989 Pink Floyd did just that. And the whole year was like that: one UFO landing after another.

Václav Havel once described people living under the Communist system as 'agents of its automatism, as petty instruments of the social auto-totality'. Now, miraculously, that *auto-totality* was gone. My generation was coming of age just as the world of fanatical rigidity and predictability was suddenly exhibiting unmistakable signs of uncertainty and fluidity. We could inhale deeply the feverishness all around us, recharge off all the adrenaline in the air and know beyond any reasonable doubt that we were going to live in a world vastly different from that of our parents. We had rock music emerging from the deep underground and bringing with it not some disposable, cloned anthems of protest and procreation, but songs of startling originality, fearlessness and lyricism. And we could read all kinds of writers, including, for instance, James Joyce; Joyce who, just a few years before, was the gadfly of Western modernism, a man whose books we would burn if we were not so busy keeping the dream of socialism alive.

In those days, not infrequently, my generation could catch the look of complete astonishment on our parents' faces – a look caused, more often than not, by what they saw on the television screen. Never before had this screen given our parents the slightest surprise. And now it was showing a Lithuanian walkout from the first-ever Congress of People's Deputies, outbreaks of ethnic violence in Armenia and Azerbaijan, Soviet troops clashing with pro-independence protesters in the Georgian capital, and people (mainly, it must be acknowledged, balding men but also, increasingly, some women politicians and intellectuals) talking incessantly about reforms and democratic institutions. Censorship did not suddenly disappear, but our country stopped functioning as some kind of Masonic Temple. You couldn't not see what was going on.

It is with awe and tenderness that I recall the late-night conversations my parents had with their friends in our kitchen. I was not eavesdropping; the door was not properly shut. Besides, they talked loudly, and I suspect they half-wanted me to hear: about Lenin and his top-secret syphilis; about Chernobyl; about the Molotov–Ribbentrop Pact (and what a farce it had been, all those lives it hadn't saved in World War II); about what was happening now in Georgia, Azerbaijan and, of course, Afghanistan; about privatisation and the 'real' motives of Gorbachev. Such conversations were apparently going on all over the country; it was like the lid on a boiling pan had been lifted. And, of course, if the kitchens belonged to Jewish or mixed households then one topic towered over all the others – what do we do now? To leave or not to leave. How many Soviet Jewish families managed to avoid asking themselves just that? Even when they were resolutely on the side of staying, as my parents most definitely were in the beginning, convinced that this was their country and they had no business in the so-called 'Free World', glorious though it was, their certainty was undermined as more and more of their friends, relatives and colleagues departed. The slamming of doors started timidly, and within a year or so gradually turned into a cacophony. You woke to it and went to bed with it, knowing that this was a mass exodus the likes of which you had never seen in your life.

Some were going because they believed in their heart of hearts that this country was a concentration camp and no price was too high to escape it. Some wanted to find out what it was like to be a Jew – not an undercover, assimilated, de-clawed

Jew of the Soviet make, but a fully-fledged, unashamed and unapologetic Jew of the Western world. Others, like my parents, initially hopeful and emboldened by the reforms, grew increasingly disappointed, eventually pulling the plug, convinced almost against their will that this country could not help but devour all its good sons and daughters. Nothing good was going to happen here, not now and not for a long time to come. My generation, or rather its Jewish component, was growing up with these conversations in our ears, with our parents debating their futures, our futures, behind half-ajar kitchen doors.

I say *my generation* and then I stop myself. I say *my generation*, but we are as splintered and scattered as it is possible for a group of people to be. This generation ended up inhabiting such vastly different realities that most of my friends would probably think my bohemian rhapsody to 1989 an expression of idiotic naïveté at best. Those who stayed and lived through the catastrophic early 1990s had to count the cost every day of the collapse of the Soviet Union – unpaid wages, poverty, lost jobs, lawlessness and fear: who among them would be able to hold back their cynicism in revisiting the optimism and the promise of the late 1980s? And those who left and watched from afar the Soviet Union go through all kinds of socio-political convulsions only to turn into Putin's Russia – a smaller version of the same autocratic, totalitarian, macho, insular State but with open borders and consumer goods on tap for those who can afford them: who among them would be able to see the late 1980s as a moment of unsurpassed historical transformation? So, you can understand that I am going back to the scene of 1989 with some trepidation.

★

'All is clear by now. By the time there is a government that can satisfy us, we will be well and truly gone. By the time laws are written to allow, not to prohibit, we will be well and truly gone. By the time these laws are passed, our children too will be well and truly gone.'

This is from Mikhail Jvanetsky, beloved of both my parents' generation and my own, a writer and performer of monologues that combine satire and lyricism in a way that no one else has done, not in the Russian language anyway. He wrote these lines in response to the unravelling of our Soviet world. So what to do then? 'We must hold freedom with our teeth. We must squash the great leaders, who inhabit a parallel reality and who have destroyed our youth. And, above all, we must fear nothing.'

Jvanetsky was telling us to *hold freedom with our teeth*, but the Tumarkins were leaving. We had fifteen numbered black suitcases and our visas. My parents quit work. My mother went first, leaving her engineering job of twenty years for a firm known, along with countless others, simply as a postbox – a closed organisation that did not have a listed address. For us to get an exit visa, she had to have some innocuous last place of employment with no security clearance and no access to any-thing remotely resembling classified materials. So she took a job with a newly formed co-operative, colouring prints of Lenin. My father left his academic position at the Ukrainian Institute of Technology, where he taught evening classes and worked on scientific research in hydraulics for the aviation industry. Now both of them were not only unemployed but unemployable, at least in their professional capacities. Emigration was permitted, and hundreds of thousands were leaving, but there was a price to pay. Once you made the decision and put your documents in, there was pretty much no way back. My sister, who was the first to decide that she was emigrating no matter what, and whose resolute stance on the matter was a catalyst for my parents, graduated from her arts academy and was all ready to go. I left my high school, the first of my class to walk out the door for good.

Jvanetsky was telling us to *fear nothing*, yet we were going. We feared a lot, of course, and that is why, to some extent at least, we were packing. We feared that in our neck of the woods, any outbreak of nationalist sentiment, any movement for ethnic self-determination and independence, would invariably result in Jews being seen as the root of, if not all then most, evil. Anti-Semitism officially condemned by the government, but practised by it clandestinely and viciously, seemed likely to become the opium of the embittered masses, and we did not want to stick around for that. We feared a military coup and the rapid curbing of freedoms. The Soviet Union, after all, was never the country of velvet revolutions. We feared the bitterness, cynicism and despair of people who, having experienced some fresh air in their lungs, would in all probability be sent back into the catacombs. We feared that, no matter what official decisions were made, what official direction taken, entire generations needed to die out before this seventy-year experiment would truly be over.

It was in 1989 that the worst train disaster in Soviet history killed more than six hundred people, including almost two hundred children on their way to summer camps on the Black Sea. In the southern Ural Mountains two passenger trains were on the railroad, passing each other, when a gas pipeline exploded. It turned out that the technicians who noticed a dip in pressure along a section of the pipeline turned up the gas flow instead of searching for and fixing a leak. This incident, a few months before our departure, seemed to sum up the country we lived in – a country where unthinkable disregard for human life was practised on every level, by everyone. We feared that all the exhilarating freedoms of the past few years were just like the gas flow turned up and up until there followed the inevitable deadly explosion.

We were wrong, of course, but we were also right.

Yet surely the promise of escape must have felt at least a little bit exciting to the barely fifteen-year-old me. The boy I was in love with was, in turn, in love with a girl infinitely better looking and talented, who, for her part, was in love with another boy better looking and arguably more talented than the object of my unrequited and poorly concealed affection. In this love pyramid, I was at the very bottom, flattened beyond recognition. I know most people wriggle like crazy right through adolescence, as if our teenage lives were ill-fitting woollen jumpers ready to tear and bite us, but before we left I had been feeling like a snail without a shell, pathologically exposed and vulnerable. School for me was not a bitter-sweet study in contrasts. It was like burnt toast buttered with soot. I hated most of my teachers, felt alone among my classmates and was picked on with gusto for refusing to shut up. I was also openly Jewish – a fact that was duly noted in our class journal, as required across all schools. The class journal, where our grades were entered, was kept at all times on our teacher's desk. At the back of the journal was a list of all the students' names and ethnicities – Russian, Ukrainian, Armenian and, of course, Jewish. In a class where at least one-third of kids were Jewish, only five surnames at the back of the journal had the word 'Jew' next to them. The rest, who included, ironically, a girl by the name of Rabinovich, as well as my best friend Alexandra Gourevitch, were entered as anything but. It really didn't matter what you were – a gypsy or a Martian. As long as you could find a microscopic drop of non-Jewish blood in your genetic pool, you were in business. My parents did not care for that kind of evasion.

Almost every time the teacher left the classroom to fetch something from the teachers' room or, in the case of our teacher Larisa Pavlovna, to manically inhale her hourly dose of nicotine in a little alleyway behind the school, the kids would throw themselves on this journal. First, the latest grades were examined and announced to the class; then, inevitably, the stronger kids elbowing their way to the teacher's desk, the page with all the nationalities would be opened and those unfortunate enough to be written in as Jews would be outed again and again. The outing was accompanied by name-calling and the joyous recitation, in a voice filled with triumphant, slimy disdain, of obscene little ditties that held the Jews' legendary greed and cunning responsible for all the world's ills, including the declaimers' particular list of grievances and resentments.

In situations like that, it took everything I had not to close my eyes and ears, not to curl up in a little ball, not to start laughing slavishly together with those stupid, bloodthirsty dickheads. *Filthy Jew, ha-ha-ha. The nose is dragging on the ground, oh-ho-ho!* It took everything I had to open my mouth, even if

only to let hot air come out – hot air or some pathetic fragments of sentences that no one could decipher, let alone feel
chastened by. Then, of course, the teacher would return, and
the carnival would be over for the time being. The kids did not
make any of it up, of course, not even the stupid poems. They
were simply repeating what they had heard at home, on the
street, in the school. They were re-enacting the adult world to
the best of their not inconsiderable abilities.

My home and school were two separate ecosystems with
radically different conditions, which meant I moved between
them at my own risk, adjusting as quickly as I could to changes
in temperature, different oxygen levels in the air and to the
presence of other living organisms besides me. School was the
place where every ounce of genuine passion was thwarted,
every fire inside us instantly put out. Home was the place
where my sister was making art, much of it brilliant, out of
everything she could get her hands on, just like in that immortal poem by Anna Akhmatova: 'If only you knew from what
rubbish/Poetry grows, knowing no shame.' Having grown
up with Inna's frenetic, swiftly burning version of the creative process, I have never learned to afford as much validity to
quieter, colder, more detached forms of creativity. My sister's
many friends were like her too, or so this is how I remember
them – gregarious, fiery and free.

By the time I was fourteen my aversion to school got so bad
that my parents used some ill-defined semi-medical concern to
organise a prolonged stay for me at a children's hospital, where
a friend was one of the top medicos; I put on ten kilos in a
month thanks to a lethal mixture of boredom and hormone-
based therapy that was administered mainly, I think, to justify

my stay. I am, by the way, still trying to get rid of those ten kilos, but it was probably worth it. It kept me away from school, and, shortly afterwards, we left Kharkov. Who knows what would have happened if we had stayed.

In the hospital, I watched the very first television soap opera to be shown on Soviet screens, *Escrava Isaura* (*Slave Isaura*), a Brazilian series from the late 1970s, Brazil's priceless gift to the Eastern bloc. Under the cover of this ideologically palatable story of oppression and subjugation of the poor, we were finally able to do as our Western counterparts had for decades – let ourselves become totally addicted to an unbelievable, atrociously acted character, whose unbelievable, atrociously acted suffering we could completely identify with. Never mind that we were closer to the outer rings of Saturn than to the obscure lives lived by plantation workers in South America. Looking back, I would say that it was the vast, underlying S&M component of Slave Isaura's oppression and struggle that had such addictive qualities, and explained our propensity towards over-identification with its main character. I am talking about the female audience, of course. I have no idea what my male compatriots thought, whether the heaving bosoms of the slaves, the sexual overtones of oppression and submission, the storylines pressed to their pounding absolute outer limits, worked as well on them as it did on the female citizenry.

Escrava Isaura was a revelation to me, but not in the way you might expect. It showed that art for the masses could produce great, visceral pleasure and, not only that, it could do so by wallowing in the human. Official Soviet art for the masses was concerned with the elimination of pleasure, pleasure both as a driving force of human behaviour and as an integral part of any act of art consumption. Sanctioned Soviet art was interested in the post-human, in transcending our frail bodies and our petty-bourgeois pairing and nesting instincts. It was about sacrifice, ideals, climbing the highest mountain you could possibly find, giving birth in the fields and then getting straight away back behind the wheel of the tractor. You got stories about being human from so-called 'high art' – serious literature and cinema – but the art intended 'for the people' was rarely about people as people. In it, our humanity was the beast to be tamed, an existential challenge, an obstacle to the triumph of the Ideal. Soapy *Escrava Isaura* was a simple story about being human, and it was, in its kitsch way, cathartic. Real therapy.

This then was the world I was going to, I thought, when I left Kharkov in '89; a world in which being human, making a mess out of your life was a right, an entitlement, and the theme of choice for all forms of art.

The Greek-born French novelist Vassilis Alexakis travels a lot between Greece and France. Every time he comes back to his home in Paris, he feels surprised to hear himself speak French for the first day or so. He puts off making that first phone call. When he finally calls, it is as if someone else speaks through him in his own voice. He reminds himself 'of an actor watching himself dubbed on the screen'. Alexakis, it must be said, does not have any problems with French. In fact, he has spent nearly half his life in Paris, writing his stories in French and working for French-language newspapers. Many of us are like Alexakis – different people in different languages. For us, going from the old home to the new is not merely a question of mechanics, of some kind of a cultural and linguistic readjustment. It is a much deeper process, a rewiring of sorts.

'Like everybody,' writes Eva Hoffman, thirteen when her family emigrated from Poland to Canada in 1959, 'I am the sum of my languages.' But this equation, Hoffman says, is not as simple as it looks. In a new language we start off with words that are cold and empty at first, that do not 'give off the radiating haze of connotations', words without auras, words that do not evoke. And in that new language the world around us starts off as an abstraction too – hollow, shadowy and dried-up – for 'this radical disjoining between word and thing is a desiccating alchemy'.

Yet our old language, the kind that filled and owned every inch of our old reality and lived experience, doesn't work in this new reality; it fails miserably to capture and describe it. And so as we grow a language (and grow in and into that language), our new reality grows as well. These two processes are inseparable, perhaps they are simply one and the same. Inevitably, a different, new self is forged. Yet for a writer who eventually chooses their new language as their medium, like Alexakis and Hoffman have done (both are highly accomplished writers in their second tongues), no task is more pressing than to somehow recreate 'that wholeness of a childhood language that had no words'.

One day it struck Vassilis Alexakis that his childhood and adolescence would never be part of anyone's memory in France. In this place where he lives, no one had known him as he was growing up. And vice versa. 'The only French people I've known all their lives,' he writes, 'are my children.' Alexakis

27

finds himself going between the place where most people's memories hold no pictures of him as a child to the place where he remains virtually unremembered and unknown as an adult. Reading him, I realise that Billie is the oldest Australian I have known all her life, and that now she is coming with me to a place where most people remember her mother as an adolescent, someone only slightly older than her. She is coming with me to the place that I now cannot help but see through her eyes, at least to some degree. Or rather, I can no longer tell where what I see ends and what Billie sees begins.

Which explains the urgency of our trip. The last time we were in Russia together, Billie was slightly older than her brother is now, a toddler effectively, not yet fully a child. Her memories of that trip were created retrospectively from a plentiful supply of photographs – on one of her favourites she ran giddily in a gorgeous pink dress through a park in central Moscow that was immortalised in Bulgakov's *Master and Margarita*; on another she sat expertly in her aeroplane seat waiting for take-off with the mild irritation of a seasoned long-distance traveller on her face. As to Ukraine, I have never made it there till now, with or without Billie. Right now is my last chance to go back with her and still be the centrifugal force of our journey, exercising the course-setting and veto powers. It is, in other words, my last chance to have Billie follow me around, however begrudgingly, as her mother's tail. In a year, maybe a few months, the tail will drop off, or the tail will be wagging the dog, and such a trip, if even possible, will be a different proposition altogether.

To put it plainly, I am trying to sneak in before the final severing of the umbilical cord, before Russia and Ukraine become *my*, not *our*, history. I am trying to go while a bit of *our* is still there, while we are still mixed up together, close enough to be able to infect each other with what aches and resonates deep within us.

Still in Melbourne, the closer we got to the D-day the more Billie's excitement had to make room for growing anxiety and a kind of pre-emptive nostalgia for Australia and for Melbourne in particular. On the way to the airport, she asked us to make a small detour so we could drive past her school. (This is Billie with her hereditary 'schoolophobia'.) The day before we left, my daughter walked around our neighbourhood streets listening on her iPod to the Sydney-based Whitlams and their rhapsody to Melbourne – the band's lead singer once fell in love with a Melbourne girl and, at least for that moment, with her city as well.

> *In love with this girl*
> *And with her town as well*
> *Walking round the rainy city*
> *What a pity there's things to do at home.*

Billie sang these words out loud, the rain falling around her just like in the song, and it did not take any special maternal sixth sense to see that she missed Melbourne already. I hugged Billie, but secretly I felt happy for her. Ever since we left Ukraine, I never loved another city again enough to miss it even before leaving it, especially if I had every intention of coming back.

2

VIENNA–MOSCOW

Vienna International Airport is said to be the fastest airport in Europe, which apparently means that you can whip
between international flights as if they were adjacent aisles in
your local supermarket. This morning, with five hours to kill
until our flight to Moscow, Billie and I appear to be the sole
representatives of the 'slow travel' movement in this whole
manic beehive. While other passengers rush past us to check
in or re-caffeinate, we drag our feet, wash our hands in the
bathrooms as slowly and as thoroughly as surgeons, and under-
take extensive market research to save a quarter of a euro on a
Mozartkugeln box. Billie lovingly photographs her hot choco-
late. You get the picture. Our deliberate attempt to squander
time is the calculated calm before the storm, the equivalent of

a sprinter putting her head down before the gun is fired and she is off the blocks. Moscow is the first point of call on our trip to Russia and Ukraine and, once we are on that plane, the 'slow' we are storing up will vanish from our lives for the next five weeks. We have less than a week for each of the six places in Russia and Ukraine we plan to visit, so each meeting, each stay, will feel interrupted, and that 'running out of time' feeling will follow us everywhere, eventually morphing into a state of chronic breathlessness.

Meanwhile I observe my emotional state with some bewilderment. I imagined I would be feeling something unmistakably momentous. Here I am, after all, baring my family's soul to my no longer childlike child; not to mention meeting again the lost, tense teenager I was myself when the Tumarkin family departed Kharkov almost twenty years ago. Where is the painful apprehension I should be feeling? The reckless elation of imminent self-exposure? Can I have at least one big emotion befitting the occasion? As Billie and I finally pick up our boarding passes one idea, as petty as it is pathetic, fills my mind – *Oh God, I am ridiculously underdressed.*

As we pass through the departure gate, the fashion altitude changes sharply. (I could have told you as much.) My daughter and I watch the sensible flatties that dominated much of Vienna Airport give way to an entire ecosphere of heels, to women dressed as if being guided by comfort and self-restraint in choosing their clothes was an insult to the very idea of femininity. You can always pick the non-Russians in this crowd; they are the ones who leave their killer heels, their yummy pants and their volumising mascara for special occasions, not realising that life is passing them by as they prance around in their fisherman pants and their Converse sneakers. Look at me: no heels, no frills, no feminine ostentation of any kind. What was I thinking when I opted for practical? Everyone knows that in the country of my birth women don't wear jeans, heavy boots and brown, cleavage-concealing jumpers, not even when they are called up for combat or zoo duty.

Yet since when have I been scared to defy the dress code? Since when have I needed to look the part? And what part is that exactly? Russians are spoilt, possibly more than any other people on earth, by the sheer scale and calibre of feminine charms on display in the former USSR. Not only do I want to be recognised by my former compatriots as a woman; I also want to be recognisable as *one of them*; to remove from my body and face all traces of the two long decades of my life I have spent as a migrant, as if these decades were a mask or a no longer needed accessory. Oh, the anxiety of being spotted. Recognised instantly. Found out as a foreigner. If it is not my clothes, then my accent will give me away – the way my sentences end in a question mark, the way my intonation goes up when it should go down.

God knows, I am an avid believer in individuality, but right now I wish I too were a sparkling, heel-clicking, strategically smelling throwback to the animal kingdom. I don't care if I am perpetuating the worst kinds of stereotypes; the truth is that in the country where I was born most women do not put on heels merely to go out. They go to work in them, throw out the rubbish in them, catch overnight trains and, unfailingly, trawl in them through the mud and the grey, melting snow. What I am feeling is not just the fear of the outsider. It is trivial. It is vain. It is embarrassingly small-minded. It is, above all, atavistic.

'When I knew your mum, she always wore heels. I don't think she owned a pair of flat shoes,' Ira tells me in Kiev several weeks later. Ira (pronounced 'Eera', not 'Aira') is the best friend my mum had in her early twenties, before she married my father and moved from Kiev to his hometown. For five years, between the ages of nineteen and twenty-four, Mum and Ira were inseparable. I love Ira straight away. So does Billie. Back in Melbourne, a few months after our trip, Billie wears high heels to a dress-up party, completely disregarding a spare pair of flat shoes we bring along in a plastic bag. Her high heels stay on for six hours, even for the crazy can-can dancing. At the end of the evening Billie tells me, 'Mum, I want to be like Nanna. I want to be the girl who has never owned a pair of flat shoes.'

Heels are, of course, the pointed tip of the iceberg. The tried and tested loyalty to them that Billie has found so infectious stands for something else – a way of being in the world. It is not for nothing that countless foreign men get giddy and twist their necks silly in Russia and all the former republics. And please do not tell me that it is just because many of the women look like hookers. It seems to me that no one, unless they are fifteen or come from a country where female sexuality is driven underground or downright outlawed, is startled anymore by bits of flesh, no matter how protruding or how spectacular. No, it is not the display of legs or breasts as such, but the way so many women in the former USSR dress with an acute awareness that today may be their last or most fateful day; the day in which they could be hit by a truck, or come face-to-face with the woman who stole their man a decade ago, or be spotted by a famous casting agent. And why not? Olga Kurylenko, the current James Bond girl, was talent-scouted on a train in Moscow when she was a mere teenager. You never know what might happen, so dress up, not down. 'When in doubt, up, not down': this great hungry-and-thirsty, aspirational mantra still separates Eastern Europe from the rest of the continent.

Such a way of being is not a reflection of national joie de vivre, quite the contrary. In both Russia and Ukraine there is no real social net to catch women should they have children on their own, lose their job or their husband, or have to care for chronically ill family. The monthly unemployment benefits paid to residents of Moscow, the country's richest city, are sufficient for only three days' food, according to a recent investigation by the *Novaya Izvestiya* newspaper. And that is before we talk about rent, utility bills and clothing. But at least in Moscow, most benefits are paid on time. In the provinces, delays of several months for unemployment benefits, wages and pensions are standard. The situation is very similar in Ukraine.

It follows then that most women, especially away from the big cities, will at one point or another have to find a man to rely on in order to survive. Now add to this picture the fact that in both Russia and Ukraine there are many more women than men and that, statistically, women live much longer than men, and that the majority of Russia's million-strong grey army of alcoholics are men, and you will begin to grasp the distinct overtones of social Darwinism that colour interaction between the sexes. Sometimes the hunt for a good man is really as crude as all that – the survival of the fittest against the backdrop of fierce competition for scarce resources.

The great tragic history of the emasculation of men during the twentieth century is yet to be told, but for at least one hundred years women have been the stronger sex, when it counts, in Russia. To them the idea that lipsticks and heels are tools of oppression sounds desperately foreign. For decades it was the very absence of such items from Russian stores, and the resulting need to hunt far and wide for them or to go without, that women found oppressive. They fought back and they improvised, just like freedom fighters do. In the 1950s women in the provinces substituted tooth powder for scarce face powder, petroleum jelly for lipstick, sunflower oil for mascara. And even when cosmetics became more widely available behind the Iron Curtain, the Soviet version was an inferior copy of the Western ideal. For many years eyeshadow came without a brush, and women learned to apply the colour expertly with their fingertips. And not all mascaras were created equal, as Herta Müller's novel *The Land of Green Plums*, set in Communist Romania, describes:

> Under the pillows in the beds were six pots of mascara. Six girls spat into the pots and stirred the soot with toothpicks until the black paste grew sticky. Then they opened their eyes wide. The toothpicks scraped against their eyelids, their lashes grew black and thick. But an hour later gray gaps began to crack open in the eyelashes. The saliva dried up and the soot crumbled onto their cheeks.

In her utterly unsentimental memoirs, Nadezhda Mandelstam, the wife of the poet Osip Mandelstam, remembers what it was like to be a woman in the early Soviet period:

> We all were crazy about stockings. Flimsy – made from real silk, partially rotten – they tore on the second day and so,

swallowing tears, we learned to lift stitches. And who of us did not cry with real tears when the damned heel would get broken on our only pair of favourite, beloved, silly 'pumps'? . . .

Ascetic by nature, not given to frivolities or easy tears, judged by most of her contemporaries to be truly hardcore, Mandelstam nonetheless did not dismiss torn stockings or broken heels as the trivial woes of small-minded females. She understood early on that the world of phantom gender neutrality into which women were forced, if not by ideology then by the sheer absence of basic consumer goods, was yet another way in which her country was being turned into a giant prison.

In seven decades of grey, impoverished Soviet fashion, the only colour of note – red – was so poisoned with ideological hyperbole that to most eyes it looked the greyest of greys. Soviet fashion also tirelessly emphasised equality between the sexes, suspicious of anything feminine, curve-hugging, revealing or bright. So the eye-catching, often overstated clothes on our women now is like a big, fat 'Finally!' The Taliban, so to speak, has left town. *Viva la gender différence!*

Wherever you live, clothes are never just about clothes, and in Russia and Ukraine you can peer into the recent history of fashion as into a deep mirror in which history, politics, culture, demographics and economics, all thoroughly intertwined, are reflected back at you. I find it remarkable, for example, that Nicholay Uskov, the editor of *GQ*, Russia's foremost glossy magazine for men, is a historian and a former lecturer at the Moscow State University. This well-groomed, highly educated man with a very serious IQ is one of the main Russian exponents of a universal idea – glamour.

The word means slightly different things in different places: in Britain, 'glamour' denotes charisma; in America taste, beauty and class. In Russia, *'glamur'* has come to stand for the total triumph of materialistic existence in a way that is directly and deliberately antithetical to the Communist ideology of collectivistic, asexual, ego-mortifying, flesh-denying and gender-eschewing ideology. Uskov is a particularly interesting figure to watch in action because, unlike the real zealots, he has the ironic detachment of someone who knows all too well the difference between *glamour* and *glamur*. Accused of promoting conspicuous consumption as an ideology, Uskov answered, 'In Europe when they say it was glamorous [*glamurno*], they do not mean that someone was bathing prostitutes in three-hundred-euro-a-bottle champagne . . . In Russia it is altogether different. We have a society hungry for *dolce vita*, and I find it difficult to condemn people who throw themselves with such abandon into consumption.'

A man with a vivid historiographical imagination, Uskov has clearly traced back the Russian elites' hunger for *glamur* to a need to erase from their minds and their bodies every last vestige of the communal flats, stinking toilets, grey sacks masquerading as clothing, and identical Yugoslavian furniture sets – everything denoting the shared past they have come to despise. And so to forget the taste of the old factory sausages, Uskov explains, people may need to eat, as quickly as they can, more dozens of oysters than the Duke of Westminster might swallow in his entire life. In this scenario, consuming your way out of your past is a Utopian idea.

Glamur is one of the defining themes of post-Soviet Russia, its rise could be traced back to the penetration of the Western glossies into the Russian market in the early 1990s, in an era when there was almost no Russian 'lifestyle' market to speak of. In the early 1990s, there was a famous kiosk in Moscow where you could buy with roubles (no scarce dollars required) coveted issues of *Elle* or *Cosmopolitan*, several months old. Here, suddenly, were magazines for women containing no 'practical advice' on sewing a skirt out of a curtain or making a feast out of three potatoes, no 'prose of life' that reminded women that they were expected to dedicate themselves to the job of 'making do'. Instead, the glossies were populated by ethereal beings with white teeth, glowing skin and slender silhouettes.

A contemporary Russian writer Tatyana Tolstaya defined the *glamur* embodied by these magazines not simply as an ideology of conspicuous consumption but as a transcendental way of being: 'In *glamur* there are no pimples, no ingrown nails, no intestinal colic . . . All of this has been overcome at an earlier stage of development, halfway through the transformation from a swine to a seraph, in the down-market glossies for "receptionists".' If the reader is fortunate enough, they could prove to be another Natalya Vodyanova, the fruit vendor from a provincial Russian market who became a supermodel and married an English lord, Justin Portman, emerging, in the words of journalist Anastasia Chastitsyna, as 'the first Russian Cinderella of international significance'.

But glamour is a two-way street: inevitably, the long tentacles of its Russian variant have reached back into the Western world. What began as a desperate and crude rip-off of Western consumerism is now making serious inroads into the parent culture; which is, I guess, to be expected. And so we hear on the news that billionaire Roman Abramovich has bought the Chelsea Football Club; that Rustam Tariko, the owner of Russian Standard Vodka and the Russian Standard Bank, has thrown a party for a thousand people at the foot of the Statue of Liberty; that another Russian billionaire imports *glamur* in force at his New Year's Eve party, with guest performances by Robbie Williams, Mariah Carey and Ricky Martin. (Surely just one of them would more than suffice!) Of course, any form of decadence, whatever its official name, inevitably has a use-by date written all over it. It represents a moment in time, already doomed, but a moment that speaks with unexpected clarity and eloquence about the society in front of us – where it comes from, what it wants to forget, what kinds of obstacle courses it erects between its new elites and its mere mortals. This is the society Billie and I are about to plunge into – and what a pair of *glamur* virgins we are. *Glamur* separates the country I left twenty years ago from the country I am about to re-enter, just as much as all the new borders, new currencies and new political superstructures.

Just as I cannot get used to the new Russian obsession with *glamur*, so I cannot quite get used to the country's new relationship with money. It is not as if people did not have money while I was growing up. But it meant different things in a society ideologically opposed to capitalism, a society that waged what sociologist Alla Chirikova called 'the seventy-year war against money'. Whether the top echelons were stuffing their cash in pillowcases or depositing them in secret Swiss bank accounts, the Party line was abundantly clear. In the Soviet cosmology money stood for an artificial and temporary form of economic and social relationship that was bound for extinction the closer we moved to a pure form of Communist society, to the great era of 'from everyone according to their abilities, to everyone according to their needs.' This was ideological candy floss, of course (the 'true believers' were all but gone by the time I was born into the maligned era of 'late socialism'), but it was not entirely at odds with the real world outside the Party assembly halls. Plumbers, fitters, carpenters, television repairmen or dental technicians could easily earn double their official wages 'on the side', to say nothing of shop assistants or retail managers who had access to rare commodities that everyone else wanted and, thus, could divide and conquer at their leisure. But for the countless employees of government-owned enterprises with fixed wages and 'no additional sources of income', money was not really the blood flowing in the veins of the economic system.

Yet just imagine for a moment that you were neither a Party operator nor a retail shark, just an ordinary person who happened to have a bit of dough. (Let us leave for a second the all-important question of where this money came from.) Say the roubles were protruding from your pocket and practically burning a hole in it. You were ready and willing to spend. In the West, nothing would prevent you from doing so, at least when we are talking about standard consumer goods (as opposed to, say, enriched uranium). But in an economy of undersupply, based around the idea of constant shortages, there flourished a whole world of endangered consumer species, from staples such as toilet paper and mayonnaise through more complex propositions such as winter coats or fashionable shoes to über-goods such as furniture or electronics. The presence of money was only a first step. Even if you won a lottery, you still had to go to the right place, knock on the right door, find the right person and say the right words. You still had to stand in queues. Yes, the queues. Contemporary writer Vladimir Sorokin defined the centrality of the now defunct queue culture in the USSR this way:

> People stood in line for everything, for bread, sugar, nails, news of an arrested husband, tickets to *Swan Lake*, furniture, Komsomol vacation tours. In communal apartments people waited in line for the toilet. In overcrowded prisons people queued up for a turn to lie down and sleep. According to statistics, Soviet citizens spent a third of each day standing in lines.

And once made, the purchase itself was not the final step in the complex chain of consumption. More often than not, the purchased item still had to be altered, refashioned, readjusted, taken in or exchanged for some other precious item. Even when it came to paying bribes, that most normalised form of social exchange, consumer products and services were used much more frequently than worn-out notes in sealed envelopes. In other words, who you knew mattered more than how much money you had. The economy of my childhood and adolescence was best represented not by the traffic of money between consumers and goods and services, but by a complex web of contacts, exchanges, favours and black-market transactions. 'In the society, where life was regulated not by monetary but specifically by status exchange,' writes renowned philologist Revekkah Frumkina, 'people with "non-convertiable" status – a university researcher or a librarian – had no choice but to scour the shops in search of the simplest things.'

Because both of my parents worked with their heads, as did

most of their friends, money played a secondary role in our lives and, from what I am beginning to understand now, was a source of deep ambivalence. In families such as ours, talking about money – let alone about the open and active pursuit of wealth – was a clear-cut form of vulgarity. Doing something 'for the money' made sense as an inevitable sacrifice for the sake of survival or your family's wellbeing, not as a conscious choice in the presence of other legitimate choices. 'It's just money,' we said, meaning, *Can we please talk about something that really matters now!*

Things have changed profoundly since those (metaphorically) golden times. My family left before the 1990s, before the triumphant return of Money as the Universal Idea. We left before Moscow became the city with the largest number of billionaires in the world, and before politicians and social scientists began to speak about the Market not simply as the most 'natural' economic organisation of a democratic society, but as a universal language applicable for all spheres of social and cultural life. Philosopher Natalya Zarubina says that, with time, money in the new Russia (ergo, many other broken-off chunks of the Soviet empire) became uncoupled from the traditional Western view of the self-regulating market economy as the most universal and adequate form of social organisation and a guarantee of social stability. Money came to be seen, in the words of novelist Victor Pelevin, as 'the substance from which the world is made'. Pelevin's work has achieved a cult following in his native Russia; one of those writers who are routinely described as a 'phenomenon'. Whatever you think of the man – and he is undoubtedly burdened with considerable literary gifts – the man understands the Zeitgeist. Zarubina echoes Pelevin. Today in Russia, she says, money is seen as a force of nature or as one of its elements – irrational, erupting, unstoppable, primal.

This refashioning and unleashing of Money as a force of nature have unfolded against a series of catastrophic economic crises of the 1990s that people today recall as a benchmark of survival. Economic reforms introduced by Yeltsin under the banner of 'shock therapy' were brutal. By mid-1993, as Susan Richards points out in her memoir *Lost and Found in Russia*, more than forty per cent of Russians were living in poverty, as opposed to a mere 1.5 per cent five years before. Inflation made the rouble completely worthless, prices continued to rise remorselessly, industry and commercial enterprises were collapsing. Rapid and comprehensive privatisation of State enterprises presented an irresistible opportunity for graft. Opportunistic bosses, in concert with senior Party officials, the criminal underclass and the newly emerging oligarchs, were able to take control of colossal sums of money and precious raw materials.

The newly installed owners and heads of various business structures, instead of reinvesting their first profits in their businesses as any business textbook would tell them to do, chose to dress their families in fur and diamonds, and send them vacationing on Greek islands. The workers went unpaid for months; the productivity and contracts evaporated with varying speeds, but the bosses did not care. They thought that this was capitalism and they were bona fide capitalist sharks. 'Between 1991 and 2000,' Richards notes, 'it is reckoned that $1 billion was secreted out of Russia every month.' Freedom, it seems, 'had brought nothing but poverty, corruption, confiscatory privatisation and criminality'. It also brought the emergence of the deepest divisions within the society, a civic dissolution of sorts. As Richards, a British correspondent in Russia, saw it, the leaders of post-Soviet society, whether in the Kremlin or the stock exchange or the university, failed to establish the institutions of an open society. (To which many Russians, gazing cynically on the West's own perfectly executed reverse-somersault-and-pike into the muddy waters of the post-Soviet democracy project might reply, 'Well, she would say that, wouldn't she?')

Neither Austrian nor Russian, the guy next to me on the flight to Moscow goes to great lengths to avoid eye contact. His English, which he saves for the Austrian stewardesses, comes with a heavy accent and an unmistakable reluctance. So we have here a man in his early forties who is neither a card-carrying member of the English-speaking world nor a frequent traveller fluent in the ubiquitous language of transactions. Clad in denim. Nondescript shoes. A no-name aftershave. An old iPod in his hand. He is clearly not one of the captains of industry dining off Russia's natural resources but, for the life of me, I cannot work him out.

I was hoping to get some rest on the flight or, better still, do some writing, but I cannot help myself – it's an itch I have to scratch, to have this guy pinned down. He refuses the airline snack. Ramadan? Or just too cool for Austrian Air's famous salted peanuts? Everyone else on the plane is more or less transparent. Behind us is a team of delirious-looking young athletes, big boys from the depths of the Russian provinces, falling asleep before waking to get drunk. In the last row, their middle-aged coach is waving a palmful of sweaty euros at the stewardess pushing the duty-free trolley, to entice her to come to him first. In front are a couple of Austrian and Italian businessmen, nothing flash, lower-middle management at best. There are also a few Russian women travelling alone, one carrying a bunch of ridiculously long-stemmed roses that would look conspicuous at her wedding, let alone aboard this small, run-down plane.

One of the benefits of straddling two worlds is that I can simultaneously imagine how plastic and stiff the Austrian stewardesses look to many Russian passengers, and how boorish and ridiculous the Russians look to them (the former Eastern bloc is probably the nightmare route, the Austrian Air Gulag). I am a fine case of what the writer Ariel Dorfman, an Argentinian-born Chilean American, called 'bilingual fate'. 'How to deal with this incessant and often perverse doubleness,' he asked. 'How to protect the fragile shell of the self from its bombardment by two needs and two communities, which read opposite meanings into every mouthful at every meal?'

As long as I can remember, I have always loved the thrill of illicit extrapolation, of building strangers' identities from a few seemingly insignificant details. Give me a washed-to-death bra strap peaking out from a crisp business blouse, and I am off and running. In an instant my mind starts buzzing, eager to cobble together a story. A couple on the train reading copies of the same book, Jeffrey Eugenides's *Middlesex*. A gracefully ageing silverhead from the neck up, a yobbo from the neck down. Then who on earth is the passenger next to me, the man with no qualities?

It suddenly dawns on me that I am practising my favourite game of identity-cracking in anticipation, limbering up for my time with people I have not seen in two decades. I have come to find pleasure in switching sides between mouthfuls, jumping across the table in the course of one meal, but on this trip I am all sides at once – the East and the West, the little lost girl and the mother, the philistine and the Wandering Jew. I am, to use Dorfman's words, a cultural bigamist, someone who has surrendered after a long struggle to the bifurcation of her self, while never fully banishing a fear that these two parts of me, uneven and not properly cohering to each other, make me less than one whole. Dina Rubina, one of the best living Russian writers and an immigrant to the land of Israel, said that when she first returned to Moscow she could run her hand across her chest and physically feel the stitch holding the two parts of her together. As our plane lands in Moscow, I am pretty sure I can feel mine.

3

THE SPACE INSIDE

IN MOSCOW BILLIE AND I are staying with my friends Petya, Natasha and their son, Andryusha, who is about to turn one. Petya, who is several years younger than me, is the brother of Katya Margolis, one of my dearest friends, a Muscovite who now lives most of the year in Venice. Before we left Australia I bombarded Petya with questions about how to get from the airport to their place, putting aside my traveller's pride altogether. In the face of the notoriously extraterrestrial taxi fare from Domodedovo Airport (every one of Moscow's three airports, in fact), and too much luggage to allow Billie and I to flit around like butterflies, I turned to Petya, stripped entirely of the world-weary resourcefulness I had formerly affected. He responded by sending me a Google map with thick dots and connecting arrows, finishing his email (perhaps to let me know that our friendship was not in danger because of my sudden loss of cool) with a spot of jesting, welcoming me and Billie to the couple's 'modest two-room apartment in the northern part of the capital' – a portal, so to speak, from which we could see for ourselves what contemporary Moscow eats, drinks and inhales.

The apartment is not in the centre of the capital, but it is not on the outskirts either. It is in a high-rise block, which looks so familiar to me that even before we enter the flat I experience a strange lurch in time. The contours of the present, distinctive and well-defined a minute ago, turn fuzzy, as does my sense of myself as a grown woman with a grown child in tow. 'Why is the lift so small?' asks Billie in a whisper, so Petya, who is trying in vain to fit both of our suitcases in the lift, won't hear. 'Why are these buildings so dirty, Mum?' Here is what I imagine Billie sees and smells – the foyer and lift of the apartment block are worn and dirty, covered in spit and smelling of piss. What she will soon discover is that most residential buildings in Russia and Ukraine, at least those that are not elite, are in exactly the same state of conspicuous disrepair. Actually, the use of the word 'conspicuous' in relation to the violently decaying interiors of the post-Soviet world (former Baltic republics excepted) is a tautology, like talking about conspicuously wet rain. It is no secret that most mundane, not-for-show Soviet structures are rotting alive. The mortality of mortar is on display everywhere, an existential condition, a cultural given.

I never paid attention to this kind of stuff before, it was the way things were and it never used to matter. Now, all of a sudden, it does. If Billie was not here, I am sure I would have dismissed the way my nose is smelling the stink it never used to smell, the way my eyes pick out all the things that were out of focus before. I would have brushed it off as a natural resetting of the senses, emigrant's déjà vu. But her presence is forcing the issue, no matter how much I resist. It is forcing me to confront a snake-brew of emotions – tenderness, nostalgia, longing, disgust, and something closely resembling survivor's guilt because we were lucky enough to cut and run while others were not. I don't want Petya and Natasha to overhear Billie's whispers or even the fact of her whispering at all. And just as much I don't want Billie to see me caught unawares, unsure of my reactions.

How is this for irony – we grew up with the toothache-inducing dictum of Marx (Karl, not Groucho) that 'being determines the consciousness'. Yet we were born into a world not of our making or choosing, where nothing broken got fixed, nothing decaying got renovated, where rivers of liquefied rubbish were flowing in the streets, and just about every road not manically mended just in time for a Great Leader's visit was an assault obstacle course. So what kind of *consciousness* were we meant to develop when our *being* was so degraded? Living conditions may mould the human psyche but, as the Soviet experience tells us, they actually do so in ways that are far more complex, life-affirming and unpredictable than Marx ever imagined. I want Billie to understand that people are not their crumbling foyers or their broken lifts, and I feel ashamed of giving a damn in the first place. I was not like that before.

I have never previously visited Petya and Natasha's apartment, but when I step inside the door I already know it. The box in the foyer, for the slippers that are worn inside the house. The coats hanging off the sagging rack, like a bunch of about-to-explode bananas. The big room, which is several zones at once: an office with two desks and two computers (Natasha is a philologist and editor; Petya is a computer programmer); a lounge room with a television set, stereo, bookshelves and a fold-out table in the corner; a guestroom with a couch that unfolds, on which Billie and I sleep. The second, smaller room where every centimetre of space is used to accommodate the marital bed, Andryusha's cot, a wardrobe and mirror. Objects and spaces have their day and night shifts, sometimes several shifts within a span of twenty-four hours. The washing is hung above the bath overnight. The kitchen table, meant for two, but around which five of us companionably gather in the evenings. Andryusha, I discover, plays in the slivers of space not taken up by things. And to think that just a year ago I felt the need to run from an apartment twice this size in Melbourne, because I could not bear the thought of my little Miguel, who was about to start crawling, having nowhere to stampede. In the West, people are truly like liquid that takes up its container's shape. Able to swell and spread themselves in an instant. Not in this country. 'If there is an infinite aspect to space,' wrote the poet Joseph Brodsky, 'it is not its expansion but its reduction.' Space is infinitely divisible into smaller spaces. Much more so than even an IKEA catalogue might lead you to believe. It is enough to remember the description of life in a standard student dormitory from *Twelve Chairs*, the most famous satirical novel of the 1920s: 'The large mezzanine room was cut up into long slices by plywood partitions . . . Rooms resembled pencil cases, only rather than with pens and pencils they were filled with people and primus stoves.'

The Hungarian historian István Rév wrote that Communism is 'the regime of compression: long lines, constant waiting, a limited number of extremely crowded places, people jammed in and pressed close to each other'. For some, like Vladimir Zhirinovsky, the leader of the perversely named Liberal Democratic Party which advocates ultranationalism and the rise of the militant State, growing up in communal apartments was the source of a powerful anger. As the smallest of children, he was routinely pushed around and humiliated, made to feel his vulnerability. In his autobiography he wrote of how he hated the stinking shared toilets, the poisonous cigarette smoke, the bullying. (Was he, in truth, displacing other hatreds – a sense of inferiority over his father's painstakingly concealed Jewishness?) To many others, communal spaces were not meaningless and dehumanising, despite their catastrophic lack of privacy and the seemingly intolerable level of transparency and interference into other people's lives; despite the queues to the amenities, everyone smelling each other's farts; despite people ratting on each other and whole webs of squabbles, stand-offs and strategic alliances – despite all of it. When I was a kid, these spaces constituted a different reality with its own system of meaning and its own rewards. You would never die alone and unnoticed, you would never find yourself without milk or salt, you would never feel socially disengaged or isolated. Boys who grew up here were comfortable around women; after all, they had lived in the pockets of their female neighbours, robe-clad women talking incessantly, with their tenderness, bad moods, menstruation and their ability to conjure the most delicious dishes out of thin air. Lev Rubinstein writes that Russia's communal apartment system, with its overcrowding and its own rich and complex internal dynamic, is closer to the medieval town than to the old Russian village. The kitchen figures as both the marketplace, where goods and information are exchanged, and the cathedral square: 'The eternally broken faucet does double duty as the town fountain.' The hallway with its clotheslines stretched right across functions as the main street.

'Long before collective farms and Gulag camps,' says Rubinstein, 'a communal apartment embodied the rapid mutation of Utopia into anti-Utopia.' The characteristic feature of that anti-Utopia was something akin to what producers of reality shows from the *Big Brother* franchise have painstakingly tried to recreate in their televised social experiments, by placing participants in enclosed spaces where privacy is abolished (even in toilets) and space itself has been stripped of its ability to conceal, shelter and segregate.

In writer Asya Lavrusha's story *Human Material*, an old apartment is a living creature with its own distinctive physiology, feelings and memory. The apartment was once spacious and luxurious, but after the 1917 Revolution its owner left for Paris. The flat's layout was brutally rearranged and within its walls twenty 'dead-ends' were created, each housing a family. The apartment did not like in the slightest its new inhabitants, who 'looked like cockroaches – it poured plaster on their heads, flooded them with water and once even tried to poison them with gas'. Not all apartments were so unwelcoming. In my childhood our kitchen could stretch to fit in as many guests as were present on the day. This is how most of us lived, except the top echelons, of course. We were the unrivalled masters of spatial optimisation. Folding and unfolding (and enfolding). Layering things on top of each other. Counting centimetres to ensure maximum utilisation of space. Squeezing the air out of our space. This determined the texture of our lives, the way we remembered ourselves as children; this made us who we are, whatever that means.

I feel at home in Petya and Natasha's kitchen and in every part of their apartment straight away, and not because of some kind of display of extra-special hospitality – no, hospitality is when there are guests and hosts. With Petya and Natasha we are never made to feel like guests of any kind. For a week the five of us simply share the space as one family in an unspoken, effortless state of reciprocity, without any complicated rituals of caretaking or mutual obligation. Our lives intersect when the time is right for all of us and then we eat together and talk, but no contact, no conversation is forced or pre-arranged. Our conversations never feel like manic catching up, like a gallop through our respective lives in a quest to fill in gaps. They flow anarchically and without an agenda and, inevitably, sometimes in virtually no time, they take us to the things that matter. I have met Natasha on previous visits and liked her enormously but, this time, as we talk in her kitchen, I remember all of a sudden the happiness that comes from being in the presence of a person whose every thought and word find in you the deepest kind of recognition. Like-mindedness in the real sense of the word.

When I first met Petya, years ago while he was still at school, I thought him a brilliant writer. The two of them are highly intelligent, witty and well-read, but there is nothing put-on about Petya and Natasha. I trust completely their apparent disinclination to appraise Billie and me. Sophisticated Muscovites, they do not condescend or bore us by trying to dazzle; nor do they mount ideological hobbyhorses or warm up only after they have metaphorically prodded me in the sternum for emigrating. As to the lively, generous, lovable Andryusha, he almost makes being away from Miguel feel bearable. It is not that we are worried about Miguel – we left him in the loving and capable hands of his dad, my mum and my indispensable auntie – but Billie and I struggle terribly with our first extended bout of Miguel-deprivation. Unconsciously and persistently, we gravitate towards Andryusha, taking great solace in his laughter, his warmth and baby smell, and in the strength of his resolve to take that first step without help from chairs, walls and supporting adult hands. We are there for his first successful attempt.

The rule is that you have to register your Russian visa within seventy-two hours of arrival into the country. If you are prepared to pay a bloodcurdling nightly rate to stay at some swish hotel for foreigners who do not mind being screwed or whose companies are paying, they'll register the visa for you pretty much in-house. If however, like us, you are staying with your friends or have some other private arrangement, then there are two options: you can either find and pay an increasingly rare specialised travel agent to stamp your visas (specialised means one that has set up a streamlined, self-regulating chain of bribed officials in all the right places) or you can go through the official channels, where, in principle, the whole procedure should cost close to nothing.

I call OVIR (the Office of Visas and Registration) from Petya and Natasha's home, hoping to inquire for their opening hours. The phone rings out. I try again. This is hopeless.

I get Billie to put on her already disintegrating boots, and we start walking. Once we find it, the building does not say 'OVIR', but I got the address from this year's phone book, and several people passing by have all pointed out to us the same semi-concealed structure tucked away from the street. Billie instinctively pushes her body closer to mine. I hold her hand and stroke her hair just a little bit. I did not have to bring her with me today. I chose to because I wanted her to know the difference between this bureaucracy and the kind she will spend her lifetime getting exasperated with. It is like a vaccination, only I am giving her a really big dose of the poison so she can shake off the other stuff without giving it a second thought.

Inside the building, there are no navigation aids to help people like me orient themselves – no reception area, no name-plates, no helpful signs indicating behind which door men and women with the right stamps may be hiding. The idea of wearing one's identity on one's sleeve continues to be repugnant to most official organisations in contemporary Russia. I suppose these lethargic mazes – hermetically sealed, impenetrable official spaces that infantilise visitors – are a hallmark of any engorged bureaucracy. Since there are no visual clues as to how things are done around here I search my memory, which obligingly throws up images of thousand-strong queues of aspiring migrants, my family included, at the end of the 1980s. It sprinkles fragments of conversations on top of these images: *For months we went to OVIR as to work. And then the Mayor said, 'I hope all of you kikes will leave, every single one of you.' There is no better cure for nostalgia than a trip to OVIR.*

The walls in the corridor are plastered with the latest amendments and changes to various rules and decrees, but no amount of working backwards can help me reconstruct the original regulations. I give up after five minutes and turn my attention to other people in the corridor, who are leaning against the walls with not a single chair, trying to take up as little space as possible. Once in a while, one of the doors along the corridor will open and a man or a woman with an unmistakable look of contemptuous superiority will walk out and disappear behind another door, while the people sweating out of their brains in the overheated corridor will unconsciously suck their stomachs in. I have it in me too – the stomach-sucking gene. I can feel it. I can feel my whole body shrinking and my voice acquiring cheerful timidity.

'Hesitation is akin to death,' Lenin, paraphrasing Peter the Great, famously exclaimed the day before the 1917 Revolution began. So I poke my head into the only room along the corridor that has its door ajar. The gap is not so much an invitation as a literal opening, an opportunity not to be squandered.

'Good morning! I need to register my visa, please.'

'This is a wrongly formulated request!'

'What would 'the properly formulated request' sound like?'

Silence. I am clearly being ignored. Come on, I was born in the Soviet Union, I should have acquired the inborn immunity to all this bureaucratic S&M with my mother's milk. Regroup, breathe in and try again.

'I am sorry, but I am not quite clear what you mean.'

'This is not OVIR.'

'Oh, right, could you please tell me how to get to OVIR.'

'OVIR no longer exists.'

'What am I supposed to do with my visa?'

Silence. The cockroach behind the desk shrugs his shoulders.

I am back in the corridor, shaking. Billie looks at me. I look at her. So much for developing her street smarts and a sense of proportion.

'You should go in, sit down, have a chat, endear yourself to him,' a woman who is using the wall plastered with notices to fill in an application form tells me. I thank her, take a deep breath and go back into the room. This time I sit down, take my time and look intently at the man on the other side of the table, imploring him to forget whatever differences we had in the past.

'A few years ago this is how you registered your visa. Has the shop been closed?'

'What shop?'

Wrong again. I am perpetually off-key today. Picked the wrong intonation. Too much familiarity. His irritation is palpable. I wanted to sound self-possessed so he would not be tempted to draw blood, but I totally misjudged it. Soon I am back in the corridor, seething and powerless.

Only later do I learn that a few years ago all the local OVIR offices were dismantled and their responsibilities handed to local police precincts. The Passport and Visa Department of the local police precinct is now responsible for visa registration. The guy I was talking to must have been the head of one such department, not that he would reveal his secret to me. Back in the corridor, questions jump out of Billie. She did her best to hold them back for most of the interlude. 'Why is this man talking to you like this? Isn't he supposed to help you? What happened, Mum?'

Billie, the truth is that I have forgotten how it feels to be on the receiving end of the petty functionaries' and bureaucrats' almost biological need to diminish and humiliate. If I could have only opened my mouth then, if I could have shaken off the powerless rage that gripped my mind and my body, perhaps, this is what I would have said to you: My dear Billie, imagine spending a lifetime surrounded by guys like this, meeting them everywhere you went – at university and at work, at a corner shop, in a hospital and, of course, at a police station. This guy, Billie, would be your boss, your neighbour, the principal of your school, the man who decides which taps and toilets the plumber will fix today and tomorrow, the one who issues residential permits and passports, who presides over the attestation commission of every university and college in this country. Imagine realising that this guy is as good as it gets. Because you are dealing with a mere bureaucrat, even if one of a vicious and obsessive strain, it means you have not been deported, sentenced, exiled or put into a psychiatric institution. As long as you know how to play the game, chances are that with time you can find a way to this guy's heart. Money, cognac, French perfume for the missus, favours you can pull, favours your friends can pull, someone you know knows this guy's superior or, perhaps, your kids – oh, miracle of miracles – go to the same soccer club.

Imagine being so used to dealing with the guys who bark 'wrongly formulated request' to every question you ask that you are astonished when someone in a position of authority treats you with respect and consideration. I use the word 'guys' figuratively here, you understand, to refer both to men and women, for there was little difference between the sexes, either on the giving or the receiving end. And if I, Billie, were to meet myself the way I am now, all shaken up and enraged by

the routine humiliation this guy dished out almost automatically and certainly without any special malice, I would smile to
myself and think today's Maria a complete foreigner. Just like
you, Billie, today's Maria comes from another planet. As I came
out of this cockroach's office, biting my lips and clenching my
teeth, I thought for a moment that I finally understood the real
reason why your grandparents left everything behind in their
mid-forties and took the biggest leap of faith in our family's
history. Because you see, Billie, it was never, not for a second,
about sausages and whitegoods. It was not about potholes in
the street and shop assistants treating customers as burglars. It
was not about living conditions and spending most of your life
banging your head on the wall trying to get the simplest things
done. Your grandfather and grandmother just wanted someone
in our family, bearing our surname and our features, to be
perfectly unhabituated to being screwed, to be genuinely surprised by not being shown respect. And this someone is you,
Billie, you realise it, right? On some level, it is too late for me,
because – I realise now – I could never think of freedom as a
birthright however much I believe it intellectually. But you,
your brother and your cousins are the first generation that does
not know any other kind of freedom.

To 'imagine what [Boris] Grebenshikov means to his fellow
Russians', *Wired* magazine said in 1998, 'you have to imagine [Leonard] Cohen, complete with his alternative street cred
and literary ambitions, somehow achieving the fame of Elvis
and the political clout of Jesse Helms'. A decade earlier, the

American press had greeted Grebenshikov's American debut album *Radio Silence* by calling the thirty-six-year-old musician the ultimate cross-cultural artist, the Emissary of Rock, and comparing him not only to Cohen but to Bob Dylan, David Bowie, Van Morrison and Peter Gabriel. The album tanked. It was produced on the Columbia label by Dave Stewart of the Eurythmics, and all but two of its compositions were in English, but still it evidently did not translate. In hindsight (and even at the time) this failure did not matter all that much. For one, Grebenshikov's attempt in 1989 at rock *sans frontières* was the stuff of history (we knew it). Secondly, at home, where he was the lead singer, writer and ideologue of a legendary band, Aquarium, their albums had already earned a permanent place in the library of unperishable cultural texts. Grebenshikov had by 1989 earned the right to be wrong, as well as the right to indulge, gods and circumstances willing, his own unmistakable cosmopolitan cravings.

As I was growing up, we called him by his initials 'BG'. If you put an 'O' in between the two initials you get 'BOG' – the Russian word for 'God'. I don't think this was the main thing though. At some point, most adolescents will turn into overt or undercover idol worshippers, but referring to Grebenshikov as 'BG' was much more about how we wanted to define ourselves. Having long since separated wheat from chaff, faces from mugs, musicians from marching bands, we did not need anything spelt out for us. Writer and historian Kirill Kobrin, just a few years my senior, remembers his friends speaking to each other in quotes from Aquarium songs. This was more, I suspect, than just youth culture, more than 'cool', more than pointlessly arcane. All this quoting, abbreviating and encoding was the means by which members of the tribe recognised each other, for in our country most of us were undercover agents living in the shadow of the seemingly unbreachable gulf between what we thought and what we said and how we acted.

Grebenshikov was not alone; there were many other, largely underground, bands and musicians in the 1970s and 1980s – just as important, just as brilliant, just as brave. Viktor Tsoi, the lead singer of Kino, who died in an accident in 1990 when he was just twenty-eight and was bitterly and widely mourned, possessed artistic and personal honesty and purity not matched by anyone else in the Soviet or post-Soviet rock scene. Then there was Yuri Shevchuk and his band DDT, their music like a naked electrical current – explosive, convulsive, painful and purifying. There were others just as good, just as revolutionary. But when I go deep into the memories of our last year in Kharkov, past the docking point for the frequently retrieved stories of our departure, past the crust of memories thinned out to the state of virtually pure emotions, what I hear is Aquarium's 1987 album *Equinox*:

> *They will get us only if we start to run.*
> *They will find us only if we hide in the shade.*
> *They hold no power over what is truly yours.*

I may be a self-proclaimed cultural bigamist, but even so I can't really imagine how such lyrics sound to someone born and raised in the world where the pursuit of happiness, rather than the pursuit of freedom, has been a defining quest for long enough to seem completely natural. Perhaps it just sounds like your run-of-the-mill rock 'n' roll philosophising, peppered with a tinge of totalitarian persecution mania. Most likely it sounds like nothing special. But it was special, please believe me. It was revelatory and life-changing.

Many of us, the children raised in flats with books and music, by parents who had let us know without ever actually saying it that this place outside of our kitchen windows known as 'the best of all possible worlds' was anything but, have grown up idolising dissent; in awe of those who spoke up and spoke out. But there, suddenly, was BG singing about what gets forsaken in constant resistance and rarified non-conformism, what gets lost in defining yourself primarily in opposition to the status quo. And he was singing right at the time when that very status quo revealed itself to be in a state of acute and unstoppable disintegration. The previous lines, it occurs to me now, are the flip side of Jvanetsky's defiant (and deeply ironic) exhortation to hold freedom in our teeth. Clearly, Grebenshikov was removing himself from the equation as a figurehead of oppositional culture, in fact dismantling the equation altogether. In Western terms, you might say he was doing a Dylan on us. How could we not be struck by his words, those of us who learned to read and to read between the lines at the same time? How could we remain at a polite distance from the way Grebenshikov removed all the glamour and higher purpose from the idea of lives spent on the run, of homes set up in the cracks of the established order, of literature written in codes and tongues? BG was singing about the freedom it takes to step out of the prefabricated moulds of destiny – out of the roles of the dissenter, the artist, the guru, the bureaucrat, the cog in the machine, the philistine or the man or woman in the street.

Those who paint us,
Paint us red over grey.
Colours are just colours,
but I am talking about something else.
If I knew how,
I would have drawn you
in a place of green trees
as gold over blue.

Blue was the blue of St Petersburg canals, and gold was the gold of the golden spires. Or it was the gold of golden leaves in autumn against the sky. Or the sun lost in the curls of one enchanted woman, whose proximity brings happiness, however fleeting. And the *something else* BG was talking about, was it beauty – the same beauty which Dostoyevsky believed would save the world? It is not for nothing that BG's hometown of St Petersburg was considered by many, myself enthusiastically included, as one of the most beautiful cities on earth. *Red over grey* stood for a revolutionary, underground culture undermining the turgid, cynical mediocrity of officialdom, but blue, gold and green were the colours of the post-political world, the world that was not circumscribed by ideological positions, a transcendental world of inner freedom.

Grebenshikov was singing and I was growing up. He was singing, and we were leaving. In those final months in Kharkov, his words bared every nerve ending inside me, but, in a strange way, they also soothed me. After all, freedom was all we had now, and BG was assuring me that this was more than enough. For years after I arrived in Australia I listened to *Equinox* and to the new Aquarium albums I copied from fresh arrivals. I needed BG badly. I was nostalgic as hell, of course, but I also depended on Aquarium to help me orient myself in my new life.

My parents wanted my sister and me – and the children they hoped we would eventually bring into this world – to be free people. They did their bit, much more than their bit, in fact. They left the only home they had known. They took us out of a place where they believed the very notion of freedom was rendered absurd and laughable. It was our solo from now on. In Australia, I needed Grebenshikov to remind me of what real freedom felt like, as opposed to the absence of external constraints. It surprised me at first. Here was a country that allowed its citizens to choose where they lived; where the Market, not the State, was the biggest source of censorship (a fact that was very hard for citizens of an ex-totalitarian nation to see in their first few years, such were its charms); where you would never find three generations thrown together in a single room crisscrossed with partitions (unless, of course, they were black Australians or refugees). Even the bureaucrats smiled and behaved themselves, on the whole. The first officer from social security my family encountered astonished my parents (and me, for that matter) by sporting differently coloured earrings (blue and green). Libraries were filled with new, or at least new-ish, books. Shops were filled with gleaming produce (to Australians, fresh fruit and vegetables were obviously a God-given right). Driving on city roads did not bring on instant contractions. Ideology did not seem to be playing first violin. Australia looked like Grebenshikov's archetypal country of *gold over blue against the green*. (Only it was not. No country ever is.)

★

Towards the end of Day Two in Moscow, Billie and I filled our wallets with American dollars and took two trains in silence to the specialist travel agency, which occupied a rented room in an institute to do with some kind of chemical materials or processes. Here the new and the old Moscow met. We walked in through the entrance, which was surrounded by large stray dogs oozing aggressive desperation. We paid, we thanked, we walked back respectfully past the dog army, and the next day our stamped passports were waiting for us. Of course, we told Petya and Natasha about our friendly bureaucrat who spoke in riddles, but we made a point of not making a big deal about what happened. What happened really? Nothing happened. Nothing of any note.

4

ENEMIES OF THE PEOPLE

No, NOT A MATRIARCH, that is not the right word, but there has to be a term to describe this woman past her ninetieth birthday, who carries within herself not simply the weight of nearly a century lived to the bone but also the essence of dignity and strength. There are many people who do not consent to turning into frail little daffodils in their old age, many of them remarkable in their own way, but Marina Gustavovna is a different species. Even if you knew nothing about nothing, you could tell this much about her: here is a woman who has not been bent much less broken by the dog of the Soviet century, with its absolute contempt for human life, for the bonds of families and friendships, and for the singular gifts of human mind and imagination. Who would have thought it would be so easy to see that, having lived through her country's autogenocide from its very start to its agonising finish, the grandmother of Petya and Katya has remained, in some profound sense, intact.

Marina Gustavovna sits at the kitchen table, as straight as a little pine tree, methodically cutting out the rotten bits from a pile of small, misshapen apples. The rotten bits by far exceed the good, edible parts, but she is determined to salvage whatever she can. What is that expression 'one bad apple will spoil the whole bunch'? It was obviously born in a culture with an unlimited supply of apples. I recognise the salvaging instinct. I have seen it in all the women in my family who came before my sister and me – before the generation that stopped taking every sliver of material reality to its absolute utility limit. Things are not immortal, of course, but you never give up on them for, in the right hands, they can have multiple lives and afterlives – a piece of cotton is made into a sheet, then refashioned into a curtain, then turned into some fabric nappies and finally becomes a dishwashing cloth. Satirist Mikhail Zadornov writes that only in this country were carpets darned, torn shoelaces tied up in a special way and laced back into shoes, laddered stockings used for everything from making tea bags to storing onions (onion can breathe in stockings – a crucial point), sealing holes in window frames and straining cherry conserve.

Billie and I first sat in this kitchen with Marina Gustavovna a decade ago when we sought refuge in her apartment after a close encounter with a large rat in a flat just around the corner, the flat where Katya was then living with her two young daughters. For a woman long in pursuit of the meaning of courage, it did not take much to turn me into a certifiable coward. And so as certifiable cowards do, I woke Katya, who had barely had time to close her eyes since the night before, and made her give extended chase to the rat with a long-handled kitchen broom. Standing on top of a table, refusing to come down, I watched the rat, which was completely unperturbed, and noted the precise contours of Katya's rib cage illuminated by the thin, white cotton of her nightie (a mother of two, she weighed less than a prepubescent girl). The next morning, Katya wisely packed me and Billie off to the family apartment and Marina Gustavovna. Rats abandoning the sinking ship? Well, yes, you might say that.

And now, ten years later, Marina Gustavovna's fingers slide across the photo frames in search of what her eyes can no longer tell her – which one of her family is looking back at her now from this or that picture. 'Come on, Billie, have a guess how many grandchildren and great-grandchildren I have. Come on, I am waiting.' Marina Gustavovna's voice doesn't do the nonagenarian squeak-squeak. It has no bald patches, is full-blooded even at its quietest. Though its pitch does rise noticeably when I, not having paid sufficient attention to an initial stern 'no', continue to insist on helping clear the table after a cup of tea. 'No, I am fine, thank you.' I forget that Marina Gustavovna does not suffer fools gladly, particularly polite ones. I forget who I am talking to.

Ten years since our last meeting, Marina Gustavovna is increasingly betrayed by her body, which collapses on her, sometimes when she is alone and, what's worse, in all kinds of public places. But her physical frailty does not mean that she no longer is able to tend the precious intellectual legacy of her father, Gustav Gustavovich Shpet, one of the most significant

Russian philosophers of the early twentieth century. She pops up in a documentary film about Gustav Gustavovich, in newspaper articles, in the footnotes to prefaces and afterwords framing various editions of his once largely forgotten body of work. She was in Bordeaux in 2008 for the international conference that commemorated him as one of the most seminal figures of Russian intellectual life in the decades preceding and following the 1917 Revolution. And for many years now, Marina Gustavovna has been making her way to the Siberian town of Tomsk, where her father was exiled, for the annual readings dedicated to his memory.

His name may have been largely forgotten for most of the twentieth century, but Gustav Gustavovich was once widely known and admired. A professor of philosophy at the University of Moscow, a brilliant lecturer and a feared polemicist, he introduced into Russian intellectual life Husserl's phenomenology with its emphasis on subjective experience and structures of human consciousness. Coming from a family of the impoverished Polish aristocracy, Gustav Gustavovich belonged to the tradition of philosophers known as polymaths, *homo universalis* – he spoke seventeen languages, cared deeply about theatre and arts and was well-acquainted with leading actors, writers and poets of his time.

He was, in other words, precisely the kind of man who was never going to be Lenin's cup of tea when the Revolution came, not with his aristocratic roots, rabid cosmopolitanism and his appraisal of historical materialism as suffering from 'poverty and narrow-mindedness'. 'Down with syntheses, integrations and unities! Long live separation, differentiation and disorder!' Gustav Gustavovich wrote in the early 1920s in

Aesthetic Fragments. This might seem an appropriate statement from a philosopher urging on his new nation engulfed in revolutionary violence, a nation determined, in the words of *The Internationale*, to wipe the slate of the past clean. No. Shpet was actually sounding like a class enemy, suggesting, if you were to read between the lines, that philosophy's role was not to present a unified worldview intolerant of any difference or opposition, but to move towards a greater understanding of humanity precisely through the study of friction, disorder and paradox.

In complete opposition to the emerging philosophical monoculture, Gustav Gustavovich believed it utterly wrong for philosophy to channel ideology – after all, at its core philosophy was science, not 'morality or a sermon or a worldview'. Thus the separation of philosophy and ideology (just like the separation of Church and State) was a prerequisite for social advancement. Not surprisingly, considering how seriously he took the pursuit of knowledge in any field, Gustav Gustavovich was a sworn enemy of amateurism, his views on the matter a complete twist on Lenin's famous dictum about every cook having the capacity to govern the country. (Lenin used *kukharka*, a feminine version of 'cook', to emphasise his point.) 'My dad,' Marina Gustavovna once commented ironically, 'was very strict when it came to scientific pursuits. He could not stand amateurs. He was much more tolerant towards a cook or a *kukharka*, than towards an engineer or a doctor holding forth with their opinions on philosophy.' Shpet never hid his aversion to the omnivorous and know-it-all dilettantes desperate to have their fingers in every pie. In no time, those dilettantes would come to take over the country Shpet had refused to abandon.

As an unambiguously non-Marxist philosopher, he was

supposed to be expelled from the Soviet Union on the so-called 'philosophers' ship', which sailed to Germany in the autumn of 1922, carrying some of the country's most prominent philosophers, writers, scientists and engineers. The famous Russian philosopher Nikolay Berdyaev, another professor of philosophy at Moscow University, was aboard, as was Nikolay Losskiy, the professor of philosophy at St Petersburg University (the former professors, that is). The mass deportation of the nation's intellectual elite was, to a large degree, a preventive measure – while its members were not openly opposed to the regime (the ones who were had by that stage exiled themselves voluntarily), they were seen as dangerous because of their innate intellectual autonomy and potential power over young minds. So dear was the deportation project to Lenin's heart that even the stroke he suffered in May 1922 did not stop the Great Leader's close involvement in painstakingly compiling the lists of those to go. Trotsky too thought that the deportation was an altogether humane gesture on the part of the Soviet government. 'In view of the fact that the professors and their ilk have not been able to make peace with the Soviet regime during the last five years,' he wrote, 'they must be regarded as enemies.' In other words, they would have to be put up against a wall and shot in the event of a coup or a serious conflict. Shpet's name was on the list, and he had to use every scintilla of influence at his disposal, including his friendship with Anatoliy Lunacharsky, the first Soviet People's Commissar of Enlightenment, in order to stay.

Soon enough, however, Gustav Gustavovich's philosophical ideas were attacked in the papers for being 'infused with reactionary mysticism', meaning that as far as the leadership was concerned, they belonged in the now overflowing dustbin of history. In 1929 it was Shpet's time to be dismissed from academia. Between 1929 and his arrest in 1935, no longer able to pursue academic research to which he had dedicated his entire life, he translated Shakespeare, Byron and Dickens, as well as classic intellectual texts such as Hegel's *The Phenomenology of Spirit*. He was one of a pantheon of brilliant translators the Soviet Union produced, more by accident than intention. Some of the best writers and philosophers, unable to publish their own work, survived by turning out heartbreakingly magnificent translations of foreign classics (as well as good translations of countless mediocre texts). Many of us, who came to a reasonable mastery of one or several foreign languages either through intense education, emigration or both, have struggled to read these classics in their original languages, and not for deficiencies of vocabulary. I know I am not alone in discovering that Boris Pasternak's translations of Shakespeare's tragedies (*Hamlet*, particularly) and of Goethe's *Faust* could make the originals themselves feel like translations – distant echoes of life-changing masterpieces. Pasternak, who Gustav Gustavovich knew personally, was one of the most famous of these translators. From the 1930s this was how the future Nobel Prize winner for literature made a living for himself and his family.

Marina Gustavovna was finishing school when her father was arrested in 1935 and given his first, initially lenient, sentence of five years' exile in Yeniseysk. Yeniseysk was a place in the Krasnoyarsk region of Siberia, to which exiles had been sent since well before the 1917 Revolution. From the Decembrists, the unsuccessful Russian revolutionaries of 1825, to the anti-tsarist dissenters and agitators of the early-twentieth century, they all came here. The Revolution and the subsequent purges, of course, had inflated the numbers of political exiles, as well as those deported on the basis of their undesirable ethnicities (Lithuanians and Germans, for instance). It also turned the town's much-admired cathedrals into boiler rooms, garages, factories and residential quarters for the special deportees. By the end of that year, in response to pleas from influential friends, Shpet was transferred to Tomsk, another Siberian town with a centuries-old tradition of exile. (One of the founding fathers of anarchism, Mikhail Bakunin, had been sent there in the nineteenth century.) But Tomsk had the distinction of being a university town, and Gustav Gustavovich could once again work. A good thing or a bad thing? 'If he had not been transferred,' says Marina Gustavovna, 'maybe he would have survived.' She was there in Yeniseysk visiting her exiled father when he learned of the transfer. She had just finished high school but could not get into a university course because of her father's arrest as an Enemy of the People. As Solzhenitsyn wrote in *The Gulag Archipelago*, the nearest relatives of political prisoners were not simply a pitiful handful of shocked women and kids – they were the wife of an *enemy* and the mother of an *enemy* and the children of an *enemy*, all *enemies* in their own right. 'And one who abetted an enemy was also an enemy. And one who continued his friendship with an enemy was also an enemy.'

And so it happened that Marina Gustavovna was next to her father as they travelled by sled from Yeniseysk to Tomsk, a journey of days through the snow-filled *taiga* (forest). The young woman's mother was terrified that father and daughter would freeze themselves to death, or at least catch a chronic illness, but somehow they both got through in one piece. Marina Gustavovna speaks of those few days on the way to Tomsk with unmistakable warmth. 'The wolves were howling, the little bells on the sleighs were ringing – it was absolutely wonderful,' she says. She was just a teenager then, the same age as I was when I came to Australia. Still essentially a girl. To this day Marina Gustavovna counts herself incredibly lucky to have been next to her father in that moment and as I begin to realise the depth of her loyalty to her family, a word comes into my head and stays there for the whole of our conversation – *nobility*. It occurs to me that Marina Gustavovna's family, from her father to her great-grandchildren, has not given this world a single plebeian soul. If we are to grasp anything of Marina Gustavovna's character, her pride in being next to her exiled father needs to be measured against the way in which the very notion of familial loyalty was under sustained and brutal attack in a world where survival demanded continual betrayal of yourself and those around you, where the fabric of so many families was soaked in blood and finally worn out by secrecy, lies and betrayals.

In 1937, the year of the Great Purge, Gustav Gustavovich was rearrested in Tomsk and this time given ten years without the right of correspondence, the ominous sentence that meant either camps (if you were lucky) or a secret execution. Thirty-seven was the worst year of Stalin's twenty-nine-year-old reign. About this reign, Solzhenitsyn wrote in *The Gulag Archipelago*, 'Just as there is no minute when people are not dying or being born, so there was no minute when people were not being arrested.' Those arrested were not limited to a particular social class or ethnicity: 'Any adult inhabitant of this country, from a collective farmer up to a member of the Politburo, always knew that it would take only one careless word or gesture and he would fly off irrevocably into the abyss.' Thirty-seven was the crescendo. Between 1937 and 1938 more than one and a half million people were arrested in the largest wave of mass repressions to engulf the Soviet Union. More than seven hundred thousand of them, including Gustav Gustavovich, were shot. For decades Marina Gustavovna and her family were told nothing about her father's fate. In 1956 his widow received a fake death certificate in which Shpet was shown to have died in Tomsk in 1940 from pneumonia. But it wasn't until 1989 that the opening of the State archives yielded the details of Gustav Shpet's death: 'Executed, 16 November 1937.'

To Billie, Marina Gustavovna is just an old woman – kind of interesting, warm and humorous, but a relic nonetheless. She jumps when Marina Gustavovna says in good English, 'I do not speak English.' Old people in Russia speaking English; for a moment, Billie is genuinely surprised. But then Marina Gustavovna confides that the key to foreign languages is to master just a phrase (*I do not speak English*; *je n'ai pas beaucoup de français*; *ich bedaure, mein Deutsch ist sehr schlecht*) and then everyone you encounter is likely to treat you with tolerance. So I cannot make the spell last for Billie. I want to whisper, 'This is not an ordinary woman, can't you see!' For a moment, in Marina Gustavovna's kitchen, the generational gap between my daughter and me feels like a dark, infinite abyss. No matter what I say in my pathos-filled, twentieth-century-history voice, Billie cannot see who is in front of her. In this apartment at the very heart of Moscow, metres away from the Mossovet and Satira Theatres and the Tchaikovsky Concert Hall, Billie sits down at the old piano. She plays what she usually plays – Tori Amos and Coldplay. How alien they sound inside these walls. Not in Adorno's 'no poetry after Auschwitz' kind of way, no. And not in a vulgar popular-culture way. It is just that here these songs, which evoke places and times that make no sense in the world of this apartment, sound thin, flat and inconsequential in the extreme, like a mobile ringtone underneath a cathedral dome. Momentarily I feel ashamed. Ashamed for both of us.

As Marina Gustavovna tells me the story of her father, I think of the words of Nadezhda Mandelstam: 'Anybody who breathes the air of terror is doomed, even if nominally he manages to save his life.' Marina Gustavovna does not look doomed to me at all, even though once her lungs must have been full of that air. I ask her what happened after her father's arrest: Did people cross the road to avoid meeting his family? Did the phone stop ringing? Did they feel, in Solzhenitsyn's words, 'in the hustle of a big city . . . as if they were in a desert'. I wait for Marina Gustavovna to start telling me the stories of silence and betrayal I have come to expect, but instead Marina Gustavovna looks surprised by my questions. No, she says, she does not remember being abandoned by those really close to them, nor does she remember her family walking away from other families with repressed members. (The Shpets's plight was hardly unique.) 'If someone were arrested,' Marina Gustavovna says, 'we would come to their place the next day. Of course, we wouldn't talk politics, but we would come.' What are these words worth? Actually, they are worth just about everything. Nadezhda Mandelstam, whose husband, the poet Osip Mandelstam, would outlive Gustav Gustavovich by a year and a month, wrote in the second book of her memoirs *Hope Abandoned*:

It is possible to tell thousands of stories about the fear sparked by the arrest of someone we knew, but I remember a nine-year-old girl who, upon hearing about the arrest of one of her parents' friends, approached the bookshelf in a businesslike manner, picked out several books belonging to the one arrested and tore out several sheets with his name. Those sheets were immediately thrown into the fire. This girl had seen how her parents would destroy all traces of such acquaintance [with those taken away] – letters, diary pages with the addresses and phone numbers.

Mandelstam could not keep the efficient, all-seeing nine-year-old girl out of her mind, believing later, as rumours suggested, that she grew up to become an informer. This girl, after all, was the rule, rather than an exception. When a member of a family was arrested, it was as if the whole family was infected by the Black Death. Any contact with the third party, however fleeting, could be fatal. In order to protect their own families, most people stayed away from those infected, ripping pages from their diaries and throwing them hurriedly into a fire. The best were tortured until the end of their days by the terrible choice between betraying their friends and protecting their immediate family. This is how the system worked at its peak: by sucking everyone into its circle of all-encompassing paranoia, fear, distrust and betrayal. Almost everyone.

Valeriya Mikhaylovna Gerlin is a friend of Marina Gustavovna and her family. She met and married her husband of forty-two years, the late Yuri Aleksandrovich Aikhenvald, in 1950, in the

Kazakhstan city of Karaganda, which Solzhenitsyn called 'one of the jewels' of the Gulag nation. Like Siberia, Kazakhstan served as one of the primary sites of camps and exile; it was for this reason both the newlyweds had been sent there. Karaganda was the location of Karlag, one of the country's biggest labour camps, which held around a million prisoners and exiles over the years and which, by the beginning of the 1950s, occupied an area as big as France. Yuri Aleksandrovich's grandfather, a well-known literary critic and philosopher, was on that very philosophers' ship that Gustav Gustavovich Shpet managed to escape. Yuri Aleksandrovich's father, an economist, was shot in 1941 as an Enemy of the People. Yuri Aleksandrovich himself, a poet, translator and literary critic, was only twenty-three when he was arrested for the second time in 1951. Following this arrest, he spent several years in a psychiatric institution, having faked his own mental illness (even writing bogus literary works that called for and celebrated the total destruction of humankind), convinced that his plea of insanity was the only way to survive. After the death of Stalin, Aikhenvald was rehabilitated and, alongside Valeriya Mikhaylovna, became a high school teacher of Russian language and literature in Moscow, both of them regarded by many of their students and contemporaries as teachers 'from God'. Both were forced from their teaching positions in 1968 for signing a petition.

In one of his most influential works, *Don Quixote on Russian Soil*, Aikhenvald tells a story about the close friend of his family by the name of Lyalya Breitman, whose family suffered terribly during the purges of the 1930s. One of Breitman's brothers died in the Russian Civil War after the Revolution and the other was already under arrest when in 1937 her husband, who had once held a very high position in the People's Commissariat of Finances, was arrested too. By the autumn of that year Lyalya was living with her aged mother, two of her young children, the two-year-old daughter of her sister who was a victim of the repressions and the four-year-old daughter of another sister who was in jail. One day Lyalya was visited by two young men from the NKVD (People's Commissariat of Internal Affairs, the forerunner of the KGB). They were, Aikhenvald writes, 'polite, with nicely combed hair and with "Ready for Work and Defense" badges on their jackets'. The polite young men took Lyalya's passport away and replaced it with tickets for the whole family on a train to Astrakhan. The train was to leave the following morning; the family had less than twenty-four hours to pack before their exile. The young men from NKVD warned Lyalya that if the family was not ready to go, they would be put on the train forcefully and without any luggage.

At this time, Aikhenvald writes:

The two-year-old Nastya was on her tippy-toes trying to get the big kettle with the boiling water from the top of the wardrobe; the four-year-old Bellochka was weeping loudly because the younger of Lyalya's sons was refusing to play dolls with her, while the older son was helping the grandma pack in fabric shopping bags multiple volumes of the *Great Soviet Encyclopedia* with their bright red, golden-lettered spines – the family had nothing to live on, and this magnificent edition was being taken to the second-hand book dealers.

The details of that day Lyalya Breitman remembered for as long as she lived, as you would remember 'the details of a nightmare that has tortured the person to such an extent that he could no longer wake up from it no matter how hard he tries'. Miraculously, the Breitman family managed to beg a favour from the wife of an old acquaintance of the family, Nikolai Yezhov, once a simple guy with eczema and a weakness for the poems of Esenin, but by 1934 head of the NKVD. He would give his surname to this darker than dark period, which would come to be known as the *Yezhovzhina*. But in this case, utterly uncharacteristically, perhaps for a moment 'softened' by his wife's tearful pleas on behalf of Lyalya, he spared the accused, allowing Lyalya Breitman's family to avoid exile.

The scene that Aikhenvald paints was replicated in countless households, minus the miraculous ending. The Soviet century was the century of mass relocations, deportations and exile. Whole peoples were uprooted and families were systematically torn apart. 'What could people take in memory of their past?' writes historian Irina Sherbakova:

What could they save and keep, these special deportees, Gulag prisoners, evacuees, and those who were bombed or forcefully taken to Germany? What could they take except their photographs and documents that survived by miracle? What family relics are kept in millions of Russian families that had '24 hours to pack' and were shipped to Siberia, what valuables? A Zinger sewing machine, a copper mortar . . .

In her Moscow apartment Marina Gustavovna takes me and Billie to one of the glassed shelves and points to the little doll sitting on it. 'This is my mother's doll,' she says. 'It was headless for a while, but we have found the head, sewn it back on, got the doll sorted out. I made a dress for her myself.' I cannot hide my disbelief. In the course of the twentieth century, family as an idea, an institution, a dominant form of human sociality, was to be made completely subservient to the State if not, for all intents and purposes, redundant. The heirlooms of individual family traditions, the objects and stories passed from genera-tion to generation, were meant to be replaced by the uniform mythology in which Stalin, or Lenin, was the patriarch presid-ing over a large family of Soviet people. Yet this doll, which physically connects five generations in the Shpet family, from Marina Gustavovna's mother to her great-grandchildren, tells a different story. And in this story familial ties not only survive but also prevail over all kinds of pseudo-communities meant to eventually eliminate them – from the collective farm to the ubiquitous Nation itself.

As I speak to Marina Gustavovna and Valeriya Mikhaylovna in October 2008, all across Russia, State and regional archives are closing their doors to independent historians. Access to invalu-able archival documents is disappearing in front of researchers' very eyes. School textbooks are being rewritten. Independent historical organisations such as the Memorial society are raided, kept under constant surveillance and repeatedly threatened. Historians are beginning to be arrested (first were journalists, now it is historians' turn, then writers, right?). There is no question of the current government's apparent determination to rehabilitate the Soviet regime by all means necessary. Yet again history is asked to service the ideological needs of the

State. ('We can do it the easy way or the hard way.') And, all the while, the clock of historical truth is ticking madly as the last of the eyewitnesses of Gulags and Stalinism die of old age, one by one.

As I speak to Marina Gustavovna and Valeriya Mikhaylovna, the government-owned television network Russia Channel television broadcasts the final shortlist from a nationwide search for the historical figure who best represents the Russia of today. This program, *Name of Russia*, conducted under the auspices of the Russian Academy of Sciences (no less!) and modelled on BBC-TV's *100 Greatest Britons*, started out with five hundred potential candidates. Now I watch the announcement of the final twelve with growing astonishment. Two literary giants (Pushkin and Dostoyevsky), one medieval leader (Nevsky), one nineteenth-century general (Suvorov), one lonely scientific maverick (Mendeleev, of periodic table fame), four Russian monarchs (Peter the Great, Elizabeth II – the only woman, Ivan the Terrible and Alexander II), one pre-revolutionary statesman (Stolypin, prime minister from 1906 to 1911) and, among this not-too-alarming populist mishmash, Vladimir Lenin and Joseph Stalin.

I watch the program dedicated to Stalin wondering how on earth his inclusion in this list could be justified. After all, we are dealing with the country's mainstream institutions – Russia's major television channel and its most eminent academic body – not some lunatic fringe à la Zhirinovsky. (In a comparable contest in Germany, no Third Reich figures were allowed to be nominated because they had long since been recognised as criminals. Not so in Russia.) The program presents Stalin as a flawed and ambiguous character (*flawed* must be the euphemism of choice for the early twenty-first century). Yes, viewers are told, the man was known for occasionally pillaging and plundering, but let us not forget that he also turned a backward, agrarian and deeply dysfunctional country into an industrialised superpower. He was making an enormous omelette, so can we please stop counting the broken eggs? Then, of course, the extra-heavy weaponry is wheeled out – the Stalin-led Soviet victory in World War II. As achievements go, you can't beat stopping Hitler from enslaving Europe and wiping the Soviet nation off the surface of the earth.

I am back in Australia by the time the results of the competition are announced – Alexander Nevsky, Russia's legendary medieval political and military leader is officially 'The Name of Russia'. He stands for a 'strong' and 'victorious' country, feared by its neighbours, intent on consolidation, but he belongs safely in the distant past. Stalin comes third. (Strong rumours suggest that the organisers had resorted to tampering with the votes to avoid the scandalous possibility that the Soviet leader would finish at the top of the list.) You could argue that such contests unleash the lowest common denominator – of course they do – but they also cannot fail but capture the Zeitgeist. In Britain, *100 Greatest Britons* was won – predictably enough – by Winston Churchill, who beat out William Shakespeare, Charles Darwin and Princess Diana, among other candidates. But the millions of votes Russians cast for Stalin would have simply been inconceivable in the late 1980s and early 1990s. By 2008, seventeen years after the collapse of the Soviet Union, things had clearly changed.

★

In *Hope Abandoned*, Nadezhda Mandelstam tells a story about her Western friend who after the death of Stalin said, 'Any one of our poets would agree to be one of your poets.' 'With all that it entails?' Mandelstam asked in return. 'Yes,' the friend replied, 'poetry is serious business where you are.' Oh how Mandelstam deplored these words. How angry they made her feel. How on earth could the ordeal her contemporaries had to go through be enviable? 'I do not envy a dog run over by a truck or a cat thrown from the tenth floor by a thug.' The suffering did not elevate, it stripped humanity right off people. I do not envy Marina Gustavovna, God forbid, though I admire her intensely. I do not envy Valeriya Mikhaylovna Gerlin. Between them, these two women have seen and heard just about everything possible – one met her husband in a psychiatric hospital, the other sat next to her father on a sledge that was carrying him from one place of exile to another where ultimately he would be shot. I do not want to claim their stories, what happened to them and their families, what happened to millions in the country where I was born, as stories of redemption. They are not and never will be.

I write for a different reason: after his expulsion from the Soviet Union in 1974, two decades after the death of Stalin, one of my favourite poets Joseph Brodsky was never able to see his father and mother again. Alexander Brodsky and his wife, Maria, died in Leningrad, banned from travelling to the West to see their son. In his 1986 essay dedicated to their memory, Brodsky wrote:

I write this in English because I want to grant them a margin of freedom: the margin whose width depends on the number of those who may be willing to read this. I want Maria Volpert and Alexander Brodsky to acquire reality under 'a foreign code of conscience', I want English verbs of motion to describe their movements. This won't resurrect them, but English grammar may at least prove to be a better escape route than the Russian from the chimneys of the State crematorium.

I too want English verbs, English adjectives and nouns to describe Marina Gustavovna and others like her (although there are no others like her). I too want English words and phrases to express out loud, for myself, for Billie and her brother, Miguel, and for those who may read these pages, my wonderment at how it can be that after everything she has been through, everything she has seen, Marina Gustavovna remains one of the least cynical people I have ever met. 'Human freedom,' Yuri Aikhenvald once wrote, 'does not consist in the choice of an action, but first and foremost, in the choice of a reality.' I read these words and I cannot think of anything I could possibly add to them.

5

MOSCOW METRO

THERE IS A BLIND woman in the Metro. When I say Metro, I want you to read between the lines. Don't worry so much about the magisterial architecture and the famous Art Deco embellishments. Don't think about Stalin in 1941, as the German Army was getting dangerously close, gathering his generals at Mayakovskaya Station to commemorate the anniversary of the 1917 Revolution. What you should imagine is a collection of people in an enclosed space, who by virtue of their sheer numbers, their intersecting trajectories, and their readiness to squash and be squashed, have merged into a cyclonic wave, Category 5 or higher. Sometimes the wave just throbs, sometimes it crashes and breaks, but only one thing happens to those in its way.

The Moscow Times tells us that the city has some thirty-five thousand residents for every kilometre of rail track, a figure equalled only in Tokyo. This is three times the number of people per kilometre of track in Paris and close to double the figures for London and New York. In Tokyo attendants have to push people onto the trains. In Moscow people do it for themselves. It is amazing just how quickly you abandon your genteel manners and start throwing your elbows and chest around. I thought I might have to give Billie a talk about how there is no shame in pushing, how in fact the whole system is held together by everyone agreeing tacitly to push and, yes, there is a certain etiquette to it, like asking, 'Are you getting off at the next?' before forcing your way to the doors, but how, in the end, it is all OK. But Billie has no need of this little motherly chat or for my permission. She just does it like a pro, totally unperturbed, and she has a natural advantage – that teenage facial expression in which boredom wrestles with contempt, and, by God, it makes her look right at home.

The blind woman wears dark sunglasses and has a stick in her hands. She is standing on the opposite platform to us, perilously close to the edge. How did she get inside the station past the violently flapping doors that slap you, the seeing one, straight in the face unless your outstretched arm is travelling well ahead of your body? Was she helped through the size-eight gap between the turnstiles by one of those invariably female attendants deep in middle age, the ones I have never seen do anything but emit shrill cries at the sight of young men jumping over the barriers? And what about those escalator journeys, the length of an average act of intercourse, how did she make it through one of them?

Our train departs; the last we see of the woman is her back

turned towards the track. She is standing quite still; no one comes near her. It seems almost suicidal for her to be there all alone, as if she were standing at the edge of a cliff. There is a village not far from Moscow, purpose-built for the blind in the glory days of the USSR, but now in total decay, along with the great Socialist dream of engineering self-sufficiency for the disabled. Living in the ruins of the Empire is hard enough for people with eyes, legs or arms intact, but for those whose bodies have failed them in some way, recent history must feel like one day's journey into night. A few stops later, a legless veteran of some no longer identifiable war is pushing his way through the crowd of legs on something resembling a cheap skateboard, his stumps wrapped tightly in layers of plastic. In keeping with its survival of the fittest philosophy, Moscow Metro has virtually no lifts and no ramps for the disabled. This man, who was once a warrior – or at least a hired gun – is now a beggar, although no one is giving him anything, not on our watch anyway. Able-bodied Russia pretends she does not see the second Russia, even though the population of the latter is probably close to seventeen million. 'The disabled are citizens of Russia,' says writer Anton Borisov (paralysed since childhood, he knows what he is talking about), 'but not of the majestic oil-gas-nuclear-cosmic nation like the rest of the Russian population. No, the Russian disabled are citizens of another Russia – impoverished, worn-out, tear-stained and humiliated.'

In the underground interchanges, the kilometres of tunnels that connect the city's train systems, women in long, bulky coats display wind-up toys. Cats chase their own tails. Squirrels and bunnies hop around. Plastic soldiers perform a commando crawl with their rifles at the ready. Selling toys here is like putting out a spread in the middle of a six-lane highway. This is not commerce, this is not doing the best with what you have – this is desperation. An old woman in a headscarf, an archetypal figure, Russia's equivalent of a semi-naked African child covered in flies, re-sells newspapers a hundred metres from the official kiosks. Her profit margin must be in the domain of nanomathematics. I wonder whether she is doing this so as not to beg.

As we shuffle along the crowded corridors, Billie's eyes almost pop out. Close to the exit, a woman is holding a hand-written sign: 'Diploma, Degrees, Certificates', ready to fold her business at a moment's notice. Forgery is rampant in Russia, but it is not legal. Not yet. You can buy anything here, I explain to Billie, a degree in Medicine, Architecture or Science, school diplomas, work history, medical certificates. In the West education is for sale too, more often than not through online virtual institutions, which promote their wares by urging us to 'get a degree without those hundreds of hours wasted studying, attending lectures, doing assignments'. In Russia, you still get direct-to-the-public forgery so, if you are lucky, you will deal with Syoma or Igor, not some world-class university registered to a PO box in Columbus, Ohio. How reassuring that there are still real people you can deal with.

The Metro is swaddled with kiosks purveying everything from pirate DVDs to bread, theatre tickets, books, underwear and the sort of jewellery that falls apart within ten minutes of purchase. After a series of suicide bombings by Chechen terrorists a few years ago, then President Putin tried to outlaw these mercantile dens of iniquity, claiming that they made it virtually impossible to maintain control and security across the city's transport network. Clearly, his plan did not work. The kiosks are everywhere, alive and well. As to control and security, they are more often than not subverted not by terrorists, but by appointed enforcers of the law – the police themselves.

In 2004, a nineteen-year-old student was travelling on the Metro when he witnessed a young woman rather crudely apprehended by policemen. Some newspapers subsequently claimed that the woman was his friend, others that she was a stranger, but the point was that German Galdetsky saw with his own eyes that the woman was taken away for no reason. Outraged, he decided to intervene. Thanks to Galdetsky's insistence, the young woman was allowed to go, but it turned out that while in the hands of the police she had been sexually harassed and threatened. Galdetsky, who could not believe that something like that could happen in broad daylight in the heart of his city's train system, embarked on an independent investigation. Which is how someone not yet in their twenties came to uncover a ring of Moscow policemen allegedly sexually assaulting young women travelling on the Metro. Unsurprisingly, after he had gathered a sufficient body of evidence to make his accusations public, Galdetsky was shot in the head by unknown gunmen; miraculously, he survived.

That same year a young man from Central Asia was shot in the face by a Metro policeman, who had stopped him for trying to jump over turnstiles. That the police in Russia are at least as dangerous as criminals is a well-known fact and, on so many levels, the Metro is a perfect place for the exercise of this institutionalised lawlessness. On reflection, it is hardly surprising that Billie and I would have the first and biggest fight of our trip right there.

★

Travelling inevitably involves friction. The rubber hits the road, and generates heat and aggravation. Given that Billie is a girl who can't shut up, and that her mother is only marginally more restrained, it is not surprising that the question of speaking and not speaking emerges early in the trip as the main source of friction between us. Billie could rally troops with her English, but her Russian will not get her out of a bus. While she understands pretty much everything, her active vocabulary is tiny, and her accent may be charming but it grates on even Billie's musical ear. Furthermore, in Russia there are all kinds of unwritten rules about children taking part in adult conversations. 'Do not answer when grown-up officials ask us questions,' I repeat time and time again. Customs and immigration officials, police, train conductors, Metro attendants. 'But what if I know the answer?' says my truly Australian child.

'It is not about who knows the answer, Billie, please, let me handle the officials. And one more thing – don't speak when we hail a car so they won't smell any foreign blood and won't feel tempted to rip us off.'

'What am I supposed to do then?'

'Why don't you listen to your iPod? It may be better than pretending that you are mute or, even more unbelievably, very shy when it comes to strangers. On the bright side, you can speak on overnight trains. We cannot hide who you are for twelve hours at a stretch.'

It does not take long for Billie to feel overwhelmed. A few days in Moscow and she wants to go home. I do not quite know what I expected. 'I always feel uncomfortable being with people I don't know well who all speak Russian,' she tells me, 'but the whole country . . . the whole country speaks Russian . . .'

Well, yes.

Today's trouble starts when Billie starts acting as if she does not know me. When I challenge her, she explodes. 'Everyone on these trains is looking at us, Mum. Can't you see? We look like freaks to them.'

'No one gives a shit, Billie, come on! You are exaggerating.'

'Mum, I want to go home. I want to be in a country where everyone speaks English, where I don't feel like a total idiot, like an idiotic foreigner.'

'But, Billie, if we stay away from countries where we look like idiotic foreigners, the whole world will become so unbelievably small.'

'I don't care. I want go home. I am not ready for this trip. I don't want to go into the Metro again. I hate Moscow. I hate being here.'

At this moment, I could add 'Me too.' For some reason that I cannot quite articulate, Moscow, a city I have been to at least half-a-dozen times, feels distant and frenetic to me on this trip, but if I make any concession to Billie now what will become of the rest of our trip?

'Moscow is an amazing place, Billie, and we haven't even scratched the surface. Once we are out of the Metro, you'll feel fine, trust me.'

Billie's voice goes up a few thousand decibels. Her face is getting red and starting to crumple.

'Mum, if I get lost, I'll never find my way out. I don't know where we live. I don't know who to ask for help, or even *what* to ask them. I don't know how this Metro works. My mobile is not working. I cannot speak or read Russian. I want to go home. You are driving me insane. I want to see Nanna. I want to see my friends. You are making me crazy.'

She strides out ahead of me, as if wanting to get lost in the crowd of commuters, as if daring me to let her go. I run after her, totally dispensing with my parental doctrine of non-appeasement, begging for some temporary peace, at least while we are Metro-bound. This is not one of the worst fights we have ever had, but it is a real blow to my fantasies of a superhuman bond forged between us on this trip, of shared revelations, synchronised cathartic tears and previously unheard-of levels of mutual acceptance. Of course, our row feels that much more debilitating because we are away from home, away from separate rooms we can storm into, away from spontaneously erupting ceasefires and all those invisible, unsung technologies of defusion that fill any home space inhabited for long enough. We have no choice but to stick together for the rest of the day, wisely keeping any possible eye contact or verbal exchanges to the bare minimum.

When we fight, Billie and I are like two cocks, throwing all we have at each other. We may start out slowly, quietly, whispering and whizzing, but invariably we end up sacrificing discretion and hurling words at each other in measurable decibels. After our fights, especially the recent ones marked by new levels of intensity, I often think (somewhat despairingly) of anthropologist Clifford Geertz's famous description of a Balinese cockfight: 'Every people, the proverb has it, loves its own form of violence . . . its look, its uses, its force, its fascination.' This strikes me as very accurate, this idea of controlled eruptions of violence as an opportunity to reflect hard on the stakes and undercurrents involved in sustaining any intimate or social relationship. It's not as though Billie and I stage our fights – you need only see us in action to dispense with any such notion – but I do think our fights allow us to witness something fundamental and true about our relationship as mother and daughter. Because our tempers are evenly matched and Billie has never been really scared of me, neither threats nor reasoning usually works for us. We do not necessarily fight dirty, but it is rare for us to arrive at a clean resolution. Rather we work through escalation to explosion and then, depending on the scale of the damage done, to silence, remorse or, just occasionally, liberating laughter. Our fights lay bare not the social conventions that encourage our co-dependency and make us behave in a particular way towards each other, but the real, clumpy, sticky glue that holds us together.

Why do we go to the Metro (other than because the traffic at street level is ten times worse and, quite frankly, other options are too expensive)? Do we go to learn what humanity looks like in bulk, bottled up and in a desperate rush somewhere? Back in Melbourne after our trip, I read Billie's neat summation of our time in Moscow leading up to the fight:

I have a question, please raise your hand if you enjoy being dragged after your mum through houses of people who you never knew existed, pushed into trains with impossible volumes of people and kicked out of them, walking in endless circles trying to find a florist and many other excruciating activities whilst desperate to eat and rest. If you answered yes, you would have thoroughly enjoyed my life in Moscow. But I, unfortunately, am a completely different person and would have rather cleaned cow droppings for a year than have endured what happened.

Could I imagine when I planned this trip that Billie and I would come undone so quickly, that a few too many hours in the Moscow Metro would rattle her to the extent that she would be dreaming of cow droppings? And if I had any intimation of the speed with which our solidarity would disintegrate, what exactly would I have done differently? For me, Billie was always the non-optional part of this trip. If I longed to make clashing or at least disparate parts of my life feel closely and meaningfully connected, then the work of connecting made little sense without her. I needed her to come with me, for better or for worse, not simply because I wanted her to know where her mother came from, but because I wanted her to feel, alongside me, the pull of our family history, to size up for herself the true measurements of our past, or perhaps of any past – its depth, its reach and its towering presence in the present.

6

GLUBINKA

TOWARDS THE END OF our time in Moscow, Billie and I take a train south-east to visit a young friend – another Katya. When Billie and I first met her in Melbourne four years ago, the eleven-year-old Katya was in town on some kind of exchange with a humanitarian flavour. She was taken in by an Australian family with several kids of their own. I knew the mother and, by all accounts, the family were genuinely nice and hospitable, and just as genuinely clueless about what it meant to host a person from a world that shared little beyond the basics with their own default one. It should be mentioned too that the girl came from a culture that did not exactly inspire confidence, having all but cornered the market (Nigerians, eat your heart out!) on bridal and internet scams. To the host family it had seemed self-evident just what they needed to do with this scrawny, shy Russian girl with little English, who came from a small town with an unpronounceable name and a population not significantly larger than that of Geelong. Feed her, buy her some clothes with a generous helping of glitter and show her the wonders of Western civilisation, starting with Chadstone Shopping Centre – a no-brainer really.

For her part, Katya was meant to be grateful, easygoing and visibly bursting with excitement. And it was very much in her nature to be just that – to show deep and instant recognition of any expression of genuine kindness from others – but Chadstone outings made her cry. Family barbecues and Monopoly face-offs made her cry too. The host family grew more and more uneasy about her stay, unsure why their good deed was unravelling in front of them. Whichever way you look at it, it was not their fault that they mistook Katya for someone she most certainly was not. How were they meant to know?

It was at this point that the mother asked me, as the only Russian speaker of her acquaintance, to talk to Katya so that she could explain her sadness in her native tongue. And this is how it happened. First we talked on the phone. Then we met. Then Katya moved in with me and Billie at my parents' two-bedroom unit in suburban Murrumbeena, which was already stretched to the limit by our own temporary occupation. Billie and I were there because I was on my own and trying to write my first book. We needed all the help we could get. And so did Katya. On reflection, it may be that Katya was the closest I had ever come to love at first sight (not counting Billie and Miguel, of course). At eleven she was clear, poised and luminous – already fully formed as a person. She continuously emitted warmth, yet she needed warmth too, a lot of it, constantly circulating, flowing back and forth. And she had the most affecting smile, gentle and reserved, which she never deployed to get her own way or to cover up things. That was what struck me most, how she did not seem in the least bit interested in temporarily cuddling up to people coming into her orbit. She felt deeply and understood loyalty. And this is how she loved us, almost from the very beginning, even from the time before she came to live with us.

Young Katya was a competitive swimmer in a nation famous for its coaching philosophy built around an unquestioned belief in spilling the blood of the new blood. The minds and bodies of the next generation of athletes needed to be ripped apart and then pieced back together by the coaching staff, in accordance with strict specifications. Katya seemed lodged deeply inside that system, training every morning before school, yet she had neither the skin of an elephant nor the rigid, efficient self-centredness of many young athletes. However her coaches tried to mould her, there were huge chunks of her they did not get to. It was particularly clear when you looked in her eyes. It was not just me, my mum could see it too.

While Katya was crying, other girls who came to Australia as part of the same delegation were busy fleecing their host families with varying degrees of skill and forward planning. You did not have to look very deep into their eyes to see, beaming straight back at you, itemised product wishlists. These girls too were homesick, and I'm sure some of them felt genuinely warm and attached to their hosts but, unlike Katya, they were on a mission, not prepared to leave Australia empty-handed. To do so would have been the height of extra-moronic idiocy.

Who on earth could blame them for growing up with street smarts the size of one of those double-door fridges they advertise on television ('Life's good') or for being spurred on by a piercing sense of desperation and injustice to fight for their slice of an imaginary cake resplendent in its coveted sweetness (or at least for their share of crumbs)? They all came from provincial Russia where, after the collapse of the Soviet Union, wages routinely went unpaid for many months, drinking started the moment that shops' doors creaked open and, typically, one large industrial enterprise provided the livelihoods of most of the population. In this sense, many of their hometowns were both one-horse *and* one-company towns. It is not hard to imagine what happened to them if the industry that fed them imploded, as it did post-Communism, more often than not in a blink of an eye, leaving thousands unemployed and unemployable. During our trip I asked my cousin Marina in Dnepropetrovsk about all the people fishing on the famous river of Dnepr, wondering if fishing (even in the cold autumn months) had become the city's favourite recreational pastime. It turned out that several plants had just closed down. And Dnepropetrovsk is not a small place by any stretch of the imagination, but the third largest city in Ukraine with a population of over one million. This is what can happen to major industrial hubs when, almost overnight, an empire is no more.

So far be it from me to speak ill of those girls who came to Australia with Katya. They lived in the shadow of big cities that sucked most of the air out of the atmosphere – Moscow, of course, being the biggest and the greediest of them all. Should you make your way out from the urban giants and middle-weights, even one hundred or two hundred kilometres, the irony of Moscow being considered for several years the most expensive city in the world would acquire a bitterness almost impossible to shake off.

But I want to go back to the contents of Katya's eyes, because there was something in them I could not walk past. People often call this quality 'innocence'. I have my doubts about this word, for it can sound flimsy and circumstantial, as if it refers essentially to the very top coat of paint that with time will inevitably get stripped off. But what if it is not the varnish, but something underneath, much closer to the core? Something that determined, for one, the degree to which Katya could not be bought or sold. In the amount of time that has passed since our first meeting in Melbourne, many people – adults, not merely shape-shifting adolescents – could routinely forget to love and remember each other. But Katya would not let it happen. She loved and remembered us with the kind of fidelity that marks our first and, often the deepest, real friendships. Being in Russia and not seeing her was not an option.

Kursk Station – or Kursky Vokzal, as it is known in Russian – is the largest of Moscow's nine railway stations, the so-called southern gateway, the eternally pumping 'Ukrainian artery', able to accommodate eleven thousand travellers at any one time. For decades, this was my family's 'home' station – the site at which we were decanted into the national capital, and from which we departed back to Kharkov. It was immortalised by Venedikt Erofeev in his prose poem *Moscow to the End of the Line* (*Moskva–Petushki* in Russian), one of the undisputed classics of twentieth-century Russian-language literature. Written in 1969, the poem was published outside the Soviet Union and circulated by samizdat until at the end of the 1980s it appeared, abridged and significantly distorted, in a Russian journal with the memorable name of *Sobriety and Culture*. You would be hard-pressed to imagine a more fantastic launching pad for this long-banned work, since its protagonist is always drinking, looking for a drink or nursing an intense yet gratifying hangover.

The protagonist, Venichka (a diminutive of the poet's given name), inevitably ends up at Kursk Station every time he traverses the capital – sober, drunk or desperately hung-over. 'Go on, anywhere. It's all the same where. Even if you turn left, you'll end up at the Kursk Station; or straight, all the same, the Kursk Station. Therefore, turn right, so that you'll get there for sure. Oh, vanity.' It is from there Venichka takes a train to Petushki, where his woman and child are waiting for him on the platform. A small town in the provinces, Petushki is his Arcadia. ('Perhaps there is such a thing as original sin, but no one ever feels burdened in Petushki.') This rail journey is the centrepiece of the poem, for en route Venichka drinks unimaginable quantities of richly varied alcohol (unimaginable to Western readers, at least), showing equal appreciation for aftershave and skin lotions. As he drinks, he holds sparklingly intelligent and lyrical conversations, primarily with the voices in his head, which come to him as angels or the Lord God himself (and this in Soviet Russia, the biggest nation of atheists on earth. I hope you are getting the picture). Venichka's dialogues and monologues are pure pastiche, laden with allusions and quotations bent out of shape or artfully fabricated. He draws inspiration from anywhere and everywhere: Marxist–Leninist tracts, the Bible, classical mythology, Dostoyevsky, Pushkin and Shakespeare.

Venichka is not the stock Russian alcoholic as understood in the West. He drinks not for pleasure but only in order to be able to reside in this world; as the philosopher Michael Epstein says, 'like a sober man, but one who is sober from the other end, not before drinking, but after it'. *Sober from the other end* – exactly. There is, of course, as Epstein points out, a quality in Venichka of the Holy Fool, a type dear to the Russian heart, with an angelic-ness 'that does not rise above the world in white garments but flips head over heels down into the most indecent gutter, drowning in the charms of this earth'. If we are to not dismiss out of hand the idea of the *mysterious Russian soul* (philosopher Nikolay Berdyaev wrote a whole treatise on the subject before he was put on the infamous philosophers' ship), if we are to forgive its messianic overtones, its exaggerated claims of unique spirituality reared on suffering, its infectious hyperbole (I'm thinking specifically of Churchill's 'Russia is a riddle wrapped in a mystery inside an enigma'), then perhaps Venichka can be our spiritual guide to it:

> Oh, if only the entire world, if everyone in the world were like me right now – timid and shy and unsure of everything: of himself, of the seriousness of his place under the heavens – how good it would be! No enthusiasts, no heroic feats, no obsessions! – a universal faint-heartedness.

Now that going to Kursky Vokzal has reminded me of Erofeev's poem, I cannot get it out of my mind. In the end, what is most affecting about *Moscow to the End of the Line* is its tone, which is

not irony, not parody, not black absurdist humour and not car-
nivalesque. Epstein describes it as 'trans-irony'. 'If irony inverts
the sense of a straightforward, serious word,' he writes, 'then
trans-irony inverts the sense of irony itself, resurrecting seriousness,' but a different kind of seriousness, unchained from
literalness and linearity, from pathos and heroic profundity.

In Melbourne, before we came away on our trip, I found
myself thinking a lot about irony, because it seems the default
register of so many fictional and non-fictional contemporary
accounts of modern-day Russia, most particularly from expat
writers of my generation (yes, myself included). Irony also
makes an appearance when the quality media of Russia find
themselves engaged in the task of reflection and commentary.
I remember an article in *Kommersant*, a daily newspaper, which
responded to a survey showing that fifty-four per cent of Britons were dissatisfied with life in Tony Blair's Britain by inviting
the dissatisfied to emigrate to provincial Russia. 'In any central
Russian district, life, by British standards, is unseemingly cheap
and remarkably laid back. By 11 am most of the working population is becoming "traditionally" relaxed.' As to the weather,
'Thanks to global warming this difficulty will solve itself.'
I laughed when I read it; the amount of irony that could be
squeezed out of the premise was infinite. Oh, the hilarity of
sending all those stockbrokers from the Home Counties to the
desolate, filthy, ignorant, alcohol-infused Russian provinces,
from which every person, dog and cat with half a brain is always
trying to escape. I laughed until I felt sick of my laughter.

But something is wrong when thinking becomes unthinkable without irony. And it is too easy to be ironic about
provincial Russia. Here, and in the former Soviet republics,

province has always been a culturally complicated place, imagined with equal fervour as the epitome of decay, bigotry and soul-gnawing hopelessness, *and*, at the same time, as the true haven of human decency, kindness and spiritual authenticity. This duality is hardly unique, of course; just about everywhere the periphery is demonised and deemed valorous all at once. Yet I love the way the somewhat disparaging English-language 'backwater' becomes in Russian the unexpectedly tender '*glubinka*' – the diminutive for depth.

Furthermore, now that we are going to Katya, being ironic about where she lives feels somehow underhanded, like I am withholding something. I cannot do that. And so as we get closer and closer to our destination of Stary Oskol I remind myself of Erofeev's voice, in which irony is not eliminated but co-opted into a new and precious kind of seriousness.

Erofeev, who drank like a fish himself and died from throat cancer barely a fifty-year-old man, became indistinguishable in the popular imagination from his most famous protagonist. So much so that when a monument was built to commemorate the anniversary of the writer's birth, it was a memorial to Venichka the protagonist, not to Venedikt the author. I have read about the monument but, despite craning my neck as Billie and I run to catch our train, I cannot see any sign of it in the square in front of the station. I learn later that the railway authorities, fearing quite rightly that the monument would become a pilgrimage site for booze artists and poetry-reading radicals, would not agree to its erection there. And so the monument stands now in no-man's-land, neither near Kursk Station nor in Petushki, tucked away in an obscure Moscow square.

★

Dear Diary,

My first trip on an overnight train released all of my homesickness and though I was tired, I was very happy. I felt so calm and serene. I laughed at the stupidest stuff.

After our first few days in Moscow, I have been starting to dread this train journey. Gone is my conviction, previously unshakable despite being untested in battle, that Billie would love overnight trains, if not as much as I do then enough to let them wash over her and give her a much-needed taste of stillness in the middle of constant movement. For months I have been fantasising about Russian train journeys, the sense they give of travelling in a dream. But as we clawed our way through the Metro to Kursk Station at the perfect median point of the after-work peak, I felt little but apprehension. Because if Billie hates trains too, we might as well go home.

Fotunately, we find ourselves alone in a four-berth cabin. This is a real blessing. The train to Katya is the height of luxury, at least by my standards. God knows, it is much more expensive than I had counted on – we are paying more for it than for two Melbourne–Sydney airfares. We could have gone much cheaper, of course – could have bought tickets to the *platzkartnuy vagon*, where there are no doors and the four bunks in the doorless compartment are complemented by two additional bunks in the corridor. The money saved would not have been worth it. No doors meant total absence of privacy and I had to be careful to ration Billie's culture shock. But to find ourselves with an entire cabin to ourselves is unprecedented, undreamed of; I don't think I have ever travelled like that in my life. We wait until the train starts moving to make absolutely sure there is no last-minute arrival knocking at our door, no over-perfumed bleached blonde, no greying man with a fried drumstick in a foil wrap. And then comes a jolt and we are off. Within minutes Billie's face begins to relax, her glow and soft-ness returns. My daughter's face is no longer the cold grey of antagonism and discomfort; it is pink, flushed and excited. And so, all of a sudden, out of the blue, we begin to talk and laugh. And the more we talk, the less we need to talk, the more lan-guage itself – thick, curvaceous, delivered first in outbursts and then in a continuous, unstoppable flow – becomes our ether. And in this ether that dreaded feeling of observing each other from the opposite sides of the barricades seems, for the moment at least, to have dissolved without a trace.

I think I can see Katya. The train has not stopped yet, and Billie and I are at the window, our eyes pulling us forward, willing us to arrive before the train does. At first Katya is a moist patch of condensed air, then she is a tiny square of blurred colour the size of an acid trip, and then finally she is there human-sized – the girl we said goodbye to four years ago, only now in a taller body with long golden hair so clean it shines through the permanently dirty window glass. When I imagined this moment – our reunion against all odds – for all the violins in my head, there was also a fear there that I could not quite shake off. The fear was of Katya (yes, even of our Katya) becoming unambiguously a product of her place and time, a girl in a tight synthetic skin, all made-up and clued-up. There were so many young women out there like that: shrewd, strategic and categorically down-to-earth. Perhaps it was the down-to-earth bit – a consensual, wholehearted cohabitation with one's limited and limiting circumstances – that scared me the most.

I knew, of course, that the distance covered from the ages of eleven to fifteen was so vast that there was no telling who would be waiting for us on the platform. Still, growing up and growing into some kind of a prefabricated biography template were two different things, and observing the latter is something I have always found to be one of the saddest things in the world. No matter how powerless and dependent on the mercy and decency of others they might be, children belong to the world of 'who is to say', of 'stranger things have happened', of 'wait and see'. They are the heralds of the great indeterminacy of life. But what a struggle it is to retain a sense of your future not being foreclosed by your proletarian suburb, the school you were sent to, the idiocy of losing your virginity to an arse-hole, your father and mother splitting up at the worst possible moment or dragging themselves through the fog of a shared existence in your name. The script does not really matter. So what if you are the golden child of a wholesome, well-adjusted family in which everyone is still married to everyone else, and your apartment always smells like apple pie and sounds like a philharmonic hall. You still have to fight for your life not to become the sum total of your circumstances, not to follow the path laid out, stone by stone, by other people's hands.

Hugs, more hugs: we are on the platform now. I can see it there straight away, even before she says anything, even before she smiles – Katya's luminosity, quiet and peerless. Nothing has changed. It is all still there. What an antidote it is to the closet cynicism masquerading as common sense, that tells us not to get carried away with our leaps of feelings and faith, to do risk-assessment before getting on planes and trains to see people who may turn out to be figments of our imagination. I turn to Katya's mum, Nina, who is visibly moved by the great cocktail of tears and intertwined arms, and hug her. We are two strangers hugging, two adult women who have no idea what the other one is really like and whether we will like each other at all. But there is no sizing up, no checking each other out, only an unspoken exchange of gratitude. In the space of that hug, Nina thanks me for stepping in when she was too far away to take care of her daughter and I, just as silently, thank her for the way she brought Katya up.

We drive through town to Katya's flat, and it is on Katya's soft bed, within minutes of our arrival, that Billie has her sweetest sleep yet. Throughout our stay Nina serves us the kind of food that requires the very best ingredients, hours of preparation and meticulous planning. This food is a sign that in this home we are guests of honour. Both Billie and I are relieved by the absence of must-see attractions. Stary Oskol: founded in 1593; powered by the mining, metallurgical and smelting industries; current population about two hundred and fifty thousand; average age thirty-five. For an outsider, a double outsider really – an expat urbanite – it is hard to stave off depression while walking around such a place.

Evgeniy Grishkovets, a much-loved contemporary play-wright, himself a boy from the provinces, says that these small Russian towns are all essentially the same. He has been in very many of them; he knows what he is talking about:

Sometimes you would walk along the main street of such a town and all of a sudden you'd catch yourself looking into one first-floor window, and it is clear that in front of you is a kitchen. And the curtains are this colour . . . and wallpaper . . . and lampshade – orange, plastic – and near the window is the back of a man . . . And you know everything already . . . what they are talking about, what is in their fridge, what is on their table . . .

Yes, that's how it feels even to one who has not lived in this country for two decades. 'It is as if you gathered the dust, which forms into small rolls in the hard-to-reach corners under the bed, and stuffed your mouth with it.'

I see Nina on the balcony of the family's ninth-storey apartment, with folds of grey sky above her head. For one moment, the sky looks like the autumn sea and I imagine Nina and the whole family living in a warm seaside town somewhere far away from Stary Oskol. It is a futile fantasy, I know, even condescending perhaps, but I imagine how different her life could have been if she was not sent here after finishing her university studies in chemistry, one of the 'young specialists' assigned to a *burning* industrial project X.

Nina is a chemical engineer, her husband a metallurgical engineer; here is one more engineering family just like ours. Engineering was once a profession of considerable prestige, but by the 1970s and '80s when I was growing up, its devaluation was almost complete. It seemed almost like a default job for the Soviet Union's urban, tertiary-educated middle classes: four engineers for one technician was a normal industrial ratio. And there were the countless jokes, in which the figure of a 'simple engineer' stood for social ineptness. Certainly, few professions were paid lower wages.

There comes a moment during our stay: Billie after a shower, her hair in a towel, one of her legs resting on Nina's lap, Katya's hands around her hand. I am embarrassed. Must we involve a cast of thousands when it comes to a mere toenail, broken and now bleeding? Yet there is something about this minor medical intervention that feels like home, like the very essence of my childhood. The mother as a 'Jill of All Trades'. The soothing seriousness with which a trivial medical problem is treated – witness the great display of iodine, antiseptics and bandaids next to Nina. 'Mum always wanted to be a surgeon,' says Katya. 'Let her do it.'

But Nina seems happy, even contented, though it was not her decision to make her life in Stary Oskol. Here she married, had Katya and her older brother. She watched the town grow. The place was really desolate when she first arrived. It is much greener and prettier now. She did not have to choose it to love and accept this place. God knows, I have mutated into such a different breed. To me the freedom of choice, the ability to move from one city to another, and to walk out of the wrong job, is fundamental to my sense of self and the way I live. But being here I cannot help but wonder what would have happened if we had stayed in the world of *playing the hand you are dealt*, instead of moving to the one where the pack is constantly reshuffled in search of aces. Katya's family is not much like my family was before we left, but there are certain recognisable fundamentals that trigger in me, quite unexpectedly, the realisation that our current nomadic existence is merely the sequel to a much more settled time, when we could not conceive of any other life but the one we had in Kharkov. These days I can only imagine my family in disassembly and reassembly modes, stretched across continents, always missing half of its members at birthdays. But how could I ever forget that we all started out in a very different place, a place from which our current life seems unimaginable? And that we are, in some kind of unknowable and volatile ratio, both the people we were then and the people we are now?

Having fast-forwarded through hours of swimming competitions, we are watching a home video of Katya's first-ever day at school. September 1 is the start of the academic year and an official state holiday, the 'Day of Knowledge'. It has always been a big deal, but especially since the events in Beslan, Northern Ossetia, when over a thousand people attending school celebrations were taken hostage by terrorists. How it all ended is well-known, although it will probably be forgotten unforgivably soon: by the end of a bungled rescue operation, more than three hundred and fifty people were dead, half of them children.

In the video little Katya's hair is short, the way it was when we first met. She is wearing a white bow almost the same size as her head. Her back is extra-straight. Serious, solemn and eager, she is going to school as if to a cathedral. Amid flags, balloons and flowers, made-up and dressed-up mothers and camera-wielding fathers jostle for position. The first-graders are triumphantly walked in by the teachers while the rest of the school watches on. A boy from the final grade symbolically carries a ponytailed girl from the first grade on his shoulders while, with proudly shaking hand, she rings the school bell for the first time this school year. The unbearable triteness of the principal's speech welcoming the new students into the school family is followed by a student concert filled with equally trying music, dance numbers and long poems so bad they come close to rivalling the epic industrial poems about the ecstasy of exceeding production targets. But watching all this school kitsch, I, a longstanding enemy of schools, have to work hard to hold back tears. This is not just some outbreak of nostalgia. My tears are not just for my own childhood but for Katya, on the video so touching in her nervous eagerness, her sense of the occasion and the way she is all alone, separated from her family, at the mercy of her teacher who seems pre-emptively exhausted by the demands of the job. Other kids on the tape are just as touching, like little chicks taken out of their pens and placed in the middle of a highway. I look at Billie, hoping for something. She is not entirely uninterested, but she has the 'sitting through someone else's home video' face on.

If this is my *Double Life of Véronique* moment, then make it times two because as much as being with Katya makes me ask what would have become of me if I had stayed in my old country, it makes me wonder even more acutely what Billie would have been like if she were born here. God knows, my loud-as-an-air-raid-siren Billie would have lost a few decibels. She would not have had her theatricality – all the dramatic excesses, the poses and the monologues. ('We are a bunch of outspoken, emotional people,' she says of her friends.) She would have learned that emotions are essentially private matters, not events staged outwardly. She would have known things about things she did not care about because she would have been educated in the system that did not flirt with its students, that did not fear insisting and imposing on them. She would have lived with the heavy realities of economics and politics on her back, not separated from them by the wall of liquid crystals framing her television screen, by her mother's alleged ability 'to take care of things', and by the limit of her imaginative engagement with the world of hard facts. She would not have considered the world her oyster (assuming, of course, she does now).

In Katya's room, Katya and Billie hug, whisper and laugh. They speak English to each other – Katya has private English lessons on top of the school program and she loves the idea of finally practising her English with a native speaker who can talk all day and night. The love they felt for each other four years ago in Melbourne requires little nudging to re-emerge. 'We must love each other or die,' Auden wrote in *September 1, 1939*. His poem about adults as scared as children is following me around in Stary Oskol. I was Katya's age when we left for good. Katya's vulnerability, purity and strength remind me of what must have been at stake for me then, how high those stakes must have been. It is most likely, I admit, a massive case of identity confusion – at different moments, and sometimes all at the same time, I feel like Katya *and* like her surrogate mother *and* like the crystal ball into which she can never see clearly (but which carries within itself the knowledge that life cannot spare indefinitely people like her). In Katya's presence I feel old for knowing what I know *and* young for feeling every emotion as a direct ray, the kind that does not slide off your skin but goes right through undeterred. This bout of identity confusion is only deepened by my immigrant story: as someone who left,

I know both *here* and *there*; as someone who is no longer a child, I know both *now* and *then*. As I think of Katya's future, fighting off a pretty standard list of apprehensions, I remind myself that I was never an adult in this country so I never got to lead a life of my own making here. I have no idea what I would have made of it.

Katya brings me back not only to myself as I was then but to Billie now. How big experiences are when you are twelve or fifteen, how deeply they enter us, how piercing the sense of loss — of home, of our idea of home, or of our innocent belief that we will never have to tear ourselves away from people and things we love. Before we all leave for the train station, Katya's father polishes his shoes with great thoroughness. 'Let's sit for the road,' he says, just like my father used to say every time we were about to go on our summer vacations. We all sit down in the hall. One frozen frame, one held breath before getting into the car together for the last time. May our journey be smooth and forgettable. May we come to our destination serene and refreshed. My stomach tightens. I see Billie's face being gradually taken over by the pre-Katya greyness. I am too afraid to look at Katya.

Dear Diary,
When we had to board the train I tried to make a joke and we all laughed, but when the train started with a jerk, it jerked our hearts and that was it — the train moved. My heart tore in half.

Two decades before my twelve-year-old daughter writes these words in her diary, my best friend stood on a platform, just as

Katya does now. My best friend, Sasha, who turned sixteen on the day of our emigration of all days, and who I still love twenty years later not with a gentle, nostalgic love but with a strong, painful, irritated love of the present moment. Sasha's face was the only thing that felt real in this whole business of leaving for good. Her face, and the music of 'The Farewell of Slavianka', a pre-revolutionary march dedicated to the plight of Slavic women seeing their menfolk off to war and once regularly performed at the departure of posh (*firmenny*) trains to Moscow. This time it is Katya, not Sasha, who stands outside the window of an overnight train to Moscow. And inside the little cabin, peering through the burgundy curtains (so unexpectedly *fin-de-siècle*), I hold hands, not with my older sister whose devastation I am too self-absorbed to notice, but with Billie, whose tears, as round and perfectly defined as soap bubbles, fall every few seconds on my hands and on the little table covered with a cloth that matches the improbable curtains.

Train departures are a particular kind of leave-taking, the most cinematic and certainly the most undisguised and unlubricated. The elaborate, anxiety-provoking rituals of air travel inject an anesthetic between those who leave and those who have come to see them off. The train goodbye is like a rough and violent cut without a sedative or even a gulp of whisky. You can hear and feel the tearing. And then there is always the spectre of other train journeys, of millions across Europe taken to concentration camps and Gulags in cattle trains.

It is Katya's, not Sasha's, eyes that I see from the train window now – so mature, so pure. She will be fine, of course. She is a powerhouse, this girl – beautiful, smart, determined and entirely humble. Her parents love and support her. Her school thinks her a hero as she keeps winning all kinds of regional competitions in Russian, English and God knows what else. She will be totally fine. It is not like we are abandoning her to a pack of wolves. I can tell this to myself all night long, but I know what I feel. Leaving Katya does not feel bitter-sweet or exquisitely sad, it feels like a non-elective cesarian. At first Katya is a full-sized figure, holding onto her mum, both of them crying and laughing at once at Billie's brave but stupid joke. Then she is a pulsating rectangle of colour and light in the distance. Then she is a tiny pebble swallowed up by the railway tracks.

7

MOTHERS AND DAUGHTERS

No matter what, my mother was always sacred to me . . . When I can hang on, this is where I leave it, but more often than not, I hammer the nail until the wall bleeds: *. . . but I am not at all sacred for you.* It is the voice of maternal desperation speaking, though have I not peaked a few years early? What room am I leaving for emotional bribery in (God forbid) any really serious teenage crisis – methamphetamines, pregnancies and member-ship in extremist political organisations? I grew up knowing implicitly (because this is how my parents and their friends were) that you should never try to wrestle recognition or respect out of anyone, let alone your own child, so to demand an acknowledgement of my maternal sanctity is a new low. But with Billie, I am already in the valley of lows, and we are just starting out – at least, this is what everyone keeps telling me, with the kindest intentions of course. I know, I know, but can't you see, I am waiting for a miracle.

Before I turned fifteen and we left for Australia, I remember my mother getting it wrong only once, when she peremptorily dismissed an honest, if bizarre, ache in my chin, when what I really needed was comforting reassurance. And I remember as well her deliberately hurting my feelings only once, saying to me in exasperation, 'Your sister was right. Demons do lurk in a quiet pond.' I *was* a quiet pond because, unlike my older sister and, later, Billie herself, I was not in the habit of enlarging my emotions to ensure that they could be detected from the outer reaches of the sky. As to the proliferation of demons my mum diagnosed, she was referring, quite legitimately, to my use of the family's painstakingly procured Yugoslav wall unit to re-enact a recurring fantasy of being a teacher (a good teacher, you understand, not like those shrivelled-up, bitter women who dominated my later years at school). The back wall of this unit was hidden from the general view, but not from the eyes of my mother, and, in a moment of weakness, I forgot myself and used it as a blackboard, on which I drew words and equations with a slippery piece of precious white chalk shaped like a cigarette butt, all the while making warm and witty elaborations on my imaginary lesson to the imaginary class before me.

The bit from my mum's pond sentence that really hurt was the affirmation of my sister's longstanding suspicions that behind my comparatively placid exterior (placid at least compared to hers) there was a litany of vices and flaws every bit as hair-raising as a seasoned recidivist's. She was right, of course, if somewhat premature in her assessment. My demons first surfaced somewhere around the time of our emigration and, by the time we settled in Australia, you could barely see the pond for all their splashing. And though for several years I tested my mother's patience in earnest, she did not budge, she did not 'lose it'. So one light dismissal and one deliberate hurt: this is all I can remember of my mother's crimes over my formative years (over all the years, in fact). Which is quite remarkable, especially considering the long list of my own maternal transgressions, and that even before Billie officially becomes a teenager, she looks set for a full submission to the Hague tribunal.

When I want to damn someone in front of Billie I say, 'He was the kind of a person for whom nothing is sacred, not even his mother.' The purpose of this statement is twofold. First, it is what I think. Secondly, I am sending Billie subliminal messages. Is she getting them? Probably she is, together with all the other glorified guilt trips that have not worked for a long time, if ever. As a mother, I want nothing more than to be like my mother. Yet our trip home is a constant reminder that I am nothing at all like her. (Such journeys of self-discovery are not recommended for parents in denial.) I remember, when Billie was young, thinking that parental disappointment was more destructive than simple anger and hurt, and promising myself to stay well away from it at all costs. Both my mum and dad were always like that, at least with me: total strangers to the outward expression of their disappointment. So I never felt like I let the team down – myself, yes, all the time, but not the proverbial team.

And after all that, on this trip I do nothing but channel chronic disappointment. In no small measure, this is because I am looking for Billie to be awe-struck, inspired, blown away – actually, any one of the three will do. Not only that, I am waiting for her to articulate these feelings with highly charged words to match the occasion or to let me know, in subtle, silent ways that only I – her mother – can understand that her universe is expanding, her nerve endings are abuzz and that her heart is barely able to contain all the emotions she feels. Instead, in front of me is a tired, hungry, bored little animal who constantly wants to sit, eat and go home. This little animal is my daughter, brought on this trip by her mother, for the purposes of – let's say it here and be done with it – some sort of transformation. Yet more often than not this daughter's eyes slide away from cathedrals and boulevards to displays of pastries in kiosks; her legs cannot carry her anywhere without aching; and her mind, her beautiful mind, is preoccupied with the demands of her flesh and with wanting all these things orchestrated by her mother to end, the sooner the better. There is no lift-off, no second wind, no energising burst of curiosity.

She is not five anymore. There are no excuses. What would my mother do? Oh, forget it. I explode.

'Why do you look like that? Don't any of these things get to you? Don't they mean anything to you at all?'

'Mum, you just want me to react in a certain way. You just have expectations of how I should react but I am reacting in my own way.'

OK, yes, she has every right to react in her own way. This is not a crime. No question.

'But why this bored, fatigued, unhappy facial expression? Do you realise that you look like this all the time, Billie?'

'This is what happens when I feel scared or embarrassed sounding like an idiot in this language. I turn inward, Mum.'

This time she does turn away and inward, her anger made glossy by tears.

There is a cacophony of voices in my head, all the embarrassing, unbearably trite things I am trying not to say to Billie – *Not by bread alone, Billie . . . Not until we are lost do we begin to understand ourselves . . . She who can no longer pause and stand wrapped in awe . . .* Sage Wisdom 101. I ache with disappointment. I promised myself I would never become like this. And here I am scraping the bottom because my daughter is not having epiphanies at the time and place of my choosing. Billie does not deserve the tragic eyes of her mother, dark with undiluted grief for a daughter who is no longer marching to the tune of her mother's drum (or not marching at all, for that matter). No one deserves eyes like that, certainly not Billie. She certainly does not deserve this trip to be turned into some kind of moral education boot camp. I need to back off. The days of moulding and shaping are over.

Sheila Munro recalls her mother, the Canadian writer Alice Munro, telling her what she remembered of herself as a daughter. 'I always talked back,' Alice told Sheila. 'I wasn't a nice child. Being nice meant such a terrible abdication of self.' Sheila remembers not wanting to hear her mother say those words. For she herself was a nice child – compliant, obedient and eager to please. What did her mother's words mean then? 'Did I abdicate my self?' Sheila wondered. I think of mothers, daughters and all the infinitely complex webs of self-abdication. As a Dr Seuss poem Miguel is fond of says, 'Oh, the thinks you can think up if only you try!' Perhaps it is much easier to respect your kids' choice of clothes or friends, their need for privacy, their social networking, than to respect the fundamental autonomy and legitimacy of their actual selves, because there is always a danger of really not liking them once you accept them as fully formed human beings. As long as they are not done, our parental fear and vanity conspire to persuade us that we still have a big contribution to make (in fact, it is our responsibility to make it) to our children's self-begetting.

But am I not the link between my mum and my daughter – genetically, culturally, spiritually, whichever way you look at it? And if so, have I dropped the ball; have I failed to transmit something essential from one to the other? I do not mean cultural traditions, stuff them, I mean something almost on a molecular level – the way our engines run, the sources we draw from, the way we automatically reconfigure ourselves in the presence of other people's needs and bursting worlds. The easy self-effacement, the ability not to listen too closely to the constant, self-important humming of our minds and bodies always hungry for something else.

It comes up again in Kiev, a week or so after our visit to Katya. How could it not when we stay with Ira, the best friend of my mum's youth, the one who is in spirit so breathtakingly close to what I have always considered to be my mother's unique blend of dignity and irreverence, humility and sharpness. Ira, who reminds me so much of Mum in the calm self-possession that infuses her total disregard for ceremony and convention. It is on noticing how quickly Billie tires out and how easily she gives in to her discomforts, that Ira – the warm, kind, ironic, tough Ira who sees everything – tells us the story of my mother and her high-heeled shoes.

'Your mum and I, we often did not sleep at night, we went for long walks all the time, and she would always have her high heels on. We would walk day and night. Once we decided at nine in the evening to go from a collective farm where we were sent, through the forest, to Kiev. We reached Kiev at nine in the morning. We threw out our shoes along the way, they were useless, and this is how we walked through the forest at night. Cars would stop and offer us a lift. We were very young, but we were very proud and we wanted to do it all by ourselves. After this walk, we could not take a step on the ground for three days without our feet hurting.'

In those days, in summer, city professionals were routinely sent to the collective farms to assist the nationwide harvest effort; Mum and Ira, who worked at the same institute in Kiev, were already good friends when the Long Night of the Stilettos took place. So the set-up for Ira's story is as ordinary as they come, but the story itself I find elating. My mother – strong, proud, light-footed, determined, with an unstoppable supply of laughter, and, what is the word I am looking for . . . yes, free.

'We used to like putting an apple in our pockets and going for long walks; once we walked to the construction site of a hydro-electric station, fifteen or twenty kilometres away. Got there easy and made friends there and then. We could easily walk for an hour and a half for the sake of getting a small cup of coffee. At the time, there was only one place in Kiev, on Khrezhatik, where you could get a cup of coffee like that. Usually, black international students would be there, and us, that's all.'

I do not need to strain my imagination to see my mum with a Newton's apple in her pocket, or the way she and Ira did not pussyfoot around anything, the way they enjoyed nothing more than *not* taking things easy. They have not changed really,

Mum and Ira, not in any essential way. Mum's legs might hurt too much to withstand a high-heeled hike in the dark, but both she and Ira still find much irony in how easily and willingly people turn themselves into fragile, self-limiting organisms. Both of them seem to lack almost entirely the deep attachment to comforts that some people are born with and many cultivate with age, and in that way you can say they are stoic, only their stoicism has no hint of martyrdom or self-elevation. It is a simple, laughing stoicism of two people who never came to take themselves too seriously.

In Margaret Atwood's *Significant Moments in the Life of Mother*, the daughter speaks of her own perception of her mother's youth:

> I used to think that my mother, in her earlier days, led a life of sustained hilarity and hair-raising adventure . . . Horses ran away with her, men offered to, she was continually falling out of trees or off the ridgepoles of barns, or nearly being swept out to sea in rip-tides . . .

The mother was always just a broken zipper away from acute public embarrassment. And even though the daughter later came to understand that the mother had only told stories of things gone blissfully awry, of near-death experiences that with time had acquired a euphoric ring to them, thus leaving out 'the long stretches of uneventful time', this storytelling, or rather what it conveyed about the narrator, became central to the daughter's understanding of who her mother was. 'Having fun has always been high on my mother's agenda,' says the daughter, as much fun as one can handle. And having fun was integral to my own perception of my mother. Could that be why, in real-life stories of women's grace under fire, stories which have obsessed me from a young age, I have always been drawn most powerfully to women who laughed, danced and wore mascara through some of the bleakest moments of the twentieth century? I think them inherently heroic: the ones in London running to dance halls during breaks in the Blitz; the ones in besieged Sarajevo spending their last money on lipstick; my dear friend Sabina Wolanski, the only one from her family to survive the Holocaust, who went dancing every night after the end of the war.

The mother in Margaret Atwood's story tells countless 'having fun' stories, but as her daughter knows:

> What she means by this phrase cannot be understood without making an adjustment, an allowance for the great gulf across which this phrase must travel before it reaches us. It comes from another world, which, like the stars that originally sent out the light we see hesitating in the sky above us these nights, may be or is already gone.

To Billie, the fun my mother had in such abundance as a young woman does come from another world. If my daughter ever tries to see her grandmother as someone who really knew how to be young, she inevitably will have to walk across this great gulf not just of time but also of culture, history and geography. But for me no adjustments are necessary. When Ira speaks, I do not need to go far. I am there. Or, rather, I wish I were there. And I wish I could take Billie there with me.

★

125

Dear Diary,

Because Mum wanted me to have a good last time in Moscow so we met up with the sister and mother of close family friends in Australia, who gave us a tour of Moscow. Probably the thing that had the most impression on me was statues called 'Children, the Victims of Adult Vices'. It had two golden children who were blindfolded (to the future) and around them were thirteen statues representing thirteen horrible aspects of adults. Drug use, prostitution, theft, alcoholism, idiocy, being two-faced, making fun of people, not caring about the past, child labour, poverty, atom war and the most important one in the middle – indifference.

Lest you be swept up in the pathos of Billie's writing, I must tell you that she writes 'empression' and 'horrable', among other things. This is because she is in a hurry to capture the whole vortex of emotions and impressions, you may say. No, this is because she cannot spell for nuts. In Russia, bad spelling is a notorious sign of poor education or, at least, of a damning lack of ability; never the fashionable attribute of a big-picture creative person. I am an avid admirer of Billie's prose, but I cringe on seeing words slighted and unceremoniously knocked about, exchanged for their phonetic approximations and for words that look like their body-doubles but bear only the vaguest family relationship. Sometimes I want to throw one massive *'J'accuse'* in the face of the education system that has instituted the complete abandonment of language and grammar as one of its foundational doctrines – a system that I, for one, have resisted with annoyingly limited success in my attempts to disabuse my daughter of her belief that spelling is for losers. Could this carelessness with the mechanics and maintenance of one's language be a form of a victor's syndrome? With English the planet's de facto meta-language (at least for now), you might say its native speakers are born with a linguistic silver spoon in their mouths. There is such a thing as linguistic privilege. I know, I have tried to sneak in and claim it too.

More often than not I get Billie to read her diary entries out aloud so I do not see her words on the page. This is a largely preventive measure: sometimes the urge to correct gets too overwhelming. When I do give in to it, Billie squirms as if during 'Body, Mind and Soul' class at school. To her, my straightening of her writing is a violation, yet another form of the elaborate non-listening at which her mother excels. It is as though I am in her room, making her bed, going through the clothes on the floor, choosing what to throw out and what to keep. And all she wants to do is to slam the door in my face. 'Go and fix up your own things, Mum.' The child, as they say, has a point.

But back to our final day in Moscow. 'Mum, this is a masterpiece,' Billie says, now fully awake and rummaging furiously through her bag in search of a little-used camera. The sculptural ensemble 'Children, the Victims of Adult Vices', which inspires forbiddingly high praise from my daughter and makes a lasting impression on me as well, was given to the Russian capital as a gift by Mikhail Shemyakin, an artist and sculptor of world renown. Shemyakin was kicked out of the Soviet Union in 1971 for his involvement in the wrong kinds of art projects, but not before being thrown into a psychiatric hospital (yes, *One Flew over the Cuckoo's Nest* all over again). After ten years in Paris, he moved to the United States, and there his monstrous renditions of adult vices and his angelic bronzes of blindfolded children were cast.

The materials for the sculptures, and their transportation to Moscow, were paid for by Rosneft, one of Russia's oil giants. But as we stand in front of the sculptures, still blissfully unaware of all the behind-the-scenes machinations (blissfully because this kind of awareness, in Russia at least, does nothing for your art appreciation), Billie and I are in a synchronised state of awe. The grotesque figures of vices are hard-core, unsparing. A voluptuous toad covered in warts, baring her cleavage, has the word 'Prostitution' engraved at her base in Russian and English. Drug addiction comes at us, dressed in a tailcoat, a Count Dracula figure with a syringe in his hand. The pig with a sickly sweet expression on its face holds a sack of money with its long piano fingers; behind its back is a sack inscribed with the magic word 'Offshore'. Theft. Alcoholism is a double-chinned, bleary-eyed Roman god sitting astride a barrel with nothing to cover his protruding stomach and man breasts. Clad in long monk robes, Pseudoscience has its eyes fully closed, while it holds the strings of a two-headed dog puppet, no doubt the end result of some kind of cloning experiment gone terribly wrong. At the very centre is Indifference, the biggest vice of them all according to Shemyakin. Eyes closed, fingers blocking its ears, another set of hands crossed on the chest of a coffin-like body.

Billie takes photos of each vice – I want to say 'lovingly', but this must be the wrong word. She looks mesmerised, but also relieved and vindicated, as if Shemyakin has understood precisely what she has been feeling on this trip, as if the maestro himself has heard her cries for help. Perhaps if these figures were paintings, they would have lost much of their impact, but as sculptures they pack a serious punch. Massive objects in the public sphere, they are imposing, permanent and thickly material. I would have been surprised to come across these figures anywhere, really – in Paris, New York or Buenos Aires – but the surprise is amplified tenfold here in the former home of totalitarian kitsch, where for seven decades the hollowed-out sculptural form serviced only one client. The monumental fetishism turned the figure of Lenin, in particular, into the equivalent of a village well, signalling the presence of some form of human settlement. These monuments were produced assembly-line style to several recurring and, soon enough, instantly recognisable templates. Lenin: sitting, standing, looking, peering like a visionary towards far-off horizons. Lenin: next to or atop an armoured vehicle, symbolising not the young nation's industrial might, but its Zero Hour – the historically verifiable platform from which the start of the Revolution was proclaimed. There was a story when I was growing up, perhaps not even a joke, of a statue of Lenin in which he sported one of his distinctive visor hats on his head while holding a spare in his hands. It was only a matter of time before different parts of different versions would be accidentally welded together, creating a sculptural oxymoron of sorts.

Billie and I walk around Shemyakin's sculptures, drinking in details, not wanting to leave. Unlike Billie, though, I am growing more suspicious by the minute. My daughter was not born yesterday either, but she was born in Australia, which means she is unlikely to ask herself, *What's the catch?* every time she is presented with something unexpected, something out of the ordinary. I have spent decades freeing myself from the what's-the-catch syndrome, which seems to be almost genetic here, passed down from generation to generation, and present here with me today. It does not take much digging to discover that the sculpture so deeply antithetical to, so mocking of, the taste of the previous regime was commissioned by a commissar of today, Moscow's mayor, Yuri Luzhkov, who personally approved every single element, every representation of every vice. In fact, Luzhkov was so committed to the ensemble that he overruled a commission composed of city planners, architects, artists and arts experts who recommended finding another location to the one Luzhkov favoured, the historical square on Bolotnaya Square, which not only has one of the best panoramas of the city and the Kremlin, but is frequented by children of all ages.

In reality, many members of the commission did not want the sculpture erected at all, but they knew better than to look a gift-horse in the mouth, especially a horse so close to the heart of the city's biggest cheese. Nor were highly charged debates about the monument confined to the members of the commission. Doctors and psychologists warned of the sculptures' disastrous psychological effects on children's fragile and impressionable psyches. Letters to newspapers asked, not without reason, why a square designed for rest and recreation had been turned into a site for shock therapy, and whether the sculpture was going to create a new category of children as victims of adult urban improvers. But Luzhkov, no stranger to unilateral decisions, was fanatical in his desire to make Moscow one of the truly great world cities.

As everyone in Russia knows, Luzhkov's favourite architect is Zurab Tsereteli, the Georgian-born head of the Russian Arts Academy. Tsereteli must come second only to Putin in the number of jokes occasioned by his seemingly unstoppable gigantomania, his love of kitsch on a grand scale and his legendary workaholism. No one, it seems, is safe from another one of Tsereteli's creations appearing at a park near them. *The medals for the Sochi Winter Olympics will be created by Zurab Tsereteli. During the medal ceremonies, the athletes will be standing next to the medals.* It was the public outcry over Tsereteli's massive Peter the Great, one of the tallest statues in the world, which led to the creation of the Commission on Monumental Arts, the body which tried unsuccessfully to steer Shemyakin's lurid sculpture towards a less conspicuous location. The Western world too, I should say, has not been spared Tsereteli's lavish generosity. A stretch of Jersey City waterfront across the Hudson River from the site of the World Trade Center groans under a ten-storey, one-hundred-and-seventy-five-ton, nickel-surfaced teardrop entitled *Tear of Grief*, a Russian government gift to the grief-stricken courtesy of Zurab Tsereteli. Another of his subtle sculptures, *Good Defeats Evil*, stands outside the UN headquarters in New York. It's a mystery how such tastelessness on a grand scale is given prominence in the public domain.

In a famous short story, writer Boris Akunin suggested that Tsereteli was, in fact, an alien with telepathic abilities. How else to explain his unique ability to cast a spell on authorities, no matter how ludicrous his ideas and how strong the opposition to them. I feel more than slightly affronted when it turns out that Tsereteli even tried to erect one of 'his' monuments to my favourite poet, Joseph Brodsky. His plan occasioned a mass internet campaign under the banner 'Save Brodsky'. (The poet had been dead for more than a decade, but horrified fans could well imagine him turning in his grave at being immortalised by the sculptor.) Mikhail Shemyakin is of course no Tsereteli, except that politically they have the same 'cover'. But Tsereteli does set the context for viewing any new sculptural addition to the cityscape of Moscow and for grasping the persistence of the tradition of the Artist Laureates or court artists, which, of course, reaches its apotheosis in the Soviet period. His 'reign' has undoubtedly contributed a great deal to the overwhelming air of cynicism that these days greets the emergence of the next sculptural 'masterpiece' in Russia, no matter who it is by. Shemyakin's ensemble of vices tightening their grip on the angelic children is enclosed by a cast-iron fence and guarded at night by security after repeated attacks by vandals. The last straw apparently was when the copper strings connecting the statue of Pseudoscience to the two-headed dog were sawn off. Billie and I visit the sculpture during the day, so we do not have to bribe security to see it. Billie fills her diary with the photographs of vices – one vice per page, while, quietly, I feel a growing disease about the public life of Shemyakin's ode to children.

And so I keep digging. It turns out that in 2007 it was in Bolotnaya Square, at the side of Shemyakin's grotesque figures, that the first official (and much-reported) gathering of children's movement Mishki (Teddy Bears) took place. Mishki's full name is 'Youth Organisation for the All-Round Development of Personality, Patriotic and Moral Education of Children and Youth'. Scary. At the time of Mishki's big entrance, Yulia Zimova, its twenty-year-old founder, told journalists that the movement's aim was to teach children pride in their town and country, responsibility, independence and concern for others. It almost sounds like a harmless version of Scouts, if only the movement was not set up by members of Nashi – a youth organisation with strong funding and ideological links to the

Kremlin, and conceived as a Russian response to the Ukraine's 'Orange Revolution'. Journalists predisposed to be critical of the current regime, who do not share Nashi's personal loyalty to Putin as Russia's saviour, often refer to the young members of the movement as 'nashists'. In fact, the references to Fascism and Hitler-Jugend abound, as well as to the Soviet-era youth groups such as the Octobrists, Young Pioneers and Komsomol.

What does Nashi want? The full and swift restoration of Russia's greatness, of course. Its membership wants people to be swollen with pride for their country. They want the rest of the world, America and Britain in particular, to sit up and listen (shaking in fear will be the next step, of course, all things going to plan). They want a 'clean', 'strong' and 'united' nation, and that means sweeping the country with a big, long broom to rid it of all kinds of scum – ethnics, democrats, prostitutes. In some of the most notorious incidents involving the group, Nashi harassed the British ambassador to Russia after he attended an opposition rally, picketing the embassy and disrupting the ambassador's public-speaking engagements. They also camped outside the Estonian Embassy to protest the relocation from the centre of the Estonian capital of a statue commemorating the loss of Russian and Soviet lives during World War II. Nashi do not limit themselves to ideological warfare, either: the movement offers paramilitary training to give its members important 'life' skills (breaking up opposition rallies, for instance).

And so Shemyakin's sculptures, so dear to my and Billie's hearts, work brilliantly within this militant, ultra-patriotic vision. Nashi and their Teddies are committed to protecting Shemyakin's blindfolded children from the adult chimeras that encircle them. In fact, the youth movements call on young people to take destiny into their hands so as to ensure they do not become victims of adult vices – bingo! Does it only happen in this country that absolutely everything can be turned on its head and smeared with enough dirt and cynicism to last anyone a lifetime? As a phenomenon, Mishki is both obscene (forced political participation of children is illegal even in Russia, to say nothing of being deeply immoral) and unintentionally hilarious, especially in its infantilisation of the political sphere. At the time of Mishki's inception, Putin had just been re-elected Russian president, and Mishki asked him, in all seriousness too, to become the head of their movement, the Chief Teddy Bear. The leaders or guides of the movement, most of them at university studying to become teachers, are called 'vozhatye' – the same name was once given to young pioneer leaders. They operate within a farcical and stringently upheld internal hierarchy. A guide able to organise ten events with children is a Restless Bear (a species known for its legendary aggression, a fact clearly lost on the movement organisers but, then again, maybe not). Polar Bear unites children from ten apartment buildings, while at the top of the hierarchy is the Brown Bear or Megasuperbear, who has been able to solve children's problems at a town or city level by, for instance, organising the construction of a playground. The children themselves are also divided into all kinds of bears. The oldest are Olympic Bears and the youngest are Tiny Teddies. (I am not joking.)

Mishki's slogan is 'Thank you, Mr Putin, for our stable future', which caused Lev Rubinstein to note that this time Putin had outdone even Stalin. In Stalin's times, the slogan was 'Thank you to Comrade Stalin for our happy childhood'. It is, of course, so tempting to think of Putin as the direct heir to

Stalin, and his brand of neo-totalitarianism as a far more moderate, modern and ideologically savvy version of Stalin's iron fist, but I am persuaded by writer and journalist Dmitriy Bykov who writes, 'In the case of Putin we are dealing not with the cult of personality – since the personality barely manifests itself and, plus, it is hermetically sealed from strangers' eyes – but with the cult of substance.' That substance, Bykov notes, is virtually impossible to define. It encapsulates 'collective expectations which are greater than any kind of logic', the dreams and wishes of the mob. Putinism, in other words, 'is a phantom of mass self-hypnosis'. Putin's rule is not comparable to Stalin's cult of personality because Putin is not a personality but the archetypal *man without qualities*, the medium for the masses.

What does it all mean for me and Billie? Is Shemyakin forever ruined for us? Am I meant to hold him responsible for providing a nice scenic backdrop for the lowest kinds of bigots who are turning children into zombie-like teddies, because frankly he should have known better? He knows what this place is like. I have not read a single intelligent defence of Shemyakin's sculptures beyond an article on a Kremlin website, in which some sociologist or psychologist lamented Muscovites' 'disproportionate response' to the introduction of new monuments. Why is no one of any credibility defending Shemyakin? Is it because his work is completely compromised by Luzhkov's intimate patronage? Is it because people are sick of auteurs claiming their living spaces? Does it all stink of unbridled narcissism? Are people wary of any artistic statement insisting that children's bright future is under threat unless we all immediately commit some kind of collective exorcism? Perhaps, most importantly, should I tell Billie even a quarter of this? Because if I do, I will be cold-bloodedly destroying in the name of her political and cultural literacy the one thing she has really responded to. I do not want my daughter to be a clueless tourist admiring toxic landmarks, but I would hate for her to be ridden with suspicions, always looking for the ulterior motives, for some dirt that you can inevitably find if you scratch any kind of surface around here. I do not want her to keep asking, 'Mum, what's the catch?' The truth is that I cannot kill Shemyakin for Billie. On our return to Australia, she shows the photographs of the sculptures to anyone who cares to see them. 'Mum and I loved the whole thing,' she says. 'We thought it was a masterpiece.' And to that I keep my mouth shut and nod rather uncharacteristically because, if the truth is to be known, we did love it – what else is there to say?

> *Dear Diary,*
>
> *Happy birthday to me. I am on my way to St Petersburg. I am home-sick again and I don't practically know how to explain how I am feeling because it all sounds clichéd . . . I'd love to quote Dorothy and say there is no place like home and tap my ruby slippers three times and be home, but it sounds too much like a fantasy book . . . I guess there are no words for some emotions. Actually there are no words for most emotions . . .*

I have timed it so that Billie will turn twelve on the train from Moscow to St Petersburg and that she will spend her birthday in the city that used to be my favourite in the whole world (the whole world of course being limited to the Soviet republics, as I had never travelled abroad). Like Billie, I was twelve when I first came to St Petersburg (still Leningrad then) with my mum. This trip was by far the best vacation experience of my childhood and adolescence. No school, my beautiful, fun, kind Mamma all to myself, St Petersburg's breathtaking beauty seen for the first time – *there are no words for some emotions. Actually there are no words for most emotions . . .* 'Euphoria' is one word. The sensation of the trip being blessed in every way. And central to it all the connection with my mother: strong, comforting and liberating. My mother away from work, stove, my father, and my sister. My mother without a care in the world. My mother not having to say once, 'No, not now, not possible.' And this city, this magnificent city so unlike other Soviet cities, so unlike poor old Kharkov where we lived, which looked by comparison like a purpose-built container for factories, institutes and drafting departments. St Petersburg was a city as an ideal, pure form. A city first and a place of residence second. We were there during the famous white nights – a few weeks in summer when darkness never comes; the night is banished and the city streets are filled with people at all hours.

Neither my mum nor I had ever seen anything like this in our lives – we were awe-stricken and gloriously insomniac, synchronised with the city.

I told Billie a lot about St Petersburg as she was growing up – how beautiful it was, how unique, the history, the white nights, how before we left for good I desperately wished we lived there. I told her the wonderful words of BG's song about a better place, which I always imagined as his native St Petersburg: *a place of green trees . . . gold over blue.* I told her about my friend Marina, who I met on my trip with Mum, and who has remained a dear and loyal friend to me right to this day despite us living in different cities and, then, on different continents.

I wanted Billie to spend her twelfth birthday with Marina and her family, to spend it in St Petersburg. If anything was going to help her weather the homesickness, the likes of which she had never felt before (Was she too young to feel it on our earlier trip? Was much less at stake for her then?) it would have to be this place. I did not want Billie to see St Petersburg when she was thirty. It would be too late then. And, no, I was not trying to plunge into the same river twice, this time as a mother not a daughter. Such ventures usually end disastrously, even I know that. But I needed the symbolism. This was our family history, all broken up and fragmented, but, despite it all, it had its axes of symmetry, moments and experiences recurring through generations, leitmotifs of some kind. Our history was cyclical as much as it was linear and in it, in different decades, my daughter and my mum got to walk the same streets with me by their side, giggling and intoxicated.

8

ST PETERSBURG

ALTHOUGH I FELL HEAD over heels for St Petersburg the first time I saw it, in theory at least my feelings could have gone either way. Just as there are 'cat people' and 'dog people', so there are 'St Petersburg people' and 'Moscow people'. 'No other city in Russia has inspired so much abuse,' the renowned philologist Vladimir Toporov wrote of St Petersburg. 'So many condemnations, reproaches, hurt feelings, regrets, lamentations, so much disappointment.' There it sits on the country's north-west border, facing out across the Baltic Sea to Scandinavia, a city that on maps looks as though it has defiantly turned its back on the rest of Russia and its face towards Europe, which in a way is exactly right. Its construction on an estuarine swamp, a site utterly unsuited for a large human settlement, let alone for a capital of Empire, has been called a tragic mistake. Peter the Great created the city in 1703 as an *hommage* to his favourite European cities, pronouncing it the new Russian capital and insisting that his entire court move there, which is how the whole Moscow versus St Petersburg thing started. To a nineteenth-century descendant of those nobles, one of St Petersburg's most illustrious sons Fyodor Dostoyevsky, the city was a 'Finnish swamp' – a rotten, slimy place.

Toporov died in 2005, but it is safe to say that the opposition between St Petersburg and Moscow lives on, and will for a long time. Within this opposition St Petersburg is a doomed abstraction, an artificial, profoundly non-Russian city built in a mosquito pit and uniquely unsuited to human life, while Moscow is warm, organic, vital, real, embedded in its location, a deeply authentic Russian urban centre. Or Moscow is a semi-Oriental village, good for commerce and little else; and St Petersburg is a unique haven of civilisation and culture, one of the great European cities. Numerous fans of Moscow naturally object to these sorts of exceptionalist claims for their rival city. In fact, St Petersburg poet Elena Shwartz probably summed up the truth best when she wrote of how she had fondly imagined her hometown as a unique country – 'West thrown into East, encircled and alone' – only to discover that 'St Petersburg has long since been flooded by Russia'.

It is summer holidays. I am fourteen and staying in St Petersburg with my friend Marina. This is essentially my farewell tour; in a few months my family is leaving the country, unless

something goes terribly wrong with our plans. My first independent trip ever, this should be the absolute pinnacle of
everything, but neither Marina nor I are able to forget for long
why I am really here. In my teenage head I secretly fantasise
that I was born in this city where seemingly everyone I've ever
really admired came from – my literary idols, Joseph Brodsky,
Anna Akhmatova, Osip Mandelstam; my rock 'n' roll heroes,
Boris Grebenshikov and Yuri Shevchuk. 'Russia's offspring
who looks nothing like his mother. Pale, skinny, European-
eyed passer-by.' This is what Shevchuk, ripping through words
and sounds as always, sings about his hometown, Marina's
hometown.

Yes, it's true I am jealous. Marina takes me around this place
with such an air of easy confidence, and I can't help but wish
that I were the one ushering her around, pointing far and wide,
in the interstices of reverent silences brilliantly quoting everyone from Pushkin to Nabokov to Brodsky (I already know
them all by heart). Brodsky said that the strongest emotions of
his childhood and adolescence were inspired by Leningrad's sky
and by the idea of infinity that the city embodied. Despite the
overwhelming imposition of architectural form – grand, geo-
metrically overdetermined, and assertively European – from
certain vantage points St Petersburg seems to him to be closer
in essence to an ocean or a steppe. The city feels unbounded
and uncontained, as if round any corner an empty vista full
of possibilities might open up before me. Brodsky said that
Petersburg's spaces and their interrelationships had made his
head spin. My head is spinning too, even more than it did on
that first visit to the city with my mother.

I walk with Marina down to the broad River Neva, along

the broad Nevsky Prospect that inspired novelist Andrei Bely to imagine the whole of St Petersburg as 'the infinity of the avenue raised to the nth power'. And yes, I am feeling this 'nth power'; I am feeling Nevsky Prospect's 'centripetal all-engulfing force', which is how Grebenshikov defines the essence of the city's main avenue, an essence which he believes has not changed since Dostoyevsky's time. I have had to give up my fantasy about moving to Leningrad when I finish school. It is too late for these kinds of indulgences. But I can run to earth the traces of Grebenshikov. I am determined to find the building where he lives. We are told to scout a certain inner-city locale by a DJ we meet at a Palace of Culture. (Palaces and Houses of Culture are a Soviet version of community centres, well-surveilled hubs of 'cultural leisure' complete with much-sought-after theatre and performance spaces and uniquely suited to channelling and sublimating people's potentially dangerous 'surplus energies'.)

We walk along Perovskaya Street, sticking our heads into every building on the way (oh, the golden era before the inter-com, when blocks of flats and even posh apartment buildings were enchantingly porous). We recognise 'our' building by the fans' scrawl, which covers the staircase walls from the ground floor right up to the top where Bob (as BG likes to be called; the man is an Anglophile) lives in a communal apartment. I have never seen so much graffiti in my life, all of it purpose-ful and, on the whole, well spelt: a dense maze of Idolatry 101, fragments of Aquarium songs and philosophical maxims that seem to engage each other in one of those longstanding con-versations that need no one to continue them. With time, it will become fashionable to regard these walls with obligatory irony, as if apologising for the lack of sophistication, for the crudeness of this altar. Only Grebenshikov's mother will tenderly copy the inscriptions from the walls, to include them in a book about her son, as a tribute to all those people who loved her little boy with such a naïve, childlike desperation.

Outside BG's door on the fifth floor, his fans are known to wait for him at all hours of the day and night, not giving up the hope that their idol may share a brisk glass of port with them in the hall (they will supply the beverage, of course), or tell them something life-changing, or simply smile appreciatively, in recognition of their loyalty and impeccable taste, on the way to taking his all-too-human rubbish out.

Somewhere between the second and third floors, Marina and I take a brush and a tube of gouache paint we brought from her place and add our own lines to the wall. A slightly reworked quote from his lyrics, nothing arse-licking, don't worry. I have contemplated our inscription for days: *Borya, always remain in a place of green trees and gold over blue*. *Borya* is neither the cool, knowing, for-insiders-only *Bob* nor the overly deferential *BG*, it is an informal version of Boris – this is, I imagine, what he would have been called before becoming *the* man about town. As Marina and I are about to put the lid back on the squeezed-to-death paint tube, we hear the creaking of a door followed by a wail of an exasperated neighbour: 'What are you doing ruining the walls? Have you no shame! Get rid of this crap or I'll call the police. Don't you know? He does not live here anymore, you fools. He never comes here at all.'

'Did the grumpy neighbour call the police?' I ask Marina twenty years later, all too aware of how quickly the tissue of my memory grows over all the gaps. 'No,' she replies without hesitating.

'Did we clean up the graffiti?'

'Of course not – are you kidding!'

'Do you remember how our lines looked on that wall?'

'Yes, they looked good – nice and fat. I saw them a few years later in a documentary about Grebenshikov and St Petersburg's underground culture. They were filming him going up the stairs and the camera caught our bit of the wall. Of course it has all been cleaned up since then. All the buildings near Nevsky Prospect have been completely renovated and refurbished – they are all now offices and exclusive apartment blocks for the *nasosy*.' (*Nasosy*, which means 'vacuum cleaners', is unflattering St Petersburg slang for the new rich.)

On reflection, I now see that 5 Perovskaya Street was my first visit to a real site of pilgrimage, although perhaps some classical pilgrimage components were missing. For one, I would have never knocked on BG's door and would have genuinely dreaded the prospect of coming face-to-face with the phantom man at the top of the stairs. I know now that the very act of paying respects to the phantom man himself was not what was ultimately at stake for me and Marina. (After all, isn't the real purpose of any pilgrimage a communion with other pilgrims, rather than the communion with a dead or living deity of one's choice?) What was at stake was the need to seal our friendship before I left the country. Climbing up those stairs together with Marina felt like a rapid and irreversible solidification of our friendship, like a more mature version of a childhood ritual in which we used to cut our fingers and rub them together, bleeding and sticky, in the literal creation of blood ties.

All these years later, I still suspect that I am a St Petersburg person, that if something had happened in those last months of 1989 and my family had not been able to emigrate, I would have somehow made my way to this city. Of course, I have never lived in St Petersburg, so what would I really know? I never woke up and went to sleep in one of its countless decrepit communal apartments, never came to see with painful clarity that this was a place of magnificent facades and rotting, neglected interiors. I never had to contend with its legendary climate – legendary for producing only sixty or so sunny days a year. And then there's the weight of its history – the barbaric creation of the city on the bones of the people, thousands of whom died draining the swamps at the whim of the Emperor Peter; the 1917 Revolution germinating and finally exploding in the city; the nine hundred days of the Blockade, which, after the camps, is perhaps the most unbearable aspect of the Soviet Union's World War II legacy. And my heroes of the city, look what happened to them: Mandelstam perishing in one of the transit camps ('Petersburg, I don't want to die yet'); Brodsky forced to emigrate; Akhmatova compelled to live with the grief of not one but two slain husbands, as well as with chronic poverty, persecution and harassment, her only son imprisoned for over a decade. So, what would I know? And still, I often fantasise about being a disgruntled resident of St Petersburg, the kind who once in a while cannot wait to escape from the city to some simple, sunny place, only to come back and 'to swallow at once the cod liver oil of Leningrad's river lamps'. (Mandelstam here again, a few years before his death.)

★

Marina is waiting for us at her apartment, ready to light twelve candles as soon as the door opens, as if she knows how much Billie needs to be fussed over, how desperately my daughter needs a big production to be made out of her birthday – with people listening intently for her steps, 'Shh, shh, was that the lift?', with the candles lit just in time, with 'Happy Birthday' sung uproariously, as if it was not at most nine in the morning. Marina's husband, Misha Senior, who met us at the train station, enters the apartment first, followed by our two suitcases – 'gigantically enormous and impossibly huge' (sounds like that Jonathan Safran Foer book, but it is merely the suitcases' description in Billie's diary). I see Misha's tall musician's frame bent under the weight of the larger suitcase, the contents of which I can no longer account for, except to say that three megabooks by Australia's own Isobelle Carmody, weighing at least five kilos, are stuffed in it. They are Billie's fiercely negotiated provisions to be stretched over five weeks on this trip. She cannot do without these books because she cannot read in Russian. In her golden bilingual childhood Billie spoke excellent Russian, knew the alphabet and was just getting into reading when she started primary school and the wall-to-wall English of her new surroundings first sidelined and then pretty much ousted her other 'native' language. Shortly after I simply gave up on the unrewarding task of forcing Billie to maintain and improve her Russian – in the words of the Russian saying 'I broke all my teeth on the difficulty of it' – and look who is crying. (Answer: I am the one who is crying, she seems totally fine with her Carmodies.)

Billie, this is my dear friend Marina I have told you so much about. Marina, this is my daughter, Billie. Here we are. Within the same four walls for the first time ever. Every meeting like that, across even one generation, feels like the undoing of a curse. It should be the most basic thing in the world for your friends to know your kids and for your friends' kids to take you and your presence for granted, to recognise your voice on the phone even before you finish saying hello: 'Mum is not home, Auntie Maria. Have to go. Bye.' But this is precisely the knot that emigration unties, this kind of assumed inter-generational mingling, assured in perpetuity for those who never leave the place they grew up in. Or at least, this is the knot that emigration used to untie. It does not have to be like that anymore, now that the era of the migrant ship is over, and walls between East and West, North and South have crumbled. Today's migrants know that coming back for a visit (even for good, perhaps) is just a question of money and dealing with rampant, greedy, sadistic bureaucracy. But back in 1989, when we left, things were different. My mum thought she would never see anyone again – not her friends, not her sister and not her father. (She turned out to be wrong about the last two.) When she was finally inside the train with many of her friends on the platform weeping and waving, well of course the train was then delayed for fifteen minutes, suspending them all at this point of the irreversible tear. It was, Mum says, probably the deepest and the sharpest grief of her life. So understand that in 1989 our goodbyes were not provisional. To have this sense of permanent rupture undone, for my daughter to be locked in a hug with Marina, for me to give Marina and Misha's nine-year-old son a respectful peck on the cheek (real boys don't hug) – this is the revenge of the emigrant, the 'Flight of the Bumblebee', and the triumph of human will, all at once.

Dear Diary,

My imaginary Marina was tall, long-legged, had long wavy brown hair and, unfortunately, was dressed in a very doll-like patriotic Russian costume. The real Marina was small, with straight black hair and most definitely was not wearing the patriotic Russian outfit!!! The one thing my two Marinas had in common was warmth.

Misha Junior had met me five years ago when I was last in St Petersburg, but I am sure he remembered little if anything of that visit. So I could not but wonder how *imaginary Maria and Billie* were meant to look and sound like in his mind, in what way we were meant to wear our made-in-Australia tags. What, by the way, would a *patriotic Australian costume* look like – and would it involve a pair of thongs? The 'imaginary Marina' as an ethnic Barbie doll, now this was funny. I had no idea that all this time in her mind Billie was dressing my childhood friends in folk costumes embroidered with symbols of nationhood, as if they came from some kind of 1980s Soviet Embassy reception. But Billie was right about one thing: with people like Marina it feels like someone is gently blowing warm air onto your frostbite. It is a feeling of gradual thawing out. The warm meal; the clean, crisp sheets; the warm water in the shower saved just for us. Drop by drop, the Russian airport as the state of being is expunged. This is what Marina does.

Marina is a broadcaster, a born one at that. Proud woman of the radio waves, heard regularly on Eldorado station, St Petersburg's home of retro radio, she is capable of communicating everything from gravity to bemusement by an imperceptible change in phrasing or register. My fellow Scorpio Marina, born in a country where women were supposed to be people, citizens, mothers, workers first and only then women; yet, just like my own mother, Marina is something I have never learnt to be: a woman first, and all else second.

For many decades, the official Soviet rhetoric of equality and emancipation was maintained against a backdrop of actual startling inequality coupled with an unquestioning expectation of women's readiness for self-sacrifice. Yes, there were countless women engineers and women doctors in the Soviet Union at a time when their Western stepsisters were left to contend with the 'teacher, nurse or secretary' trifecta. During World War II Soviet women did not just bandage the wounded or manufacture ammunitions, they led tank divisions and operated machine guns. And after the war it was Valentina Tereshkova, with her perfectly proletarian roots (her father was first a tractor driver and then a slain war hero), who became the first woman in space in 1963. The 'glass ceiling' may have been well and truly broken for Soviet women, but the shards of the shattered glass lodged themselves in every aspect of women's everyday existence.

Though the Constitution guaranteed Soviet women equal rights, the actual differences in their estates was revealed in a simple '*chastushka*', a folk limerick which could be loosely translated like this: 'I am a horse, I am a whale, I am a female and a male.' Soviet women were repeatedly told how far they had come compared to their bourgeois counterparts – after all, the existence of the vast majority of tragically domesticated Western women was summed up by the Three K's in the atavistic German slogan popular under Hitler: *Kinder, Küche, Kirche* (Children, Kitchen, Church). The irony, of course, was that neither *Kinder* nor *Küche* had disappeared from the equation for 'liberated' Soviet women, while the Party was to prove far more demanding and omnipresent than the *Kirche*. Women were essentially the slaves of the slaves, with little leisure to contemplate the difficulties of their two-tier subjugation. It was not a question of wanting it all, but rather of doing it all – work, children, housework, community work and sex (try doing it in a room you share with your kids and your parents). Soviet women led the world in abortion statistics because of the lack of contraceptives. Forget about time to spend on self-development! They pinned back their two-sizes-too-big tops, stuffed cotton wool in their two-sizes-too-large shoes and, after long hours at work and in queues, they constructed elaborate networks of contacts and strategic alliances so as to get their hands on a mascara or a creamy beige face powder. (They were women, after all.)

In short, the task of being a woman was socially unsupported and, in practical terms, a nightmare. And even though Marina and I came of age in the dying days of this massive gender abolition experiment, we emerged two very different people. My friend was not in two minds about being a woman, but every bit of me was. Why did all that insane ideological bullshit work on me? Why, as a teenager and a young woman, was I so obsessed with achieving some kind of phantom gender neutrality, pretending, at the age of twelve, that I did not know what perfume was? (Please!) Getting off on being treated as one of the guys? Why did it work on me, even though my own mother was the living proof that you could be deadly smart, strong and independent while being beautiful and feminine to boot? That you did not need to de-sex yourself in order to be taken seriously? That being the woman of the family could be a source of joy rather than simply the painstaking fulfilment of duty? Unlike me, Marina instinctively knew early on that happiness was essentially a private affair rarely achieved in the service of ideology or ideals, that sensitivity was not a weakness, that emotion would not undo us, and that caring for your family was as noble a pursuit as feeding the hungry. Like I said, she was a woman first.

Billie's birthday present from Marina and family is five hours of *Carmen* at the Mariinski Theatre. The Mariinski, known for most of the twentieth century as the Kirov Opera and Ballet, is in its two hundred and twenty-sixth season. Bizet's opera first played there in 1885, igniting its massive popularity across Russia. The composer Petr Tchaikovsky is said to have predicted *Carmen*'s fatal appeal when attending its premiere in Paris several years before. 'In ten years,' he apparently said, '*Carmen* will be the most popular opera in the world.'

At the Mariinski everything is mixed together: the tradition, the magnificence of the architecture, the high artistry of performers – and the petty viciousness of a group of middle-aged women behind us, who at first look so harmless and homely in their glasses and neck scarfs, like a bunch of geography teachers on the cusp of retirement. We are in the row in front of them and, it would seem, blocking their view of the stage. 'Both the girl and the boy think they are the only ones in the theatre,' they say. They are not even whispering but enunciating clearly, the dull kitchen knives of their words driven into our backs with great deliberation. 'Valya has let her hair out and all the sailors are falling over themselves': a line from a Russian folk song is meant to encapsulate the scandal of Billie's long and luxurious hair eating up the viewing space around her head. Marina stays silent, used to women like this and the constant white noise of their disapproval, which is not addressed to anyone in particular yet is voluminous and demanding just the same. But I am out of practice.

'What specifically would you like to see happen?' I turn around and face the group. 'You are clearly upset, so please tell me how the situation can be improved.' My voice bristles with the exaggerated politeness of someone ready to throw punches at the slightest provocation.

And so Billie's hair is pulled back for their viewing pleasure, but the women do not rest for long after this victory. Judging it much too minor, they move their attention to a young woman in the row in front of us, who happens to be wearing a rather ostentatious beret (ostentatious, at least in their opinion). This is how it is with the Arts: the good, the bad, the ugly, the profound, the petty, the profane, all hopelessly intermingled in one experience. In the Ermitazh Theatre, where we watch the ballet *Swan Lake* a few days later, some Russian men on the balcony wash down booze straight from the bottle with soft drinks straight from the can. The rest of the auditorium is filled almost exclusively by four busloads of American tourists, who spend most of the performance digesting their recently consumed large meals. The sublime and the ridiculous always together here, each other's faithful keepers.

Carmen, everyone knows, is based on Mérimée's 1845 novella. But what you may not realise is that Mérimée was heavily influenced by Alexander Pushkin's poem *The Gypsies*.

A non-gypsy man falls for a gypsy woman; plunged into a melancholy he cannot explain, he is led away from his settled urban life to be with the woman–wanderer he so ardently loves. And when, with time, having given birth to his child, she tires of him and falls into the arms of a younger lover, he murders her in rage and desperation. Pushkin's gypsy is the woman who calls the shots, who cannot be possessed or loved into submission. No sacrifice in the world can keep her safely near. Carmen is essentially this woman as well – the fearless, fatalistic, face-slashing, hip-swinging, hot-blooded, drop-dead Carmen. She is the highest calibre of femme fatale, capable of causing a man to forsake his principles and honour and, finally, to become a murderer.

The femme fatale was, of course, the antithesis of the Soviet woman as comrade. Straight after the Revolution the New Woman – a type embodied by Inessa Armand and Alexandra Kolontai, Lenin's close allies – was precisely the type who worked, fought and risked her life for revolutionary ideals, standing shoulder to shoulder with the man next to her, rather than using her charms to seduce and ensnare him. Any New Woman fit to become an equal member of the revolutionary society wanted equality, freedom and mutual respect in her relationships with men, instead of craving co-dependency, irrational passion and insularity. Both Armand and Kolontai were every bit the burning revolutionaries, but they were also true proto-feminists (which is more than you can say for most of their male comrades). Their radical views on the emancipation of women included a vision of women's sexual liberation in which it was perfectly fine for women to have multiple partners and enter into open marriages. They were both strikingly beautiful (which always helps, whether you're a New Woman or an old one), possessed of abundant charms and sex appeal.

Despite multiple refutations, the rumours of Lenin's long-standing affair with Armand have refused to die down for almost a century. Then there was Lilya Brik, the strikingly beautiful and unconventional de facto spouse of Stalin's favourite revolutionary poet, Vladimir Mayakovsky, and you might say more of a New Woman in the Western mould. For large periods of time Brik, Mayakovsky, and Lilya's husband, Osip Brik, lived and worked together in one apartment, in a Soviet mini-version of the Bloomsbury set. By all accounts, Brik, who was surrounded by smitten suitors all her life, loved both Vladimir *and* Osip, and the two men admired each other and managed to share her with a spirit of remarkable camaraderie. To openly live with two men – one of whom was rapidly becoming the 'loudspeaker' of the socialist ideas and ideals – was an incredibly gutsy thing to do in austere and puritanical Soviet society. Brik was routinely condemned as a perverted bourgeois femme fatale, rather than being praised as a social revolutionary. Predictably, most references to her as the poet's muse and partner were expunged from the official version of Mayakovsky's life after his suicide in 1930. Yet her life was apparently spared by Stalin himself. Seeing her name on an execution list during the Great Purge, Stalin is said to have remarked, 'Leave Mayakovsky's wife alone', and struck her name from the list.

The vision of the New Woman did not last for too long after the Revolution, because it was simply too radical and inconvenient for the men in power, and too challenging for women of traditional values to support, as Brik's case suggests. A newly formed nation already dealing with revolutions, civil wars and massive industrialisation challenges would simply implode if women stopped taking care of men, or giving birth to children, or bearing the lion's share of the so-called domestic sphere.

Despite its exciting allure, the New Woman's sexuality was markedly different from that of the traditional femme fatale who appeared in early Soviet literature and opera, reforged and recoded as a bourgeois woman with bedroom eyes and an insatiable desire for material possessions. She reappeared during World War II as a woman on the home front, having an affair while her husband fought the Nazis, risking his life every second of every day for her and their children born and unborn. The savage nobility of Pushkin's and Mérimée's gypsies, and the love of freedom above all else that defined them (Carmen: 'Love is a rebellious bird that no one can tame'), were gone. Instead, staring at us from underneath her heavily made-up and cunning eyes, was a banally treacherous seductress, a creature as familiar with the concept of true, all-consuming freedom as a broom handle in a closet.

The proud, attractive gypsies of Pushkin and Mérimée are also nothing like the gypsies I came to know in daily life. The ones I saw growing up were skilful thieves, underground merchants and compulsive wanderers. They moved in mobs, stole everything that did not lie straight and had a way of rendering our 'indefatigable' Soviet police powerless. They were most recognisable in popular images of dirty children, female beggars and palm readers (often one and the same), of golden jewellery dangling and sparkling on women of all ages – at least it looked golden to me then. The Russian language too pinned them down in no uncertain terms: a 'gypsy sun' was the moon, a 'gypsy trade union' a gathering of hobos. People were wary around them, while the Soviet state tried to tame them, settle them, put them into purpose-built factories and collective farms and take their children away. To little avail.

The parallels between the persecution of Jews and gypsies in Europe are well-known. The Nuremberg Laws of 1935, aimed initially at the Jewry, were amended to include Romany people, who by 1937 were firmly classified as concentration camp material. In the Soviet Union, gypsies were tirelessly harassed by authorities powerless to control their movement and their activities. According to the *European Commission against Racism and Intolerance*, they are still the most oppressed minority in today's Russia. Like citizens from the Caucasus, they are twenty times more likely to be stopped by police patrols than citizens of Slav appearance. But unlike other persecuted minorities, gypsies seem to have relished their outsiders' role. In his recent history of gypsies, artist and writer Nicolay Bessonov suggests that, despite all their persecution, 'there was no freer people in the whole of the Soviet Union' – free from involuntary atheism; from military conscription; from the social apparatus that forced people like sausage meat from schools to tertiary institutions to their first 'assigned' jobs, then to permanent positions few would ever leave. Gypsies made their own choices about what to do and were not beholden to their superiors. For a totalitarian society this must count for something, says Bessonov.

Anyway, back to the opera and Billie's birthday treat.

Dear Diary,
Escamillo was a chubby not too good-looking bloke who was massively undervoiced. Compared to Don José (pronounced Ho-ss-ay) he was

horrible. It made Carmen look like a lady who went for the popular guy that the (fake) peasants loved. José was amazing. Carmen was, as my mum and Marina said, 'a chick with an attitude'.

Since we met over two decades ago, Marina and I have never had a fight. For one, we have never lived at close quarters long enough to have those kitchen-sink stoushes; and as far as the big picture is concerned, from love to politics and back again, such differences as we could unearth and debate over a great distance – by way of phone calls, letters and emails – were never fundamental. So when our blow-up comes, right out of the blue at the end of a long and happy day together, with a nice dinner in our stomachs, both Marina and I are taken aback. It is Marina who starts it with what is clearly a throwaway line not intended to cause friction, most probably not even meant to elicit any kind of response. A rhetorical statement, in other words.

'Those Americans, so hollow on the inside. I have to say I absolutely loathe Texas.'

Have I heard her correctly? Unsure, I respond in a way that on reflection seems all too combat-ready, as if she is pushing on something inside me, something I cannot quite identify.

'What are you talking about? Have you been to America? How many Americans do you know?'

'You know I haven't, but I have met enough Americans. But this is not the point. Look at their culture, their movies, their music. What more evidence do you need?'

I'm on thin ice, since all through our trip I have been making rude jokes about the busloads of American tourists who seem to dog our steps. But I plunge headfirst into an argument anyway.

'I cannot believe you can talk like that about the whole people. It is like saying that all Russians are alcoholics and all Jews are cunning.'

'No, it is not. Alcoholism is external, but this emptiness, it lives and multiplies on the inside. It is their culture. You cannot mistake it for anything else.'

'You cannot talk about the whole people like that. These are personal attributes, not national ones.'

'Yes, you can. The only reason you may think you cannot is because of political correctness. But if you are honest, you can say that Norwegians, for instance, are on the whole rather primitive. They made their secondary education compulsory not that long ago. You can say that Finns are pretty calm. You should see them fish. And Americans, well, you know what I think.'

It starts off all bemused and civilised and ends in shouting. Misha Senior has to pull us apart, make us stop talking over each other. He knows, all of us know, that this conversation is unlikely to end well with either of us crossing the floor. It is best to end it now. He looks on like a boxing referee at the end of a round, anxious to make sure there are no freak punches thrown when the other is not looking. Misha is a con-firmed cosmopolitan, his superior English learned initially for the sake of the English-language music tradition, which, in his view, any self-respecting rock musician should know and fol-low closely. He loves London, loves the English mother tongue, and the music born and bred in that British milieu. I have no idea where he stands in this argument, for he never tells us. And lest Marina comes across as a case study in banal insularity, let me say now that she has travelled widely and possesses plenty of what is known as cultural awareness and curiosity. Her position, in other words, is in no way a reflection of horizon-deficiency. I know that much.

However contentious Marina's pronouncements may sound to me, I recognise how lame my retorts must sound to her. They even sound lame to me. Am I a victim of political correctness, a spouter of crusty slogans, a 'bleeding-heart liberal', as those damn Americans might say? The same words pronounced elsewhere, about the utter fallacy of reducing a nation to a person (usually an infuriatingly flawed person), would seem safely self-evident, but here, in Marina and Misha's apartment, they sound grandiose and self-righteous. I wonder too, after calming down a bit, to what degree the intensity of my response comes from grappling with one particular tradition central to anti-Semitism and, perhaps, to any kind of xenophobia. This is the tradition of condensing the whole Jewish people into a singular grotesque image, which is then held responsible for the suffering of the Russian people – a cunning and ruthless Jewish moneylender of the nineteenth century, or a Jewish revolutionary of the early twentieth century embracing all things Soviet with an eerie zeal. Variations of those stereotypes have existed in Europe for centuries, and now they have a global counterpart in the figure of a cunning and ruthless Israeli settler responsible for the suffering of the Palestinian people. Is this the button that Marina pushes in me? After all, she does not actually hate anyone (probably not even Texans!); she is just generalising, big deal. There is no double standard in what she is saying either. I am pretty sure she could have a crack at the Russian people in the same expansive, all-encompassing terms.

Several months later, still trying to figure out what it was about our fight that affected me so deeply, I peer into the brave new world of the Russian blogosphere, only to discover how uncontroversial Marina's views actually are. Educated and smart people are saying essentially the same things – despite some fundamental similarities, people and cultures are different, and there is no harm in trying to capture those defining and important differences in words, as long as you are not being outright xenophobic, blindly asserting your own people's and culture's undoubted superiority.

I read these articulate and well-formulated posts, and I feel like I come from another planet. Yes, I too think that without recognising and trying to understand what is profoundly different about people's lives, behaviours and worldviews, there is no effective politics, no good literature, no enlightened conversation between cultures. And the notion of the global community itself, if it is to be more than a vast transnational zone for the exchange of goods and services, only makes sense when universal principles come together with this recognition of irreducible difference. What bothers me is the monolithic quality of the pronouncements of difference – the clash of civilisations theories, the idea of the chosen people (whoever these people are), the notion of national characteristics that Marina espouses (however refined those notions may become in the hands of a skilful demagogue). I am reminded of writer Marietta Chudakova's observation about how comfortably inferiority and messianic complexes coexist among her fellow inhabitants in post-Soviet Russia. And it's not just about

Russia of course. What about the Americans with their sense of Manifest Destiny; the French, who gave the name to chauvinism; the British with their Empire on which the sun would never set (or so they thought)? When you think about it hard enough, the human condition can sometimes seem like a giant medical chart of all these complexes – superiority, inferiority, messianic, you name it.

Perhaps if these monolithic pronouncements concerned only the question of national or ethnic identity I would disagree with them vehemently but not feel quite so personally affronted by them. But they hover around a very different kind of question too – not what it means to belong to a certain people, but what it means to be a woman. The Soviet ideas of womanhood – harsh, puritanical and deeply disingenuous – have long since been eclipsed, but there are still 'hard and fast' rules about what it is that a woman really needs. Since the end of my second marriage, most heartfelt birthday wishes I receive from my female friends in Russia and Ukraine focus on the appearance of a man in my life. Not just any man, of course, but kind, smart, good-looking, passionate, creative, with money and a strong libido, who will carry me around in his arms, having first taken the burden of solitary womanhood from my shoulders. At times my friends can stretch themselves to endorse my argument that there is no greater tragedy than a loveless, hollow marriage, and that to escape such a fate can be cause for enduring happiness – as long as they think I am on the way out to try to meet someone else.

Back in her kitchen in St Petersburg, Marina and I look away from each other. Billie, with her nose buried in an Isobelle Carmody book, does not seem to have noticed the change of temperature around her. Has she heard any of the shouting? 'Let's have a drink,' says Misha, who is half-Russian and half-Jewish (and thus simultaneously smart and cunning, and uniquely predisposed to solving 'problems' with a few shots of vodka, but not too many). We drink in silence and I think about Marina. I test my feelings about her: Have they changed? Have our life experiences pushed us to the opposite sides of the divide, turning her into a xenophobe and me into the caricature of a holier-than-thou Western liberal democrat? For half an hour or so our faces wear *Do I really know you?* expressions. Then our stiff necks start to relax. It is very hard to maintain our hurt pride and momentary outrage. There is too much love, history and loyalty between us to regard each other with suspicion.

We are still friends, and I wonder how our friendship turned out to be immune to this blow-up. If you think of it, our conversation was seriously unsettling for both of us, maybe even a deal-breaker. Friendships, I do not need to tell you, tear over less irreconcilable differences. Is it because we forgive our childhood friends much more than those friends we make as grown-ups? Or is it because we learn that we do not need our friends to agree with us or to espouse the same views on select 'big' topics? (This is what drinking buddies and professional acquaintances are for.) What we really need is for our friends to stand behind us, to have our back, to hold us, especially when we are ridiculously far away from each other.

It occurs to me that I have never really asked how it was for you in 1989, Marina. I was so preoccupied with my own grief. I ask you now, and you reply:

I remember so well the cold wind on the Neva embankment. And you got on your knees to say goodbye to the Neva. The cold I felt was inside of me, from the thought of seeing you off into nowhere. I really did think that I would never see you again. I could not imagine then that this country would stop existing, and that there would be instead a new country with international passports and trips abroad. I was convinced then that all I had left was writing letters and waiting for months for your replies (because of all the mail being checked).

Do you remember we met some of my classmates and I felt kind of ashamed for them? They were so uninteresting, unremarkable (forgive me my arrogance). This is the truth. And they were staying here, while you were going. I really wanted you to understand then that these people were just my classmates, they were not my close friends. This was very important to me. I wanted you to know that I was with them because I did not have a choice.

I knew this, Marina. I also knew that after I left you never contemplated the possibility that our friendship was too high-maintenance or too abstract to survive. You have found me after all those years in the pre-email wilderness, during which time both of us changed postal addresses and lost track of each other. You did not count this protracted episode of mutual disappearance as death from natural causes. You did not stop looking. I did, but you did not. What are our 'ideological differences' compared to this history, to learning from opposite ends, what Mandelstam called, 'the science of departures'?

9

LENINGRAD

I WOULD NOT BE telling you the whole story about St Petersburg if I said nothing of the war. Not so much World War II as the Great Patriotic War, the Soviet portion of the conflict, which began with the German invasion of the Soviet Union on 22 June 1941. As I was growing up, the city of Leningrad and its agonisingly long siege by German troops were inseparable in my mind. This is not, I think, some peculiar personal quirk. I was born into a world drenched in references to the Great Patriotic War (the very opposite of 'don't mention the war' culture). It was omnipresent and had certainly long since eclipsed the symbolic power of the 1917 Revolution.

The legendary 'hero city' was how St Petersburg was referred to as I was going through school. It was one of several cities granted this formal recognition by the Soviet government. (Really clever totalitarians can teach us a great deal about running brand-awareness campaigns.) In my history textbook at school, the war towered over all other topics, and the description of the Siege of Leningrad read like a series of black, pounding newspaper headlines: one of the darkest chapters of the conflict with Fascism; nine hundred days of starvation, cold and constant shelling between September 1941 and January 1944; then, of course, the horror trumped by a happy ending. Against all odds we did not surrender Leningrad (while, needless to say, 'they' did not think twice of surrendering 'their' Paris). The 'mission statement' that accompanied every mention of the siege was crystal-clear. I bet it could have been conjured up without much hesitation by every child seven-plus, even a kid shaken awake in the middle of the night.

In the endlessly repeated summations of what had happened in Leningrad and what it all meant, heroism overpowered human suffering, finally swallowing it altogether. This was what always happened. As I was growing up, the mantra of *heroism* was like a stick with which we were constantly hit over the head, rendering us incapable of making sense of the war in almost any other terms. But, in reality, the Siege of Leningrad could not begin to be contained by the story of high patriotism. It was too devastating, too confronting, too awful for that. What were people to eat when there was nothing to eat, when their daily ration was the legendary one hundred and twenty-five grams of bread — if you had a ration card, that is. But what if it was stolen, or you were not entitled to one, like many temporary residents stranded there by the war? Before their mothers' eyes, the malnourished children of the city shrivelled into dystrophic old nannas and grandpas, then died from hunger and cold. (The first winter of the siege was the worst in living memory.) One by one, people of all ages simply collapsed in their homes, on the streets and stairwells, and died on the spot, their bodies lying around until trucks traversing the city for no other purpose than this finally arrived to collect them. Officially, around six hundred and fifty thousand lives were lost in besieged Leningrad. The real figure is more than one million, and some estimates even push it close to two million. Which means, at the very least, every third resident of the city.

In the 1970s Daniil Granin and Ales Adamovich, two writers who had themselves fought in the Great Patriotic War, decided to collect stories of *blokadniki*, the name given to the survivors of the siege. Their *Book of the Blockade* remains the best account of the siege I have read to date. Initially published in a heavily censored form, it was reissued unabridged after the collapse of the Soviet Union. Granin had been a soldier on the Leningrad Front, Adamovich a partisan in the Belarusian forests. But even those experiences could not prepare them for the stories they heard. In the end they found that the heroism of the siege survivors and victims was of a domestic quality, 'an intra-family, intra-apartment' type, rather than a patriotic mass sacrifice on the altar of embattled motherland. The heroism of *blokadniki* unfolded not in the ideologically inscribed public sphere of conflict but within homes and families. Private and interior, it inevitably coexisted with other hidden aspects, far more unsavoury, that were also absent from the patriotic history of the siege: the lesser parts of human nature that sometimes could be traced to the sheer extremity of the siege experience and sometimes to people's rotten insides, as in the case of some privileged cadres who kept themselves warm and fed at the expense of others, or of the scum who killed people for their ration cards. Inevitably, there were cases of cannibalism too.

After everything they had heard, exhausted and made ill by the stories of people's suffering, Granin and Adamovich became convinced that during the siege people treated each other 'much more sincerely, humanely and mercifully than at the end of the 1970s'. So many *blokadniki* managed not to become indifferent to the suffering of others, despite being pushed to the absolute limit by their daily experiences. In contrast, that very indifference gradually became accepted as the social norm in the decades after the war. Heartlessness was no longer seen as a great personal failing. As they were going from one apartment to another (often the very same apartments in which *blokadniki* had lived through the siege, and which decades afterwards were for the most part in a terrible, shameful state of disrepair) they asked themselves what their book was ultimately going to be about. After circling around, Granin and Adamovich invariably would come back to the same thing. Their *Book of the Blockade* was, first of all, about the intelligentsia. Leningrad was a city with a very strong tradition of intellectual, cultural and spiritual life. The fact that this tradition persisted right through the siege is well-known. Its most celebrated manifestation is, of course, Dmitry Shostakovich's *Leningrad Symphony*, written and first performed in the besieged city. But there were other remarkable signs of this life: new theatre plays were staged, museums were opened and well-patronised, students continued their education, Leningrad radio kept on broadcasting, and a group of architects worked on the plans for the city's revival after the war.

★

Dear Diary,

Last night we went to see Leningradka – *a puppet show about the blockade of St Petersburg (Leningrad at the time). It was amazing, stunning, touching, intelligent, creative, heartbreaking, terrifying and unlike anything I'd seen before.*

'*Leningradka*' is the word for a female resident of Leningrad. The play's subtitle is 'Puppet Parable for Adults'. *Leningradka*, which fuses puppetry and cinema, is based on a real-life story about a young girl left all alone during the siege. She survived by hiding in a wardrobe and staying there throughout the siege. So as not to go insane, she made up fairy tales.

When you entered the small room, which contained seating for less than fifty, all there was was a large see-through screen, a speaker in front of it and a phone at the side, but otherwise that was all. When it began you saw an old woman with a mischievous smile, the type that says, 'I know something you don't know.' I, as a child, was sitting in the front row, and so it felt like I was in the projection with the old lady walking around the black-and-white ruins where she used to live. As the old woman continues to walk, she becomes a child again.

The mischievous old lady goes back to being a twelve-year-old girl, Valechka, in Leningrad during the war.

Valechka the child creeps through her house past her distressed sleeping mother into the hallway. Her mum is lying with her back to Valechka, but there is a shot in which we can see she is crying. Valechka creeps into the kitchen and you can see her father. Her narrative voice starts telling us, 'For the last few days Papa just sits with a smile on his face and barely talks. Mamma cries and doesn't want him to go. They don't speak to each other.'

Papa is about to leave for the front, and Mamma cannot bear to see him leave.

Valechka's father has a lolly in the palm of his hand, just one lolly, so small, for us it is nothing but for them it is the size of a day's food. The lolly is from the domovoy *– a little creature that guards their building. 'You put milk under the table, and when you wake up in the morning the milk is gone and in its place is a lolly,' Papa says to Valechka.*

A *domovoy* is a house spirit, a poltergeist that looks after a building and its inhabitants, engaging them, regularly but rarely in the flesh, in the intricate rituals of give-and-take. Normally, which is to say in peacetime, a *domovoy* manifests itself playfully by knocking, slamming doors and, when no one is looking, gobbling up treats left for him, most commonly milk.

'That night,' says Valechka, 'was the only night when I did not want morning to come.' She said that line with such pure sadness and you forgot she was just an actress . . . Next morning her father leaves to fight at the front, leaving two weeping women behind. Some unknown time later you see Valechka fill a bowl with water and walk over to the wall to scrape some of the wall into the water, making it white, like milk. She places it under the table and stays there a bit, waiting for the domovoy.

By this stage there is nothing to eat. When hunger started in Leningrad, people ripped wallpaper off their walls and ate the flour paste with which they were initially plastered.

169

Then you can see the shots of these endless planes dropping bombs in lots of hundreds, blowing up Leningrad. Bombs start blowing up near Valechka and her mum, and suddenly a bomb blows up right where they are. 'Mamochka (Mummy),' cries out the small petrified voice of Valechka, 'Mamochka, Mamoch . . . kkka . . .' Valechka can barely whisper and her only reply is cold heartless silence and more bombs, her mother's murderers. Valechka comes up to a small shattered window and opens it and whispers into the dark night, 'Domovoy, domovoy, prixodi ko mne domoy.' ('Domovoy, domovoy, come to my house.') Then Valechka hides herself in the cupboard. The image zooms out, making itself seem further away and suddenly a puppet appears. The puppet is the domovoy.

The *domovoy*, with his vast, piercing eyes and rough, greying beard, looks like a friendly janitor. His hands grip a broom. He exudes sadness and bewildered, steadfast devotion. He is visibly tired. This war is ophaning his building – those inhabitants who have not left are dying one by one. Valechka is the last one of his wards. As long as she is alive, he will not abandon his duties.

Before I saw this play I had seen rather primitive puppet plays that were not well crafted or just stupid, so I was worried that it would be the same in this play, but I was so mistaken I cannot describe it. The puppets were detailed and intricate, realistic yet out of this world. Handmade by a master with so much care and love it was like in Pinocchio – they were the creator's children. They were everything I could have dreamed of and more. I shall not continue describing the play but will tell you that the show continued and only got sadder and sadder. Other puppets are revealed – the selfish rat, HUNGER, and a Nazi soldier who opens his coat and inside is another puppet, COLD. The play was so touching that in the end there was not a single person dry-eyed.

In Russia, there is a longstanding puppeteering tradition. During the Siege of Leningrad, puppet plays continued to be performed in the city by Demmeni Marionette Theatre at 13.00 on the dot, when the punctual German military would take a lunchbreak and the bombing of the city would temporarily subside. Poet Samuil Marshak even wrote a satirical play entitled *Young Fritz*, especially for the theatre. After a long season in the city, it toured the frontline in the Leningrad region and Karelia. More than six hundred performances starring the puppets of Hitler, Goering, Goebbels and the rest of the gang were staged in the forests of the region. According to eyewitnesses, during those performances whole forests would be shaking with laughter. OK, this was during the war; but in peacetime, all those years later, who would have thought that a puppet play about the Siege of Leningrad could be so unforgettable?

As words, statistics, images, even eyewitness accounts, HUNGER and COLD have become deeply ossified, but as puppets they come to life. They are terrifying and real, but they are also small, inept and childlike. Other puppets in the show are just as affecting – a lonely tram that crosses the city; a sledge that in the siege woud have been used for transporting water and corpses; a truck carrying mandarins to the kids of Leningrad across the thin ice of Lake Ladoga via the legendary 'Road of Life' (*Doroga Zhizni*), the only route that connected the besieged city with the mainland. The ice breaks and the truck with its precious cargo sinks. The puppets are so 'intricate' (as

Billie says in her diary entry), so tiny and fragile, they are the opposite of the standard larger-than-life stories of the siege, its victims and survivors. Everything is scaled down. The large historical canvas is replaced by the intimacy of the room and the puppet play. The shouting is brought down to a whisper.

After the show, Billie can barely move. Slowly, as if she has not walked for months, she comes to me and sits on my lap, hugging me tightly and letting go of all the tears she has tried hard to ration during the performance – the room is small and, being in the first row, she knew that this was not the time or place for uncontrollable sobbing. This is the best, the tightest, the most gut-wrenching hug of our trip. We do not move for a long time. Through my own tears I see Marina watching us, moved by the way Billie has been unravelled by the story of her city. All she says when Billie separates herself from me is, 'Billie, you need to know about what happened here.' And then all of us get up, keeping that slowness in our bodies, and walk outside, carefully hanging on to each other. After days of constantly harassing Billie because of my insatiable desire to see her floored by history, pinned to her chair by some cultural artefact, affected with a capital 'A', I feel deeply ashamed of myself. All this prodding of my daughter's 'thick skin', breathing disappointment on her withdrawn face, willing her to surrender to the power of Art. *Get off her case, you fool. Stop stalking her,* I say to myself. *Love her, trust her and, for crying out loud, just let her be.*

'The heroism of defenders and residents of Leningrad, who had endured the toughest of ordeals but did not surrender our native city to the enemy, will forever remain in the memory of our people.' These words were in the history text we used at school. I repeat them to myself the night after the play, noticing something I had never noticed as they were hammered into me in my youth: the city's defenders come first, and only then its residents. The three million *Leningradtzi* are lumped together with the Leningrad Front soldiers – exhausted, undernourished and outnumbered as we were constantly told – as well as the entire Soviet people united in their 'heroic quest for liberation'. *Blokadniki* in this formula are no more than a part of the great heroic whole. The not too subliminal message is clear – without the entire nation fighting, suffering and dying together, Leningrad would have been starved to death. The suffering of *blokadniki* is diluted and dispersed. This suffering seemed inevitable and unsurprising when I learned about it at school. It strikes me now as maybe one of the greatest injustices in twentieth-century history.

The rest of the Soviet nation was not to learn about Leningrad's plight before January 1942. The official story of the siege, which emerged straight after the war and persisted more or less unchanged for decades, went as follows: Leningrad did not fall, not because of its people but thanks to the visionary leadership and the colossal assistance provided to the city by the Party and by Comrade Stalin personally. Of course after 1956 and the Twentieth Congress of the CPSU, at which Khrushchev made his famous repudiation of 'certain aspects of the cult of personality', the figure of Stalin was less often centre stage, but until his death in 1953 Stalin had to be inserted right at the heart of this and every other victorious war narrative. The Siege of Leningrad was formally recognised as an expression

of the heroism of the Soviet people, wrote Granin and Adamovich, but 'in reality, all the top officials of the city, all the
people who attempted to get the defence and provisions going
and then the evacuation; all the people who organised the work
of factories, the rebuilding of the destroyed parts of the city
and electrostations – were subjected to repressions'. This wave
of top-secret repressions against the city's leading officials and
community leaders, which occurred between 1948 and 1950,
became known as the Leningrad Affair or Leningrad Case
(*Leningradskoe Delo*). Its victims' alleged 'crime' was a concerted
campaign to oppose the city of Leningrad to the Party, the
Soviet people and to Stalin himself, drunk as they were on 'the
self-delusional' and self-congratulatory perception of the city's
achievements in the war and during the siege most particularly. To put it bluntly, in all its obscenity, they were accused of
conspiring to use the Leningrad Party cell as the basis for the
subversion of the Party's Central Committee.

'The heroism of Leningrad siege survivors,' Granin and
Adamovich wrote, 'was perceived by Stalin and his inner circle
as the expression of the city's freedom-loving spirit, its rebellious nature, its excessive, and at times threatening autonomy.'
Alexei Kuznetsov, a *blokadnik* who was the Leningrad Party
Secretary, allowed himself to get carried away in a speech he
made in 1946, in which he proclaimed that the fame of St
Petersburg had by then overshadowed the legend of Troy. He
was executed some years later. The Siege of Leningrad did not
finish when the war ended, it was transformed into a political
blockade. The 'disgraced city was surrounded by suspicion, all
initiatives were squashed, the city was not allowed to reclaim its
nobility, its achievements, its cultural significance'. Leningrad's

'inferiority complex' was created and painstakingly maintained by a series of the newly installed, plebeian-minded Party officials (most imported from elsewhere). The idea was to turn Leningrad into an ordinary regional centre; in the expression that would emerge later, 'the great city with a regional fate'. Leningrad was punished for imagining it was special and for having ample evidence to prove that indeed it was. Yet this punishment, this campaign of ostracism, paradoxically (or maybe inevitably) worked to strengthen the perception of its separate fate. For the city's intelligentsia it was one more proof (if any was needed) that their city was unlike other Soviet cities, that it was not really Soviet and not really Russian, but its own country, a universe unto itself.

In St Petersburg, the most breathtaking and poetic of cities I know, I find myself coming back to the war over and over again. I struggle to explain to Billie why on their wedding day newlyweds, as tradition dictates, carry bunches of flowers to war memorials. Why Marina is close to tears in telling us how, during the war, a group of female sappers risked their lives disarming mines plastered all over a monument to the poet Alexander Pushkin. Why in the suburb of Pushkin (formerly Tzarskoe Selo), exhibitions in the lavish tsar palaces are accompanied by black-and-white stands documenting the extent of the palaces' destruction during the war. Why Misha Senior, driving us around the city, eager to point out all the places linked to Dostoyevsky (isn't it what all the tourists want?), keeps bumping into sites and objects that intervene in his impromptu literary tour, forcing him back to the subject of the war.

Even though Misha, Marina and I were born almost three decades after the end of the war, it has left its mark on us through its continuous and omnipresent evocation. We too can say, with the historian Svetlana Aleksievich, that, 'War was always remembered, at school and at home, at weddings, christenings and wakes. Even in children's conversations. We did not know the world without war, the world of war was the only one we knew and the people of war were the only people we knew. Till this day I do not know any other world or any other people.' The 'cult of the war' has not disappeared along with the Soviet Union, quite the contrary. Indeed, the victory against Hitler, writes sociologist Lev Gudkov, remains 'the only positive reference point for the national consciousness of post-Soviet society'. In public opinion surveys in recent decades, Russians' belief in the war and the Soviet victory as the most important historical event of the twentieth century has only grown. So much is at stake in terms of national identity that every attempt to reassess the war in either general terms or through a particular episode inevitably produces a massive public backlash. In an instant, those who dare to get close and personal with the war are accused of desecrating the memory of the dead, of attacking that which is most sacred to millions of people and (this one is always a winner!) of spitting in the face of those survivors and veterans still living. The Soviet Union's victory in the war, writes Gudkov, 'does not just crown, but also kind of cleanses and justifies the war, at the same time foreclosing its dark side from rational examination'. And, equally, the dark side of the wartime leadership is foreclosed too. The victory works backwards to rehabilitate post-factum not only the war, but Stalin himself and the 'excesses' of his regime that made this victory possible – millions of his own people shot, deported, thrown into camps and dispossessed.

Russian journalist Aleksandr Minkin speaks of the cultural stranglehold of the war on post-Soviet society with wonderful simplicity: 'The victory in the Great Patriotic War is for everyone (both for the government and the people) the only available foundation on which their heart can rest.' All the remainder is 'a litany of terrible catastrophes, cruelty, famine, disintegration', but in the defeat of Fascism the nation finds true joy. Perhaps most crucially, Gudkov tells us, the Great Patriotic War in Russia has become the 'surrogate for culture – the field of meaning, in which the most important themes and scenarios of the present day are played out'. The war is central to any form of cultural and historical meaning-making. In other words, it remains the measure of most things. But when the war is 'the surrogate of culture', cultural values become defined almost entirely through the prism of 'the highly strung, ecstatic situation' and so we get, not necessarily in this order, 'heroism, self-sacrifice, national mission, the quest for redemption' and the persistent idea of Russia's special destiny in the world. (These ideas work just as well within the template of religion; unsurprisingly, religion is everywhere in the post-Soviet world.) When *the extraordinary* is deemed to be of highest value, *the ordinary* becomes not only diminished or despised, it becomes a corrupting, alien force. And so we end up with a whole nation of people who do not quite know how to be civilians, people who, in the words of Aleksievich, 'have lost the ability to distinguish war from peace, survival from life'. She writes, 'We either fought in the war or were preparing for the war. We never lived any other way.'

10

A TRAIN PLATFORM
SOMEWHERE

*Under dictatorship everyone is scared of the question and under democracy –
of the answer.*

*Under dictatorship there is more ballet and humour, under democracy –
more travel and robberies.*

As to the large-scale animal fear – just as much in both cases.

*Under dictatorship you can be knocked out from the top, under democracy –
from the bottom . . .*

*So while our freedom does differ from dictatorship, the difference is not
so stark as to be clear to a little-educated person such as, say, a writer or a
military officer.*

Mikhail Jvanetsky

THE END OF THE Soviet Empire, the death of Communism, the
birth in Russia and Ukraine of bruised democracy – it is hard to
know how to think, let alone write, about change of this mag-
nitude. Because to say 'from then on everything was different'

is firstly to say nothing, and secondly to lie. So I keep coming back to Mikhail Jvanetsky and his timeless monologues, particularly the above written in the early 1990s soon after the Soviet Union stopped existing and Soviet ballet was replaced as a popular pastime by a renaissance of crime and by holidays overseas. (Fortunately, humour proved harder to give up than *Swan Lake.*) International travel, once the preserve of the Party nomenclature and artistic and scientific elites intimate with the KGB, was by now well and truly the opium of the masses. Sometimes, the more things change the harder it is for 'a little-educated person such as, say, a writer or a military officer' to tell the difference. In the cracks and fissures of the radical break from the past, the rejected past tirelessly reproduces itself.

I turn to Jvanetsky to see what words he finds to speak about the whole tragicomedy of transition, because I trust him. He is a rare specimen, writing with the sooty owl of black humour on one shoulder and the snow petrel of open-hearted lyricism on the other. Most of all I am drawn to the pitch of his voice, to the humility you invariably find alongside the exquisite economy and clarity of his vision. Humility is a big deal to me, and I do not know what to make of the fact that I've never been able to find an adequate Russian translation for the English word. (*Smirenie* comes closest, but it has distinct religious overtones and reeks of kneeling and prostrating.) Jvanetsky's words are so precious because they do not ring with the irony of dissociation, with bitter disappointment, or anger or nostalgia – the types of emotional responses to the end of the Soviet Union that the writer Marietta Chudakova identified as dominant in the post-collapse society.

Chudakova, who at one point was a member of President

Yeltsin's Advisory Committee, takes the failed coup of August 1991 as the starting point for her reflection. The coup was indeed the turning point: the attempt by the Party true believers and KGB to go back into the heart of darkness was thwarted; people came out onto the streets to defend democracy and reform; and Yeltsin, sober, atop a tank, emerged as a hero. Within months the 'patient' (Soviet State) stopped breathing and was declared (for all intents and purposes) deceased. In another country, that defiant stand against the coup would have become the stuff of legends, marked by a national holiday, celebrated with sickening regularity, but in Russia, says Chudakova, 'It has been mocked and dragged through the mud by the majority of the population.' She notes how the first reaction against the events emerged very quickly, even before the barricades were dismantled. With a self-knowing smile, people dismissed what happened as nothing more than theatre. 'The smart-arses,' Chudakova writes, 'refuse to believe that capital-h History can take place in Russia.' There is no History here, they say, only 'political technologies' at play – staged coup, staged resistance to the coup; everything calculated, planned and manipulated. After all, what kind of History can happen here in our dump? Our '*dump*', which of course is also our '*Great (and greatly misunderstood) Nation*'. Time and time again the two ideas, which might seem mutually exclusive to a bemused outsider – the inferiority complex and the megalomania – sit rather comfortably in many people's minds. I wonder if this duality is, in fact, the essence of the much-vaunted Russian enigma. But why the urge to belittle and dismiss? When something so enormous and unexpected is happening, Andrey Dmitriev observes, 'The main actors, caught naked in the icy winds of history, hastily throw onto themselves the first clothing they can lay hands on – decrepit, often gaudy,' the kind that in the heat of the moment looks totally natural and even solemn. In hindsight, this clothing often seems ridiculous, even farcical, creating in many the desire to dissociate themselves from the loud colours of artless enthusiasm, of rose-coloured Utopianism, of unconditional and unsubstantiated beliefs in reform, Yeltsin, people power, you name it.

As an observer, not an actor in any way, thousands of kilometres away from my barely folded homeland, I was safe from oversubscribing to the beliefs and ideologies available in the wake of the collapse, safe from all the cringe-worthy outfits and from the need for sharp, high-speed U-turns. And in a way that would never be shared by my parents and, I suspect, by my sister either, I have felt bitterly short-changed by that safety.

And so I could never fully get how it happened that, only a few years after the events of 1991, so many people wholeheartedly succumbed to complete disappointment with the new order. Not just any kind of disappointment, but total, irreversible disappointment – the kind that Chudakova believes her compatriots are particularly adept at modelling. 'We were such fools [sometimes slightly softened into "We were such foolish idealists"]. Democracy – are you kidding? The Soviet Union – who told you it had collapsed?'

'We were convinced that as soon as the cannibal regime of the Communist Party bit the dust,' writes Dmitriev, 'from under its ruins there would emerge people in white clothes, pure and honest, smart and full of initiative, freedom-loving individualists yet obsessed with the idea of the common good.' And in no time, these people would erect democratic institutions, and the self-regulating market economy they would introduce would not only bring abundance, but also create a robust civic society. 'The world will witness the emergence of the New Russian Person: the real European, but with the Russian soul.'

I speak of this fantasy not to mock the Utopian idealism of those who believed that the end of the Soviet Union would bring freedom and prosperity (up to a point my family was among them), but to point out how only very few of us, so full of hope and enthusiasm in the beginning and so bitterly disillusioned later on, had any real appreciation of Western-style democracy as a historical process, a long painful road paved with arduous work, countless lives lost, terrible mistakes, hard decisions and divergent paths. And similarly, and perhaps even more importantly, hardly anyone understood that the West's freedom and prosperity were not abstractly guaranteed by the system but had to be fought for daily by normal, ordinary people like us. Even Karl Marx, of all people, could see that 'unheroic as bourgeois society is, it nevertheless took heroism, sacrifice, terror, civil war and battles of peoples to bring it into being'. Most of us nursed at the breast of Soviet history couldn't, not straight away. In the Utopia many clung to after the collapse of the USSR, democracy was like a perfectly made-up young woman in a glossy magazine, who you could not envision ill and dressed in her trackies, with a red crusty nose and puffy, watery eyes. The post-Soviet Utopian imagination, says Dmitriev, neither revered nor respected the West but simply envied it. To respect the West, he says, would be to try to understand it, not to copy it while being torn between envy and contempt.

For Marietta Chudakova, the most explicable reaction to the death of the regime was hatred directed at all those who dared to boogie on its grave. For people gripped by hatred, the collapse of the Soviet Union was, as Vladimir Putin would ultimately declare, unambiguously the biggest tragedy of the twentieth century (in contrast to its biggest triumph – the victory in World War II). Chudakova never had a problem with those who detested people like her for celebrating the end of the monstrous regime. All she felt was deep satisfaction: 'What, and you thought it would never end?' But there is, Chudakova continues, one more emotional reaction – a kind of a 'dull melancholia', a 'sickly feeling of something important missing from the air'. And this *something important* is not simply the security that complete dependency on the State offered people provided they played by the rules, it is something intangible that existed then, in *that* air, but is now completely gone. Chudakova believes it is this emotional reaction (in all its countless versions) that now represents the dominant response to the death of the regime, uniting people from different social stratas with completely different life experiences and at times opposing political views.

But what on earth did we think was going to happen? That the past, the whole seventy years of it in all of its ostentation, brutality and sheer force, would just lie down and die? 'When a system, such as the Soviet, manages to hold on in such a vast place for so long, it effectively mines the whole country,' Chudakova suggests. These landmines continue to detonate for decades on end in places where we least expect to come across them. Make no mistake: they will continue exploding in our faces.

Back to Mikhail Jvanetsky. As the Soviet Union was collapsing, he composed a letter to his late father telling him of things Jvanetsky Senior could have never imagined in his wild-est dreams:

> We are all on a high now. First of all, we have broken up into republics once and for all . . . Everyone has their own customs controls now. Because in one republic there is no meat, in another there is no fish, the third one has no bread. And we want to know what is missing where, and we want this status quo to be reinforced . . . Whichever people you have found yourself with, this is where you stay put.

Here we are on the train trying to get from Russia to Ukraine, a procedure we would have performed countless times twenty years ago without giving it a second thought, but all of a sudden we are in dangerous waters, caught breaking and entering into Belarus, of all places. Not only has everyone put forward their own customs controls, as Jvanetsky says, everyone seems to defend their borders and customs with a singular zeal. At least Ivan Petrovich Sidorov does, our man in charge of Teryuha railway border crossing.

Dear Diary,

Ivan Petrovich Sidorov, the lovely man from border control, had the pleasurable task of degrading us into less than the eye of an ant, and may I comment did his job so well that I a strong twelve-year-old girl was nearly reduced to tears. I told my mum that, as I have never met a Nazi, when writing stories about them I'll know where to get my ideas and description from.

As Sidorov marches away with our Australian passports in his hands, Billie and I play hangman. I still have that piece of paper with two words on it – *monstrous* and *beautifully*. All of a sudden the world is split into two clearly defined camps – the *monstrous* Belarus border-patrol zealot and the rest of the *beautiful* world. In a few minutes Sidorov is back. He takes possession of our remaining suitcase (the other smaller one called it a day in St Petersburg, after Misha Senior dragged it all the way from the train station) and marches in front of us. Off the train we go then, Billie determined not to shed a single tear in front of the enemy. As we step onto the platform, the kindly Ukrainian train attendant who tried so hard to help us looks devastated, as if we were two school kids abruptly removed from her class by a trigger-happy principal. 'You are wonderful,' I say to her, my one and only mindful gesture before panic and sheer amuse-ment turn everything into a blur. The train leaves. People warm and safe inside the moving train look at us through the windows, or so I imagine, trying to figure out our story. I bet no one gets even close. Billie looks at me for reassurance. 'It's good for the book,' I say.

In the station's tiny waiting room, Sidorov approaches a woman inside the ticket office, the only other representative of authority besides him: 'Taken off the train mid-journey. Here are their passports and tickets. Get them sorted.' The only other person taken off our train is a dodgy young man unable to leave the territory of Belarus because of his criminal record. He calls a friend on his mobile to organise a pick-up. Soon their conversation takes a decisively antagonistic turn. 'Listen, shut your mouth and pick me up in Gomel or I will come and shut your mouth for you,' the young man shouts; it sounds like he means what he is saying. Gomel, the nearest town to the border, is where Sidorov is sending us too, on the next train. 'In Gomel you will go to the Department of Immigration and Citizenship. Lenin Prospect 45A. At the train station you will put your luggage in the cloakroom. Then you get your transit visas. All clear?'

Nothing is clear. Department of what? What number on Lenin Prospect? Put our luggage where? Sidorov is clearly not in the habit of changing the way he speaks when dealing with civilians, or maybe it's personal. Billie looks at me again, needing her mother to show at least a hint of defiance, not to be bulldozed by this guy. I make sure that I stand straight, speak back with confidence and even irony, and, in general, show some style while Sidorov orders us around. I am so busy demonstrating to Sidorov that he is not the boss of us that by the end of the conversation I have only the vaguest idea of what we need to do in Gomel to get out of Belarus. (This must be my own maternal version of machismo.)

We are put in a *platzkartnuy vagon* – the second-class carriage ungraced by doors apart from those (thankfully) in front of the toilet; exactly the type of carriage I have decided to avoid during our trip in order to minimise Billie's culture shock. A young border-control officer is to accompany us on our way to Gomel. 'You have to help me with the suitcase,' I tell him, 'I have hurt my back.' (True, by the way, usually I am fine doing my own heavy lifting.) 'What do you have in it?' the young officer says after he picks it up. 'Books,' I answer. 'I am a writer.' I have not said this so proudly for a long time.

On the train to Gomel we eat the fried chicken drumsticks that Marina, ignoring our protests that we would be just fine, lovingly packed for us in foil. We no longer care to pretend that we are like everyone else – we are not, stuff it. People around us follow our movements and conversation with vague suspicion, trying to figure out our story: Who the hell are they? Why were they put on the train in the middle of nowhere? Why is the girl speaking gobbledygook to the mother? I have a photograph of Billie from that moment, a drumstick in one hand, sad but also beautifully composed as if in this most phantasmagoric moment of our trip she has decided to go with it.

In Gomel, miraculously, we manage to get our visas. (Well, what else were they going to do with us, really?) I don't know how or why but everything falls into place. On my insistence (this is where age and experience come in handy) the young officer takes us halfway to the Department of Immigration and Citizenship, marching like a soldier at a parade through the railway square so that Billie and I have to run to keep up with him. The department is about to close but somehow one woman finds another woman who unlocks the right office, and yet another woman takes our passports and gives us a special form to take to the special bank so we can make our visa payments – seventy US dollars for both of us, a serious sum in Belarus. The bank is closing soon but somehow we manage to get it all done, and when we run back with the receipts the department is still open and our passports are not lost. Eventually, we find the very woman who sent us to the bank, and she personally takes us to another office, where Belarusian visas are glued into our passports. The female personnel of the Department of Immigration and Citizenship are almost uniformly kind. I am pretty sure Billie will not use her memories of them to write about Nazis. Billie smiles, holds my hand and comes to the conclusion that in general women are nicer than men, at least when it comes to the border regions of Eastern Europe.

At the Gomel train station the toilet is of a squatting variety with half-doors that do not conceal heads and legs, and a bucket for used toilet paper. It certainly trumps yesterday's train toilet, the one with the dubious cloth stuffed in the wall. Billie is beside herself with horror and amusement, but all her proud resistance is gone. We pay three hundred and eighty Belarusian roubles for two squares of brown toilet paper. In the cubicle she is giggling so hard she cannot pee from laughter. 'If toilets were anything like this at Australian schools, no one would go,' she says.

Dear Diary,
Now I am in a train station in the middle of Belarus waiting for the train to Kiev that comes at 2 in the morning, that is eleven hours away. While I am writing I'm staring at the statue of Lenin and listening to Soviet music, how comical.

A milky-white statue of Lenin is in front of us; I have to get close to make sure it is what I think it is. This is what journalist Alexander Feduta describes as the Belarusian President Aleksandr Lukashenko's successful attempt if not to stop then to really slow down time. I am tempted to say to Billie, 'Look around, this is a ready-made slice of the Soviet Union for you. The Empire is long since dead but this is like its living museum.' For a moment I wonder if there was a reason for us to be taken off the train to Kiev after all, because where else could Billie see such an embodied approximation of her mother's childhood?

Since his election in 1994, Lukashenko, who is colloquially referred to as *Bat'ka* (slang for Father), has acquired international fame (or infamy). He is what is known euphemistically as a 'colourful personality', a former farm manager who styles himself as a man of the people and likes to be photographed in a combine harvester or next to one lucky cow. He is making the tiny country he leads famous too, for it is the last European dictatorship left standing. (Russia may still catch up, though not quite yet.) He cultivates friendships with Cuba and Iraq, and accuses Western countries of espionage and subversion. As we observe his crude, transparent, comical manipulations of his people we may fall over laughing but, whatever it is that Lukashenko does, it has been working for well over a decade.

Alexander Feduta, an erstwhile press secretary for the president who has written extensively about his own radical change of heart, points out that Belarus is about 'the only one of the post-Soviet states that not only does not conceal the ideological basis of its economic policies as well as the direction of its foreign policy, but is most sincerely proud of it'. Ideology, rather than shared ethnicity, blood, soil or language is the binding substance of 'Project Independent Belarus'. All tertiary students are required to complete a university subject, 'The Fundamentals of Belarusian Ideology', just as several decades before, their parents and grandparents could not graduate without completing 'The Foundations of Marxism–Leninism'. And this ideology is not strictly speaking simply neo-Soviet or neo-Communist. After all, Belarus is not a dazed former republic refusing to accept the demise of the Empire, it is a post-Soviet nation that has used parts of Soviet legacy and iconography for its own purposes. It retained the so-called Soviet middle class – teachers, doctors, engineers, who work for the government and depend on the government for their livelihood. This

Soviet middle class, to which my parents belonged, no longer exists in Russia, where even those people in the government's employ have to seek other sources of income to survive.

For the five US dollars we spend at a grocery store not far from the train station, Billie and I eat like kings. For dessert we buy crème brûlée and the Eskimo ice-cream of my childhood, which tasted like angel's tears dripped in fructose. With hours to kill before our train arrives in the middle of the night, we get a rest room – fourteen thousand Belarusian roubles for twelve hours – with two single beds and no heating (even though it is European autumn). The rest room attendant has layer upon layer of jumpers and shawls wrapped around her. In the basement, the cloakroom attendant snoozes on the table underneath her artificial fur coat. Desperate for some sleep, Billie and I put on everything we have with us, and then on top of that we don our coats, boots, hats and gloves. In this state, barely able to move our limbs, we throw ourselves onto our beds.

'How is it possible to fall asleep in your coat and boots?' Billie is puzzled and amused at once.

'If you need to sleep, you will,' I reply. 'It is not that bad actually. We have beds to stretch out on, we have warm clothing, no one is bothering us. A real traveller can sleep standing up if need be.'

'Yes, actually, it is not that bad,' says Billie. 'It's good for the book too.' She quickly gets up to take a photo of me. I look too ridiculous for this moment, drowning in my own clothes, not to be captured for eternity. One day her kids will laugh, looking at this photo of their grandma. As Billie gets back into bed I make a wish. It is very simple. If my daughter, despite the utter weirdness and discomfort of our sleeping arrangements, and in the face of everything else we have been through in the past twenty-four hours, manages to fall asleep here and now, then everything will be OK. OK not just on this trip, but in general, in our lives. I close my eyes and doze off. When I open them reluctantly, Billie is asleep.

In the middle of the night we board the train for Kiev. It is about 3 am when we approach Teryuha railway border crossing. I hear Sidorov's voice before he comes through the door of our cabin. He is ordering the train attendant – a man in his thirties – to turn the lights on everywhere. Sidorov takes our dark-blue Australian passports and, satisfied, returns them to us with a smirk.

'See,' he says, 'and you were worried. Now everything is in order. You can get to your Ukraine.'

'Yes,' I say, 'we had a great time in Gomel, cultural leisure and all.'

'Pleased to hear,' he replies.

I am waiting for something to go wrong at the last possible moment, for some other obscure bureaucratic procedure to be revealed that would prevent us from getting to Ukraine, but Sidorov is walking away from us, his hands are empty, our passports and suitcase are with us, his steps are receding and, get this, we are free, mobile and warm (the train is heated). Billie hugs me and falls asleep in an instant – no longer a hysterical novice, by now an authentic veteran of our travels into the otherland.

II

1941

As a historian I study human memory or, more precisely, its social dimensions. I am interested in how memories of the past bind us together, but also in the speed with which they can toss us onto the opposite sides of barricades. Historians, especially the ones who are not afraid to talk to people, know all too well how flawed human memory is – fragmented, unreliable and blinkered. Sometimes people unconsciously replace their own experiences with newspaper headlines. Sometimes they do just the opposite, assimilating things they have read or heard about as their own experiences. Sometimes – actually quite often – they struggle to speak in their own voices, slipping into a prevailing public idiom and all its accompanying clichés. Human memory is not only selective, it is incredibly responsive to environment.

For all my professional knowledge of memory's many flaws, I was still taken aback to discover the gaps and imperfections in my own recall of the years I spent growing up in the USSR. I had to ask Marina how exactly our trip to Grebenshikov's apartment on Perovskaya Street ended, because I could not bring it to mind at all. She, on the other hand, did not have to think hard. The colour of the gouache paint we brought with us, the words of the disgruntled neighbour, fell out of her as if these memories were just sitting there waiting for the question to be asked. I also had to ask my parents to fill in the blurry bits of 1989 and they did not hesitate – they remembered dates, names, emotions and whole blocks of dialogue. I found too that I could not remember things about World War II that I had once known by heart; possibly because having discovered the extent of lies we were told, I have dishonoured most of the historical knowledge I acquired in adolescence. (I don't know if the baby got thrown out with the bathwater, but there was plenty of bathwater on the floor.) My memory, I discovered, was just like that joke about holey cheese.

But just because I have apparently forgotten slabs of my own history does not mean I am immune to them. One particularly resonant thing I have learned in my research is that we do not just refashion memory; it also refashions us. Like osmosis, memory seeps through into the way we act and feel, without us making conscious connections between the present and the past. It is there in how we raise our kids, where we choose to live, who we drink with, whose hands we refuse to shake. You will understand, therefore, that in the Soviet Union all forms of remembering, direct or indirect, will get you into trouble. For seven decades there the past existed in the public arena as pure ideology, invariably at odds with reality, and uncontaminated by lived memory. When the public past has nothing to do with what people remember and when remembering your own past even in private is inherently dangerous, people do not simply forget or repress, they find other ways of not letting the past go.

Historian Jehanne Gheith tells a story about Mikhail Afanasievich, a Gulag survivor who kept silent about his time in the camps even when he thought he was going to die. Yet one thing he did after being released was to get himself an enormous German shepherd and name him Stalin, which, on some level, was a breathtakingly reckless thing to do. This was the first thing Mikhail Afanasievich told Gheith when they met, waiting for her reaction. 'I outwaited him,' Gheith writes, 'and he said: "Why did I name the dog Stalin? So that we won't forget . . ."' A woman called Nina, who was a teenager during the war, recounted coming home from school one day to find a seal on her apartment door. Her mother, Zoya Mikhailovna, had been arrested on charges of espionage, and they would never see each other again. Nina too was soon arrested herself and accused of being a German spy. When she was released, Nina felt she couldn't tell anyone about what happened; instead, she decided to have a daughter and name her Zoya Mikhailovna in honour of her mother. To do that, she had to marry a man called Mikhail so that her daughter would have the same patronymic as her mother – and she had to give birth to a girl. She succeeded on both counts.

But even in societies where you do not have to struggle with the mismatch between what you remember and what you are meant to remember, memories do not come out of us as perfectly formed stories about the past. They are not always conscious or intentional or contained. Cognitive scientists who study memory distinguish between declarative and non-declarative memory systems; the latter, they say, is 'hard-coded' into us and cannot be accessed consciously. The most obvious of these is 'the body knows' type of memory. Your fingers can dial a phone number that you cannot consciously recall, while your legs can take you to the place that your brain cannot locate in space. (In fact, in many of these situations, the conscious attempt to recall something could be an inhibitor.) Scientists and philosophers alike call this the memory of 'knowing how' as opposed to 'knowing that'. Another type of non-declarative memory is the traumatic memory, the kind that is involuntary in its nature, catching us unawares and pushing us off our feet. Flashback is perhaps the most familiar form of this, but there are all kinds of other types of the unconscious remembering that manifest themselves through our bodies, our emotional responses and our interactions with the world and other people.

As a historian I have come to see that a great deal of our memories occupy a grey zone between declarative and non-declarative, between parts of our life we can turn into a coherent narrative and other parts that work behind the scenes making us in some profound sense who we are. The same is true of the way memories are passed on within families. Linguist Ruth Wajnryb, who has interviewed many Australian children of the Holocaust survivors (she is one of them), writes that the majority of people she had spoken to did not remember being told about their parents' history. Being born into their particular family meant they were born knowing. Wajnryb calls this kind of memory 'an oblique knowledge, more a sensing at a visceral or subconscious rather than a cognitive level'.

This is what many of Australia's indigenous kids taken away from their parents – the nation's stolen generations – grew up with. Their true identity may have been silenced, distorted or denied, but this kind of *oblique knowledge*, this subconscious sensing of their roots that Wajnryb talks about, proved much harder to eradicate.

Like countless people of her generation, my paternal grandmother kept secrets all her life. My dad was in his late forties when he learned that she had had another husband before she married his father, and that this first husband had perished in the camps as an Enemy of the People. I believe she only told her son because we were leaving for Australia, and she did not expect to see him again. But this is not why she is on my mind now. I remember very well how she would always pick up crumbs of bread from her table one by one and put them into her mouth, and would follow me as I carried a sandwich from the kitchen to the couch, bending to pick up the trail of crumbs I dropped. At the time I had no idea about the Holodomor (literally 'death by starvation') – the Ukrainian famine of the 1930s in which millions of people died. I learnt about it only after I came to Australia, as more and more information emerged after the collapse of the Soviet Union, and as the newly independent Ukrainian government lobbied for the famine to be internationally recognised as an act of genocide. The famine was artificially induced, a direct result of Stalin's government policies, not of failed seasons. Now I knew what my grandmother had gone through, and what her obsession with breadcrumbs actually meant. Her experiences were passed on to me not as a story but as an encrypted image I could only decode years later. But I never forgot it, sensing as a child that it had some kind of unspoken meaning and history. 'Children can smell narrative,' writes Ruth Wajnryb, 'the way airport police dogs can smell drugs. And they are drawn to it in the same way.'

In my field when historians talk about social memory, they often talk about museums and anniversaries, about media controversies and sites of memory (I have written about them myself at length), about oppressive silences and collective amnesia. But when I think about social memory, about the very essence of it, I remember a passage from historian Irina Sherbakova's essay about memory in the Soviet Union. What happened in the 1920s, 1930s and 1940s, she says, was an unspoken, or barely spoken, part of every conversation. These were the memories that people 'would take out of the air, from the drunken narrative, from the eternal question – and which year are you from? (This question meant almost the most important thing – were you part of it or not, did you fight in the war or not?)' I think this is precisely it, this image of the 'air' in the room. Perhaps it was that air that changed irrevocably with the collapse of the Soviet Union, prompting the spread of the 'dull melancholia' described so evocatively by Chudakova. This vision of memory as *an unspoken, or barely spoken, part of every conversation* reminds us of how often memory is both preserved and transmitted in deeply intangible ways. This is what philosopher Edward S. Casey called 'an active immanence of the past' in our bodies, our ways of being and, of course, in the spaces we inhabit and share with others.

My parents have always been open with me and my sister. If in writing this book I had to go back to them time and time again, sitting down next to my mum with a notebook on my lap, it is only because I have not asked enough questions before and because I have not listened attentively enough. Maybe I was not ready, or maybe I thought I knew what happened. After all, I breathed that 'air' together with them. Perhaps as a historian I thought I needed to look for bigger, more important stories than that of my family. Or maybe it was just like the proverbial case of the marriage counsellor whose own family life is going to the dogs. *Historian, know thy own history, you fool.* If it was not for this book who knows when I would have got beyond my own discomfort and unease in order to ask my mum to tell me the story of her birth from start to finish in one go, without any interruptions. Which is not to say that I will have the wisdom or the skill to render it authentically here, only that my mum trusted me with this story and what else can I do now but to try to tell it as best as I can.

Early in the summer of 1941 my great-aunt Tamara, a young doctor recently graduated from Kharkov Medical Institute, was sent to work in the Ukrainian village of Dubovyazovka, not far from Kiev. She went with a child in tow. Tamara's husband (the first of several) had died in the Finnish War of 1939–1940, and so it was just the two of them now – the self-assured, outgoing, remarkably well-dressed young 'specialist' and her two-year-old daughter, Vera. My grandmother, Faina, joined her sister in the country soon after. Faina was pregnant with the child who would turn out to be my mother, and tailed by her own toddler, three-year-old Lina. Summer at Dubovyazovka meant fresh air, sun, coveted cow's milk, and fruit and veg on tap – and as everyone knew, these things, so wanting in the city, made for much healthier kids.

Faina was older than Tamara by four years, and not like her at all. My grandmother was much less inclined to hold court than her sister; she dressed modestly and was skilled at deflecting the spotlight. She was attentive and kind, and took care of things when no one was looking. There was not one showy bone in her body. Both Faina's daughters would inherit her attentiveness to others, and her distaste for publicising their own good deeds, even though they would belong to a much more emancipated generation of young women. (The drama queens only started appearing in my family when my sister and I came along.)

While Faina and Tamara, with two and a half kids between them, were in Dubovyazovka, my grandfather Iosif, who was senior assistant to Kiev's public prosecutor, remained at work. Between my grandmother and grandfather existed an unspoken but unambiguous marital contract. Just as there were criminals and prosecutors, whose worlds only overlapped when the former were caught and prosecuted by the latter, so the clearly defined domains of men's and women's work were only meant to intersect in extraordinary circumstances. Ninety-nine per cent of the time child-rearing fell under women's jurisdiction, together with cooking, cleaning and laundry (all the good stuff!). Men's work was, as you would expect, to ensure the wellbeing and security of the family. The irony was that, just like most of the young women around her, my grandmother did all the women's work as well as 'work' work – she was an economist by training – which meant that most of the time she was preoccupied and exhausted.

It was in sun-filled Dubovyazovka that Tamara and Faina learned about the start of the war, from the round mouth of a radio perched in the middle of the square near the office of the obligatory village council:

> Today at 4 am . . . without a declaration of war, German troops attacked our country, attacked our borders at many points and their aeroplanes bombed our cities – Zhitomir, Kiev, Sevastopol, Kaunas and some others – killing and wounding over two hundred persons . . . This unprecedented attack upon our country is treachery unparalleled in the history of civilised nations.

The announcement, made at noon on 22 June by the Soviet Foreign Minister, Vyacheslav Molotov, came as a total shock, not only to the two women but to the entire community. Today it may be hard to understand why, especially if you are looking at history from the other side. By that stage the war had been raging in Europe for close to two years. But the Iron Curtain that Winston Churchill would famously draw attention to in 1946 had in fact already descended, blocking or distorting most of the news from the Western front. All most Soviet citizens knew was that in August 1939 Molotov had signed the Non-Aggression Pact with Germany, and the fact of this pact, coupled with people's belief in the all-seeing and all-knowing Stalin, meant that most of them were utterly unprepared for Molotov's announcement of Germany's treacherous attack on our 'sleeping nation'.

As to the secret protocol within the Non-Aggression Pact, its existence would only be officially admitted by the Soviet Union in December 1989 (just as we were leaving). The West learned about it during the Nuremberg Trials, but my grandmother and others of her generation died without the slightest idea of all the political machinations that helped produce the defining experience of their lives. No one but a handful of people at the very top knew about the secret agreement, which gave the Soviet Union control over parts of Poland as well as Romania, Finland and the Baltic States, while allowing Germany to have a free hand in the rest of Europe. Certainly, the war in which the Soviet Union invaded neighbouring Finland (and in which Tamara's husband died) was completely dissociated from the larger European conflict. It was widely believed – in the public mind, anyway – to be a conflict between two parties, provoked by Finnish reactionaries in turn backed by British and French imperialists, and in no way a reflection of the larger forces at play. The ordinary Soviet population did not have a clue what was going on, not in 1941, and not for decades to come.

And so it was on that June afternoon in the middle of Dubovyazovka square, surrounded by others in a similar state of shock (adults mainly, many kids were said to be initially excited by the news of the war) that Tamara and Faina had to take in all this indigestible news in one massive gulp. Their country was at war. Their hometown was bombed. All connection with it was lost. There was no way back to Kiev, and that meant they would have to join the massive exodus of war refugees across the European part of the Soviet Union, all moving east to parts of Russia around the River Ural (the traditional border between Europe and Asia), or to the Central Asian republics of Uzbekistan and Kazakhstan. It also meant that my grandmother and grandfather would be separated for years.

In those first few months of the war everything happened very quickly. The Luftwaffe's bombs exploded in Kiev in the opening hours of the conflict. (Residents at first took them to be Soviet military exercises.) Within months the defence of Kiev ended in one of the most disastrous defeats the Soviet Army would experience. In military textbooks – not the Soviet ones, of course – the campaign would be immortalised as one of the biggest, if not *the* biggest, encirclements of troops in the whole of history, leading to the capture of more than half a million Soviet troops. The Soviet Army was in total disarray. In his memoirs, *We Are from 1941*, Dmitry Levinsky, a twenty-year-old soldier at the start of the war, recounted the bloody chaos of the retreating Soviet Army – no food, no bullets, no medical aid, no connection to the headquarters, no clearly defined frontline and no common strategy. Add to that the three million Soviet soldiers who became POWs at the very start of the conflict. It is simply not legitimate to apply the word 'army' to the Soviet troops of 1941, Levinsky says. While he himself did not take part in the Battle of Kiev, what he remembers of the first few months of the war – how soldiers were given two-metre puttees instead of boots, how machine-gun operators had to carry weapons in excess of thirty kilos, and how news of the war was delivered to various army regiments by messengers on foot – helps us understand why the first stages of the war resulted in such catastrophic losses for the Soviet Union.

Lest we forget, the military was under Stalin's absolute control; by the start of the war the majority of the most experienced and talented high-ranking officers were part of a different army altogether – the army of the repressed. The catastrophic conclusion to the Battle of Kiev had as much to do with politics as with the sorry state of the military. The implications of surrendering a major capital were dire (What next? Moscow?), so the troops were given orders to hold on to the city at any cost. My grandfather, in his memoirs written in Australia in the final years of his life, remembered the heightened rhetoric around Kiev's defence. He recalled an article in *Pravda*, the nation's central newspaper, declaring on 13 September 1941 that 'Kiev was, is and will be Soviet.' But Kiev *was* about to stop being Soviet – in less than a week's time – and would not be liberated until two years and two months had passed. The price paid for not surrendering Kiev until the last possible moment was enormous military losses and the severe weakening of other parts of the front, but it was symptomatic of Stalin's 'die but do not retreat' approach to war. In the chronic confrontation between political and military considerations, politics usually triumphed. Human life never counted for much in the Soviet Union, but during the war soldiers and civilians alike were sacrificed by the million with determined and heartbreaking ease.

As the recipients of tragically mixed messages, many of Kiev's civilians did not use the tiny but nonetheless real window of opportunity they had to flee. By the time they were ready to go, it was in most cases too late. For his part, my grandfather was under orders to remain in Kiev until the last possible moment. Together with the military prosecutor N.D. Vinogradov and Vinogradov's senior secretary, they managed to cross the frontline on 18 September, when German troops were already on the outskirts of town. The three of them headed for the forests of the Chernigov region in northern Ukraine, where they went underground and joined the large partisan regiment active in the area.

My grandmother, of course, had no way of knowing whether her husband had managed to escape Kiev before it was occupied. But many residents who remained there as Nazi troops marched into the city believed in their heart of hearts that Germany was a civilised and cultured nation, and that nothing too terrible was going to happen to them. Some remembered the 'reasonable' conduct of Germans during World War I and had no way of realising that they were about to contend with something altogether different. Their wishful thinking was not entirely delusional. After all, the worst had not yet occurred: it would be on the Eastern front that the German Army, specifically the SS, would demonstrate how far it was prepared to go. It is also not entirely unfathomable why a significant minority of Kiev's one hundred and sixty thousand Jews did not run for their lives while they still could. In September of 1941, the extermination camps were not yet built, and Himmler's policy of the 'Final Solution' was still some months off. The fate of Kiev's Jews, along with the mass extermination of Lithuanian Jewry at roughly the same time, was the awakening, the moment when it became apparent how 'the Jewish question' was going to be solved from then on.

Within days of the occupation, the city's remaining Jewish residents, mainly women, children and the elderly, were ordered to assemble in one spot with their belongings:

All kikes of the city of Kiev and vicinity must appear by 8.00 a.m. on Monday, September 29 1941, at the corner of Melnikovskaya and Dohturovskaya Streets (near the cemeteries). You must bring with you documents, money, valuables as well as warm clothing, underwear, etc. Those kikes who do not comply with the order and are found elsewhere will be shot on the spot.

These notices, printed in Russian, Ukrainian and German (with the street names misspelt), appeared across the city. The same sort of orders had been given at other European cities, big and small, before Kiev. But this time those assembled were not taken to ghettos or put into cattle trains bound for concentration camps. Instead, they were all indiscriminately executed at a local ravine named Babi Yar. The massacre was the first terrible milestone in what has subsequently been called 'industrialised mass slaughter of Jews'. It is a true miracle, I tell Billie during our time in Kiev, that no member of our family ended up there.

But there is something else I have to tell Billie, which is even more difficult to stomach. Anti-Semitism was not brought to Ukraine by the Nazi SS units and death squads. The republic had a tradition of Jewish oppression dating back to the seventeenth century. Ukrainian pogroms of the late nineteenth and early twentieth centuries were notorious for their barbarity, even though at the time persecution of European Jewry was commonplace. The truth is that the relationship between Ukrainian Jews and ethnic Ukrainians especially during World War II, is as painful and complex a human story as you are likely to find. Ukraine's anti-Semitism, never quite dormant, was reignited by events of the first half of the twentieth century – the Russian Revolution, the Soviet oppression of the Ukrainian people, and the fall of the Weimar Republic in Germany. Hitler's poisonous vision of Jewish Bolshevism (in Nazi propaganda the two phenomena were inseparably fused) fell on fertile ground among ethnic Ukrainians who, within a decade of their country becoming part of the Soviet Union in 1922, were forced to endure not only famine but also large-scale dekulakisation and waves of repressions against the republic's leaders and intelligentsia.

When the war came, a sizable minority of ethnic Ukrainians welcomed the arrival of the German troops – at least initially. In parts of western Ukraine annexed by the Soviet Union shortly before the start of the war (in line with the Molotov–Ribbentrop Pact), the Germans were seen as liberators. There is no question that the Ukrainian nationalist movement collaborated with the German invaders, and large numbers of those who did not actively collaborate were still deeply ambivalent about Ukraine's position. In the words of historian Vladislav Grinevich, the war was seen by many as 'the sacrificial struggle of the Ukrainian people against two imperial powers – Soviet and German – for the independent Ukrainian nation'.

In Nazi propaganda campaigns, the invading German Army was presented as the powerful ally of ethnic Ukrainians and their fight for independence, *and* as the mortal enemy of both Jews and Bolsheviks. Ukrainian collaborators, of which the *Polizei*, the dreaded 'Auxiliary Police', were the worst, persecuted and harassed Ukraine's Jewish population with impunity. My great-grandmother on my dad's side was shot by the *Polizei* in a small Ukrainian town called Lubni. Sometimes collaborators were coerced, but others volunteered their services. They were there at Babi Yar too. But there were countless Ukrainians who would not collaborate. And though the actions of those who risked their lives to help their Jewish neighbours, friends and total strangers could not undo the crimes of the *Polizei*, to remember the war, I tell Billie, is to remember these Ukrainians alongside the collaborators. Rudolf Boretsky, now a professor of journalism at Moscow State University, was eleven when

Kiev was occupied. When the Jews of his city were ordered to assemble with their belongings and no one quite knew what awaited them, his mother, together with young Rudolf, visited the families of all her Jewish friends, pleading with them not to follow the German orders but to hide instead. For the most part, her pleas fell on deaf ears. Rudolf remembers that she did not think twice of hiding a Jewish acquaintance in the corner of their room behind the wardrobe, keeping this hiding place secret even from the neighbours. His mother was a woman of admirable inner strength, but she was hardly an exception. This too is part of our history.

At the time, my family did not share the terrible knowledge of what was happening to their people in Kiev. As the city's Jewish population was rounded up, my grandfather was fighting in the forests of Ukraine and my grandmother together with her sister and the kids was on her way to Uzbekistan. There was, it seems, no clear and systematic plan of evacuation: the bulk of it was carried out through people's places of employment. As a doctor, Tamara was assigned to Uzbekistan, and this is where my grandmother and all the kids, born and unborn, headed in the summer of 1941. Most of those evacuated were women and children. The majority of men stayed on to fight (although not just men; around a million Soviet women also became combatants in the course of the war).

From Dubovyazovka, Tamara, Faina and the kids got to the train station by horse-drawn cart. My grandmother had almost no belongings, just one small suitcase containing the light clothing she had brought on her summer vacation. At the station, train after train was leaving, taking a continuous stream of people away from the front. The evacuees faced round-the-clock bombardments of both the trains and the railway tracks. If the rails were damaged and needed to be repaired, people simply waited at the side of the tracks until they could reboard. Thank God it was summer. Sometimes German planes flew low to the ground and a machine gun would methodically hunt down those who had escaped the larger artillery. Writer Evgenia Frolova was a schoolgirl evacuated from Leningrad. She remembers being inside a train that was bombed: 'Everything drowns in the hissing sound, in roar and smoke . . . The whole train is shaking and rocking. Clothing, blankets, bags and bodies are thrown off the plank beds, from all sides something whizzes by over our heads and plunges into walls and the floor. There is a scorched smell as if from milk burnt on the stove.' It was not only the bombardments the evacuees had to endure, but hunger and disease as well. To eat and to feed their children, people sold whatever they had so they could buy the produce that peasants from nearby villages brought to the stations along the way. This was how Tamara, Faina and the kids just made it to Uzbekistan. By the time they reached Samarkand, the largest city in Uzbekistan after Tashkent, my grandmother, great-aunt and the two little girls were barely alive. Not only were they on the brink of starvation; their heads were overrun by lice, even Tamara's formerly well-coiffured one.

Samarkand is an ancient and famed city, part of the Silk Road and once one of the main centres of Persian civilisation, yet nothing in its history could have prepared its residents for the arrival of hordes of refugees from Russia, Ukraine and other 'European' republics of the Soviet Union. Uzbekistan was sunny, abundant, harvest-rich, a world away from the death, destruction and hunger of Russia, Belarus and Ukraine.

Among the endless stream of wartime refugees it sheltered was the cream of the nation's creative elites, from major cinema studios, which continued to make films during the war, to the Moscow State Jewish Theatre under the direction of the legendary Solomon Mikhoels. Tashkent became a refuge for some of the country's most famous writers, including Anna Akhmatova, who was evacuated there from Leningrad. Despite the major culture shock Akhmatova experienced on arriving in Central Asia, she also discovered true human kindness.

'In those cruel years in Uzbekistan,' she wrote, 'you could meet people of just about every nationality of our country. Russians, Belarusians, Moldovans, Ukrainians, Poles and Uzbeks, Lithuanians and Greeks, Kurds and Bulgarians worked side by side at factories and on film sets. And how many orphaned children from the occupied territories of the Soviet Union found new families in Central Asia.'

Uzbekistan had not been incorporated in the Soviet Union until 1924, after considerable local resistance; the European components of the USSR were alien and unimaginable to Uzbeks as their own country must have been for the majority of refugees. Still, large Uzbek families with many children of their own took in kids and refugees of all nationalities, sharing with them last pieces of bread. There were all kinds of Uzbeks of course, just like there were all kinds of Ukrainians, but there were a great many good, decent people. The inevitable clash of cultures with all its resulting misunderstandings and friction did not kill off the human impulse to take care of others in dire and obvious need.

My grandmother and great-aunt arrived in Samarkand to find an Asian city caught up in the vortex of the vast and distant war. Writer Dina Rubina, who was born in Tashkent, reconstructs the wartime scene there in a way that honours the mythical proportions of the refugees' arrival – something much more akin to a plague than the orderly relocation of people and organisations that the word 'evacuation' might imply. 'Imagine that on some Asian city descends a million lice-ridden, ragged fugitives . . . Echelon after echelon come to the station but the city cannot take any more . . . And still the hapless crowds fall out of trains and set themselves up at the square near the station. [In that square, under the direct sun, whole families spread their blankets in the dust on the ground.] There is nowhere to set your foot, you have to look very attentively not to step on anyone. But the new ragamuffins continue arriving.'

When I read this, I can imagine the square in Samarkand where Tamara, Faina and the kids disembarked. As I try to picture other families encamped there on that summer night I know that my grandmother and great-aunt were in a better position than most. Tamara was obliged to report her arrival; she was guaranteed a medical assignment and thus stood a decent chance of keeping her pregnant sister and their kids afloat. It was, however, too late to report anywhere when they first arrived, so Tamara, Faina, Vera, Lina and my mum (in my grandmother's womb) had no choice but to spend the night in the Samarkand square. It was not that bad. Someone gave Lina and Vera a slice of bread. At least they were safe now, away from the bombs.

When they woke in the morning, the bag with all the valuables and documents was gone, and with it Tamara's degree certificate confirming her medical qualifications. Devastated by this theft but determined to get her assignment nonetheless,

Tamara went to register with the authorities. Whatever she said to them, however vigorously she argued her case, it was not enough. They sent her away. There were too many impostors out there claiming to have qualifications. Forgery was rampant. Certificates, degrees – everything was being forged. 'No documents,' Tamara was told, 'no proof.' As she walked back to the square towards her anxious family, Tamara ran into a professor from the medical institute who had marked her graduation exams not long before. It was common for people from all parts of the country to bump into acquaintances near those central squares in Samarkand and Tashkent, but Tamara's chance encounter with the examiner, who immediately vouched for her identity with the authorities, was a particularly blessed event.

On this day that had started so ominously, Tamara was assigned to the Station Malyutinskaya, a tiny *kishlak* deep in Uzbekistan, where the residents have never seen a doctor and where official medicine of the kind my great-aunt practised was as alien as they came. The word *kishlak* comes from Turkish for 'winter hut' or 'wintering place', and describes rural settlements built by the semi-nomadic people of Uzbekistan and Tadzhikistan – an idea entirely unfamiliar to urban women like Tamara and my grandma. Tamara's job was to organise a medical outpost. The family was given a room in the same building where Tamara ran her clinic. While Tamara worked, Faina looked after the two toddlers and, soon enough, the newborn who arrived in these strange and most unexpected circumstances. When the war first descended on them, my grandmother had asked her sister to terminate this pregnancy. Carrying a child at such a time was an act of pure insanity:

what chance would they all stand, the infant included? Tamara was a determined pragmatist who would have had no objections in principle to abortion, but she surprised her sister by refusing point-blank to oblige. 'No, this child will bring light,' she said, and that was that. When Tamara delivered my mother at Station Malyutinskaya in the early days of January 1942, the baby was named Svetlana; *svet* means 'light' in Russian. (Faina, by the way, was thirty-two when my mother was born; my mother was thirty-two when she had me, her second daughter; and my own second child, Miguel, was born when I was thirty-two, so I guess all eyes are now on Billie.)

All through the ordeal of the evacuation from Ukraine and their remote posting in Uzbekistan, my grandmother continued to search for Iosif. Though her efforts were unsuccessful, she managed to locate her husband's birth family. Iosif's brother was fighting at the front, and the rest of them – Iosif's mother and sister, Sarah, with her two young boys – had also been evacuated, not to Central Asia but to Chkalov, an industrial city near the River Ural. Eventually, Faina received a notice that Iosif was 'missing in action'. She knew all too well what the vague sentence stood for: 'missing in action' was code for a combatant whose gravesite could not be identified. In her mind, she buried him.

Who knows how my grandmother managed to get through her time in Uzbekistan with two toddlers and a newborn in her care round the clock. It was the war, says my mother when I ask her this question. Grown-ups routinely did incredible things to keep kids alive. As Tamara worked, Faina cooked for the family on a brazier using bricks of dry dung as fuel. The baby, my fiercely independent mother, refused to be put down on the mattress and had to be carried at all times. Once my grandmother spilt boiling water on herself and had to continue performing all of her chores with only one useful arm. The worst was the abundance of poisonous spiders, malarial mosquitoes and even scorpions. (My auntie, four years old at the time, remembers a huge one on the white wall of their room.) Such pests were notorious for spreading deadly disease. (A cousin of Tamara and Faina who was also evacuated to Uzbekistan died from a blood infection following a spider bite.) In 1943 Tamara, Faina and the kids were all bedridden with epidemic typhus. It was a miracle that they got through it without losing anyone. When malaria came, it looked like the end. Tamara, the family's doctor, was completely delirious. Everyone else was sick. Despite being terribly ill, Faina had no choice but to continue looking after the kids. It was at this moment that she wrote a letter to her husband's family in distant Chkalov. 'Save us,' it said.

How they managed to get through the malaria no one can now say. It must have been sheer luck because you can be as brave and as determined as you like but malaria does not give a toss. Tamara was not allowed to leave her medical post, so at the end of 1943 Faina travelled to the Ural region alone with the three kids. In Chkalov, Iosif's family lived in one room of a two-room apartment. With my grandmother's arrival, there were eight members of the family living on top of each other in this small space – three women and five children. At night my mother slept in the hall in a washing tub just big enough for a baby. Faina slept in the hall too, on top of a chest. In the other room lived a family of a former local ballerina Galina Valery-anovna, who before the war had had the apartment completely to itself. Contrary to stereotypes about artistic personalities in general and divas in particular, Galina Valeryanovna seemed neither bitter nor resentful towards her involuntarily acquired neighbours. She fancied herself as a fortune teller, using beans for the purpose as was then the Russian fashion, but when she offered her services to my grandmother, Faina was not interested.

Galina Valeryanovna insisted. 'Let me do it,' she said.

'I am sorry, but I do not believe in this kind of stuff,' Faina replied.

'Just let me. I can tell you that your husband is alive.'

'Why are you being so cruel?'

'Listen to me. Your husband is alive and you will see him soon.'

When my grandfather and his colleagues left Kiev in 1941 and joined the partisans in the forests, they were ordered to move into the occupied village of Nosovka, in the guise of ordinary residents, to set up an underground cell. The three of them spent six months in the village running an anti-Fascist group responsible for supplying the partisan forces with food and medical provisions. My grandfather's very first job in life had been as a wood-turner, and he had been a skilled, success-ful craftsman. Thanks to this, Iosif was able to move to Kiev from the small Ukrainian *shtetl* where he lived and, in time, to bring his parents to Kiev as well, taking full responsibility for their wellbeing. Now my grandfather's woodworking skills came in handy not only because they provided a credible cover, but also because many farmers in nearby villages were in des-perate need of a woodworker of his class; and so the trio never went hungry.

When they discovered that their cover had been blown, the

trio quickly left Nosovka and headed into the forest. The next day their house and workshop were completely demolished. Before leaving Nosovka, my grandfather accidentally became a witness to a scene that he could not expunge from his mind: two Ukrainian *Polizei* shooting point-blank a Jewish couple discovered hiding with a local blacksmith. Determined to avenge the couple's death, one night my grandfather took a platoon of partisans and set the houses of the two *Polizei* on fire. When the policemen ran out of the burning buildings, both of them were shot. Iosif was, by all accounts, a formidable leader. During his time in the partisans, he went from platoon leader to company commander and then head of the special division; after the war he was made lieutenant-colonel in recognition of his service.

At the end of 1943 Kiev was liberated, and the German forces were driven out of Ukraine. Early the following year, my grandfather started looking for his family. Told that his wife and sister-in-law were evacuated to Uzbekistan, he set out to make his way there. He knew neither their exact location nor the number of train journeys required to reach them nor, in fact, whether Faina, Tamara and the kids would still be in Uzbekistan years later. And, of course, their survival was anything but guaranteed wherever they were. Yet, just like Tamara's chance encounter with her university lecturer in Samarkand's central square, fate – or chance, although to me it does smell like fate – made Iosif fall casually into a conversation with a fellow passenger on the very first train he boarded. It turned out that the man knew Iosif's brother and his family. What is more, he was pretty certain that Iosif's oldest nephew, Arkady, was working somewhere in the city of Chkalov, so my grandfather decided to get off the train there and try to locate his nephew before continuing his journey to Uzbekistan.

My grandfather's inexplicable fortune continued in Chkalov. Perhaps this is the kind of stuff that only happens in war. At the moment he disembarked, Iosif's mother was heading home from the market where she had exchanged tobacco and vodka for some bread and lard to eat. Iosif wrote in his memoirs:

> Only 20 to 30 metres from the house, I saw my mother who turned around and ran into the house – 'Fanya, I have a son, you have a husband, your kids have a father.' No words can describe what happened when we all reunited, how many tears were shed. Even now, when I am writing these words, and more than fifty years have passed since then, I am crying.

Needless to say, Chkalov's former prima ballerina, Galina Valeryanovna, was vindicated, big-time.

Stories of the war haunted me all through my childhood, in particular the story of Zoya Kosmodemyanskaya, who quit her Moscow high school to join the partisans as soon as the war started. Tortured by the Nazis, Zoya did not give up the names of her comrades. Taken to the gallows for a public execution, she shouted (in one version at least): 'You'll hang me now, but I am not alone. There are millions of us, and you can't hang us all.' Like the generation before us, we learned about Zoya's sacrifice at school. The first woman during the war to be awarded Hero of the Soviet Union (the highest honour in the land), she was a high-ranking martyr within the pantheon of war heroes and the one who somehow had a way of really getting to me.

In my mind Zoya Kosmodemyanskaya served as a trigger for a seemingly inescapable question: *What would I do?* Sometimes this question was heavy and demanding, like a toddler in my arms who would not be put down. Sometimes it was as annoying as a buzzing mosquito circling around my head for hours. In any event, I lay awake at night wondering what I would do (almost inevitably the question morphed into *What* will *I do?*, so certain was my belief that sooner or later the Cold War would produce another catastrophic conflict). I could not help but suspect the worst about myself – unable to withstand pain, I would give up the names of my comrades. I was ashamed of my hypothetical betrayal, of the paralysis and all-consuming fear I felt at the thought of torture and death. It never struck me as ludicrous to measure myself against Zoya. This was what Zoya was there for, so we could use her as a human yardstick of sacrifices we had yet to make. Our little lives against her great death. I did not spot the substitution nor did I feel the need to scream out, in some kind of moral self-defence, 'Look around. The war is over. The Germans have long since gone home!' Since 1991 Kosmodemyanskaya's story has been challenged, not just the super-heroic part, but even her identity and the reason why she was caught by the Germans in the first place. (The story is that she set fire to a house in an occupied village with no strategic significance to the enemy.) So much about the war, the way it was blithely sold to us, turned out to be questionable at best.

Perhaps I was particularly impressionable as a child. Perhaps most kids were laughing on the inside as they took part in all of the rituals of veneration that the cult of Kosmodemyanskaya and other Soviet hero–martyrs demanded. Perhaps the teachers were laughing too, behind our stiff, uniform-clad backs. All I know is that *I* was not laughing. For all my own obsession with the subject, it never occurred to me to bombard the older women in my family with questions about their wartime experiences. I knew much more about Zoya Kosmodemyanskaya (true or false) than about my own grandmother. In my family my grandfather was a war hero because he fought; all the rest were simply survivors. I was proud of my grandfather's chestful of medals, of the bravery and leadership he demonstrated as a partisan, of the way he sabotaged the enemy and cheated death almost daily. The way Soviet society publicly remembered the war diminished the value of private memories, especially those of women who did not do anything sufficiently heroic or sacrificial (keeping your children alive did not count). When a great deal of archival and historical information that put a thousand nails in the coffin of Soviet war mythology was finally unleashed during my late teens, I felt the need to distance myself from the topic altogether, as if the child I once was, who stayed awake wondering what she would do in the hands of the Nazis, felt cheated and betrayed.

Historian S. Aleksievich writes that women remember the war differently from men:

> The women's war has its own colours and smells, its own lighting and its own sentient spaces. Its own words. In this war there are no heroes and extraordinary feats, there are only people busy with their inhuman human endeavours. And in this war they [the people] are not the only ones suffering, but also the

earth and the birds and the trees. Everyone who lives alongside us on this earth. They are suffering wordlessly, which is even scarier.

In interviewing survivors of the Leningrad siege for their *Book of the Blockade*, Granin and Adamovich also came to regard women's memory as distinctive – it was concerned with details and nuances 'more colourful and robust' than that of the men they interviewed.

I was Billie's age when Faina passed away, and I never really spoke to her about the war. It was not just that I had had my fill of heroic stories: I was too scared of causing my grandmother pain with my questions. I think I understood even then that the actual war – as opposed to the war of heroic mythology – continued to burn inside the people who went through it. It was too immense, too painful and too raw to be a subject of desultory conversation. And even as a grown woman more than capable of initiating difficult conversations, I thought for a long time that there was something cold and dishonouring about orchestrating a family history moment, at least when it came to war experiences, and so I waited for the family stories to come out on their own accord without being forced or solicited by me. God knows, it took me this long to speak to my own mother about it, not in passing, but at length, chasing every detail, slowing the story down, tracking backwards to make sense of sequences of events that seemed miraculous or incongruous or both.

The women in my family had a different war to the one I grew up imagining. I want Billie to know their war, her great-grandmother's and grandmother's war, and I am finally ready to ask a million questions. Of course I know now that, underneath it all, beyond my own difficult relationship with the subject of the war and the fear of somehow not doing the right thing by the experiences of those who survived it, I was also scared to death of immersing myself in that world of 'inhuman human endeavours'. I was right to be scared. I carry much more pain inside myself now than I did before I started asking questions. I cry a lot, and I hug my children with rib-crunching bear hugs. Once again, the war haunts me, whether it is the war my own family lived through in Ukraine, Uzbekistan and the Ural region, or the deprivations of the *blokadniki* of Leningrad. I lie awake at night imagining, not SS troopers, but Faina's story: a baby inside me and another one in my arms. Bombs explode, the last bit of bread is eaten and all our documents are stolen, while around us women just like me clutch their children, and *everyone who lives alongside us on this earth* is suffering, side by side.

12

KIEV

IN 1986 MY BELOVED grandmother Faina died. It was just a month after the catastrophic explosion at the Chernobyl nuclear power plant in northern Ukraine, and when my parents travelled to Kiev for the funeral, the grief and emotional displacement they felt was multiplied by another shock. The train station looked like it had during the Great Patriotic War, with countless children, surrounded by bags, being sent away by their parents. (A year later on a walking holiday in a Baltic forest we saw mushrooms three or four times their normal size, apparently nurtured by radioactive rain, but that's a whole other story.)

Now Faina was gone, Kiev still had my grandfather's herring (the taste of which I crave to this day), my grandfather's typewriter (the only one in our family at the time) and, of course, my grandfather himself. All of my poems of any note were typed up on Iosif's typewriter, and the very act of typing them made me feel less like a precocious Jewish girl and more like a writer. Being turned into identically sized, tightly set black letters on special extra-thin pieces of typing paper did wonders for the poems too: they got better, which is to say that in their printed form they instantly seemed to me less indulgent and try-hard. My grandfather used the typewriter for no less a creative task, even though he would not have seen it in that light. With considerable skill, he composed petitions to authorities on behalf of people who came to him: bare acquaintances or old comrades he had known since his days in the partisans, they all sought his help. My mum remembers him 'endlessly' typing those letters in the evenings.

The letters set out the circumstances of the arrests and various kinds of harassment endured by these people's relatives. They asked for cases to be reconsidered and for the innocence of their loved ones to be reaffirmed. My grandfather was the master of a clear, clean and competent appeal to the authorities – a genre of its own in a country where citizens were routinely arrested on entirely fabricated or trumped-up charges. The frequently phantasmagoric nature of accusations meant that, despite their ordeal, shocked and terrified families could still harbour hope that a mistake had been made in their particular cases. A woman from the same Ukrainian *shtetl* as my grandfather's family was arrested as part of the so-called Doctors' Plot, perhaps Stalin's last grand witch-hunt, in which Jewish doctors were accused of the conspiracy to poison the top political and military leadership and wreak medical sabotage on the broader community. Before the 1917 Revolution the tsarist *pogromzhiki* liked to accuse Jews of drinking the blood of Russian infants; with just another turn of the wheel, the vampires now became Jewish medicos. In the case of the accused woman, her brother stayed with my grandparents while my grandfather – the same man who would not tolerate anti-Soviet talk in his household – wrote letter after letter protesting the woman's innocence on behalf of her family.

This was my mum's father in a nutshell – prosecuting people by day in his professional job (embezzlers, not anyone involved in real or fictional political acts), and writing letters by night, imploring authorities for leniency on behalf of the wrongly accused. The late Faina Ranevskaya, an actress who was celebrated for her wit, famously quipped that in the Soviet Union the following three qualities could never coexist in the same person – intelligence, honesty and allegiance to the Communist Party. 'If a person is intelligent and honest, he is not a member of the Party. If he is intelligent and a Party member, then he is dishonest. If he is honest and a Party member, then he is a fool.' My grandfather was a true believer *and* also a deeply decent man, so I guess that would make him a fool. (In Australia, aged in his eighties, he read through masses of the secret documents and historical archives that came to light after the collapse of the Soviet Union, and reconsidered his political commitments once and for all.) 'Your grandfather adopted a totally inexplicable position,' Mum tells me as she remembers the convergence of his faith in the Party and his letter-writing. 'I guess it was impossible to remain whole in that world.'

Whenever I think of Kiev, the audio of my memories always includes typewriter sounds – the backspace key repeatedly pressed hard, or the little bell at the line break punctuating the unmistakable pleasure of getting physical with words. I typed and typed in Kiev, and when I did not type, I walked. You never ran out of places to go to because Kiev was a bona fide metropolis. The place had everything – venerable history, magnificent architecture, the wide, full-bodied River Dnepr, not to mention cheese and coffee in the shops. (Capital cities were always better stocked than the rest of the country.) But I have rushed over the history for the coveted cheese and coffee. Kiev was once the centre of Kievan Rus, a medieval state that was the forerunner of the Russian Empire and the portal through which Christianity entered the region. And that was another thing that made Kiev special – the sheer number of cathedrals and churches that had somehow survived the Soviet war on religion. Even if they had been violently re-purposed, many of them were still part of the city skyline. They were a feast to the eyes of a child raised on a visual diet of hammer-and-sickle monuments (even a 'godless Jew' like me).

And the other thing about Kiev was that people loved their city, just as the *Leningradtzi* loved St Petersburg. The writer Mikhail Bulgakov, son of a theologian, grandson of two priests, was born here and never fell out of love with his city. Another Kiev-born writer Victor Nekrasov ended up in the authorities' bad books precisely because of his love of his hometown and his sense of urgent, personal connection to his city's recent history and urban fabric. Nekrasov wrote most poignantly about Kiev already after being forced into exile in 1974. He was expelled for exactly the same reason that so many other writers were – for spitting in the literary well from which a vast body of the Soviet reading public was drinking. I think of Bulgakov and Nekrasov often during my visit to Kiev with Billie. They feel real and close to me, my invisible companions, maybe because there is no more of our family left in the city – only my grandmother Faina's grave.

I recognise Ira straight away, standing on the platform in a long coat next to her forty-something son (there primarily for heavy lifting). I am tempted to say that she has not changed in the twenty years since I last saw her, though I know the utter ridiculousness of such a claim. In this part of the world twenty years is enough to age anyone, but the last two decades have been like an incessant dose of heavy radiation. The story of those decades reads like a grand fable, a succession of cycles that seems to have an unstoppable, timeless logic: an Empire collapses, a New State emerges, Great Hope and Dreams of Democracy are followed by Disenchantment, Poverty and Lawlessness, then, at the start of a new cycle comes the Orange Revolution, bringing more Hope, more Dreams of Democracy and then more Disenchantment, Poverty and Lawlessness. Just as in Russia, there is a gaping wound between Ukraine's haves and have-nots. And Ira (together with her son, who these days lives with her and spends a great deal of his time looking for work) is a serious *have-not*, objectively speaking. Yet you would not in your wildest dreams describe her as embattled, let alone defeated.

Even through the train window, Ira exudes strength and light-heartedness. People with hard lives, even the ones who have neither time nor inclination to feel sorry for themselves, often look like they are labouring under the weight of a massive burden. Not Ira. She is, as I said, the same woman I saw when we came to Kiev in 1989 to say our goodbyes – just aged in Photoshop. And she speaks like the same Ira too (the woman I remember and the one in my mother's stories), in the same young voice, in the same direct, unweary, unhesitating way. Perhaps that instant familiarity I feel on the platform, familiarity which only grows during our time in Kiev, is partly to do with the fact that Ira speaks and acts just like Mum. If we had stayed and copped it, like Ira did, this is what my mum would have been like, I suddenly realise.

The other day, when it looked more than likely that we were going to be taken off the train in Belarus on our way to Kiev, I rang Ira to tell her that we were running behind. 'Hello, Ira,' I said. 'This is Masha, Sveta's mother.' (Sveta and Masha are the informal, everyday versions of Svetlana and Maria.) Of all the possible slip-ups, of all the ridiculous things I could have said to her the first time we spoke in over two decades, this was telling. 'Forgive me, Ira. I am someone's mother and someone's daughter, only I got the two confused.' Was I, am I, really confused? What would Freud say?

It has taken me unforgivably long to allow Mum to step down from the pedestal I created for her, to free her from my image of her as a superior being radiating (at an even temperature all year round) wisdom, benevolence and hard-edged optimism. Only in the last few years have I been able to let my mother assume her full separateness as a person, someone who can be seen differently by different people, who in fact can *be* different with different people. And here, almost in the flesh, is Ira – the person whose closeness with my mum, even if it was over four decades ago, means that she knew her in a way that I could never know her, that the two of them had a connection that I could never come close to having.

And, in a way, I must stand for Mum. Neither my father nor my mother have ever gone back since we left in 1989, not to Russia, not to Ukraine; my sister and I are the family's self-appointed shuttles. My parents had their own distinct reasons for staying away. Believing he was leaving for good, my father made a decision to cut himself off. It was a case of mutual, consensual rejection, he says – his country stripped him of his citizenship and his rights for leaving at the end of 1989, and he stripped his country of its centrality in his personal universe. It worked for him. He is fine. He never was a tragic nostalgic. There were people, he tells me, some of them his friends, who called the Soviet Union 'this country', demoting it to the mere status of an involuntary place of residence long before they could depart for good. He never did that. My father always said 'my country' and meant it. And the forty-eight years he lived there he counts as happy. He is not bitter. But the ties (with the place, not the people) have been cut once and for all. My father has always been allergic to ambiguity and indecision; since I have known him he has only ever done *death by one cut*. It seems clear to me that he has resolved to live wholeheartedly in Australia, to turn it from *this* to *my* country. Could he have been so interested and attentive otherwise, so invigorated by difference, so untouched by the frequently schizophrenic immigrant condition, in which an inner sense of superiority battles with outer disadvantage and inadequacy? He always struck me as a 'one-country man'.

'There is such a thing as survivor's guilt,' says my mum. She

227

is talking about what it would feel like to see her Kiev friends again, none of whom had a choice to leave Ukraine. Not being Jewish, they could not have applied to emigrate for that reason to Israel, the United States or Australia like we did. As to moving somewhere in the name of a better life, they were, on the whole, too broke for that. (One of life's little ironies is that you need money to escape having no money.) It would make my mum feel deeply uneasy to see her friends now, or so she thinks – like she won the lottery and they did not, and then she came back to brag about it. But it is not just this guilt but also Mum's lifelong fear of insincerity: she cannot bear the thought of falseness creeping into her dealings with people who were once her closest friends. How can simplicity, purity and freedom – once the hallmarks of their friendship – survive twenty years of *this kind of apart*? she wonders. For her the answer is that it cannot: 'We lived a shared life and we no longer do. I do not think we could possibly pick up where we left off. To remain real friends you have to be part of each others' lives. But when you don't have that and when you live completely different lives, your relationship is inevitably changed at its very core.'

Knowing that this is her attitude, and knowing how much she cared for the friends of her youth, I ask her what it was about my father that convinced her in her twenties to marry him and move away hundreds of kilometres from Kiev. 'He stood out amongst his peers,' she says. 'He was intelligent and well read, but also so interested in everything; every sphere, every aspect of life. He was a great communicator too, you could talk to him about anything.' My father took his work very seriously (*A man should take what he does seriously!* she thought), which is why she decided it was right to move to Kharkov. He had a job there already and there were no guarantees about what would happen to him professionally if they made their lives in Kiev. And, one more thing, he had great friends, a lot of them; he knew how to be a real friend and these were fully-fledged, strong, enduring friendships. And because of what Mum's friends meant to her, because of how deeply and passionately she was attached to them, she recognised that quality in my dad straight away and loved him even more for it.

Of course, that time in Kiev, the time of my mother's late teens and early twenties was unlike any other in Soviet history, at least before the 1980s. It was not the capital-s Sixties that the children of the West experienced. Still, the late 1950s and early 1960s were an absolutely blessed time to be young in the Soviet Union. Nikita Khrushchev was, of course, nothing like the counter-culture revolutionaries of the West. 'Small, temperamental, aggressive, prematurely balding, with a shrill voice and confused speech': this is how journalist Ilya Milshtein described him. Though he could not (and would not) give his people the Summer of Love, he gave them a few years of a warm spell, the famous thaw that followed his secret speech at the Twentieth Congress of the CPSU in 1956, in which he condemned the cult of personality. This speech kick-started de-Stalinisation, as well as a brief but intense flourishing of the civic society and the arts. In his biography of the Soviet leader, historian William Taubman called it the bravest and most reckless thing Khrushchev ever did. 'The Soviet regime never fully recovered,' wrote Taubman, 'and neither did he.'

From the Ukrainian factories and mines where he started to the Politburo where he ended up, Khrushchev was the very embodiment of Lenin's dream of a cook being able to govern the country. 'Semi-literate, with savage, almost Neanderthal ideas about culture, history, politics, littered once and for all with the Party propaganda, Khrushchev was a classical Stalinist.' (Milshtein again.) How could a man like this set into motion a chain of events that would eventually lead, decades later, to the collapse of everything that Lenin and Stalin had so painstakingly built? For this is precisely what he did. While Khrushchev himself was formed in the thick of Stalin's epoch, Gorbachev came into his own in the looser, slippery time of Khrushchev's era, at the time when, in the immortal words of poet Anna Akhmatova, 'Two Russias looked each other in the eye – the jailers and the jailed.'

The thaw allowed for the emergence of a whole new kind of people. They were called the children of the Twentieth Congress, or *shestidesyatniki* ('people of the 60s'). 'The first semi-free generation in the unfree nation, the most surprising, striking, charming generation of the Soviet people in the last century.' (Milshtein one last time.) The term *shestidesyatniki* is, of course, misleading because it attempts to encompass people who had not much more in common than their in-principle agreement that it was *freedom* that their country so painfully and devastatingly lacked above all else. But beyond this, *shestidesyatniki* had startlingly different ideas about what that freedom should actually look like and how it could blossom in their country. Some believed that all that was required was a return to Lenin (since Stalin was the original villain who corrupted Lenin's vision), while others were convinced that the system in itself was by its very nature inhuman, sadistic and bound to implode (and they, of course, could not wait). Among *shestidesyatniki* there were enormous festering divisions between the dissidents on one side and those, like Joseph Brodsky, who rejected the belief taking root among the new generation of artists and writers that they were in fact cultural revolutionaries and saviours of their people.

The West got its own serious, if widely distorted, glimpse of the thaw generation once Khrushchev started letting artists and writers and filmmakers and athletes out of the country (in limited numbers, of course). The incessantly touring Yevtushenko – a man who had everything going for him, but who ended up being one of the most scorned figures of that generation – and a constellation of brilliant writers who were forced into exile from the USSR: Brodsky, Aleksandr Solzhenitsyn, Andrei Tarkovsky, Sergey Dovlatov, Vasiliy Aksyonov and, last but not least, Victor Nekrasov whose love and knowledge of Kiev guided me on this trip. These were all people whose creative trajectories were intimately connected with what happened – or what was allowed – in those few years of the late 1950s and early 1960s. Undoubtedly the thaw did produce a renaissance – brief, doomed and divisive it may have been, but it was still a moment of untold cultural significance. Everything was blooming – literature, theatres, cinema, bard songs, even newspapers. Serious journals such as *Novy Mir*, dear to every liberal's heart, but also the newly created *Yunost* (*Youth*), of which my mum says, 'Every page was worth its weight in gold.' Stadiums were used for public poetry readings, which attracted tens of thousands. You could tell the start of the thaw, my father tells me, by seemingly tiny things, such as how some French characters in Mikhail Romm's 1956 movie *The Murder on Dante Street* were not imperialists and collaborators but genuine and courageous anti-Fascists (in other words, friends not foes).

It still defies belief that the man responsible for this artistic boom was the same shoe-stomping, corn-loving political leader who, in a much-mythologised episode, went berserk at the sight of several avant-garde artworks exhibited at the famous Manezh exhibition, calling them 'dog shit'. Or the man who in 'meetings with artistic intelligentsia' (at which attendance was compulsory, of course) referred to the now-famous sculptures of Ernst Neizvestniy as pederasty in art: 'So why do, I ask, pederasts get ten years and these artists want a medal. Why?' (Applause.) Or, for that matter, the man who was in charge of the Soviet Union during the 1956 invasion of Hungary, the 1961 crisis that led to the partition of Berlin and the Cuban missile crisis of 1962, during which the world seemed to come to the brink of outright nuclear conflict. Oh, the paradoxical nature of Nikita Sergeyevich Khrushchev . . .

While the late 1950s and early 1960s was undoubtedly one of the best times to be young in the Soviet Union, the State's unmistakable interest in fostering the passions and enthusiasms of the young could be explained in less-than-innocent terms, of course. For example: with the rehabilitation of political prisoners under Khrushchev, the Gulag population had significantly decreased, leaving gaps in the slave labour force on which the country was built. These gaps were filled by the country's young – idealistic students enthused by the heady language of 'construction projects of the century'. As one writer of the era, Alexander Ageev, commented, 'A young worker on some faraway building site costs the State a bit more than a Gulag inmate [they are fed better] and maybe even less – you don't pay for the guards, plus they are healthy, while the productivity of free labour is higher than that of slave labour.' In exchange for becoming 'the cannon fodder in "battles for harvest"', young people got their dose of romantic adrenaline – guitar songs around campfires, tents in the middle of nowhere, love under the stars. And, of course, untrodden expanses of their country tamed and transformed for the nation's benefit.

Four decades later my parents can still quote from countless poems and songs of the time – they are part of their vocabulary and, in a received way, part of mine too. 'Did you think of yourself as *shestidesyatniki*?' I ask them. 'No,' Mum replies, 'these were the people who actually did something, a pleiad of passionate people burning from within. We just devoured the fruits of their labour.' As I watch my parents remember the late 1950s and early 1960s, I see not a trace of cynicism in their attempts to distill the era; so unlike the cynicism dressed in irony's weatherproof clothing that in Russia's independent media characterises a great deal of commentary about the *shestidesyatniki* as a cultural and social phenomenon.

'You know, Masha, your mum and I spoke on the phone just the other day, and we confessed to each other that we never again had such a close friend in our lives,' Ira says on our first day in Kiev. Why cannot I get enough of Ira's stories? Of how she and Mum separated at night only to be reunited without fail the next morning, whether at work or somewhere else; how their friendship came first and everything else needed to fit around it (even Ira's post-secondary education – she went to evening classes in whatever time she had left from being with Mum). I have, of course, been treated to plenty of these stories before – their repertoire of shenanigans and all – but somehow hearing them now in Ira's kitchen with Billie by my side is eye-opening. Maybe it is because of the fact that I have only recently given up the arrogance of a child who thinks they know their mother inside out. But there's also a symmetrical pleasure in hearing about your mother when young from a woman who was young alongside her, in the company of your young daughter and in the place of your mother's youth.

Billie and I particularly like the ridiculous stories in which Mum and Ira bend rules in the name of some silly prank, or defy authorities for a laugh and still come out on top. Their practical jokes were risky and renowned for their complexity, with seemingly unreformable bachelors at work among their persistent targets (poor guys who in hindsight simply turned out to be late-bloomers). In many ways these stories compensate for much of what I know firsthand about my mum's working life in Kharkov; while not altogether gloomy, it was certainly devoid of the carefree spirit of the 'Mum and Ira' era. I think of my mum in Kharkov at the age that I am now, and I see her constantly running to work (on high heels, of course), because an entire work team was punished, their bonus payments often withheld, if one of its members was late. But the young woman in Ira's stories is my mum before my sister and me, before marriage, family, responsibilities, before the right things to do, before too much is at stake, before the onset of selflessness and maturity. One day to get out of work, Ira tells us, she let wasps that used to congregate around the vending machines that dispensed mineral water (no syrup – one kopek, with syrup – three kopeks) repeatedly sting her arm. To the queue waiting to buy a drink, she explained that wasp therapy was the best way to cure a very rare disease from which, sadly, she suffered. Released from work, Ira went to her aunt's centrally located apartment. (She lived with her mother on the city outskirts.) When my mum, infinitely entertained, called her from the institute to find out how she was going, Ira was just waiting for her friend to finish up at work, not knowing what to do with herself without her 'second half'.

'Your mother was really striking – those eyes of hers and those super-long lashes, a grey lock of hair and high heels, always stylishly dressed.'

'Did many guys at your work like her?'

'Just about every single one of them.'

I remember reading writer Zoe Heller's description of her mother, Caroline Carter, who was beautiful – not unobtrusively pretty but 'importantly beautiful'. 'Reared on her example,' Heller wrote, 'I grew up thinking of beauty as something inextricably linked to the formidable – the first time I met a *silly* beautiful woman, I was startled.' With a mother like mine, I saw beauty in a similar light. (I am sure it is obvious by now that I have never had an Oedipus complex, only an inferiority one!)

'One time we went skiing,' says Ira. 'I knew what I was doing, but it was the first time for your mum. Her legs were sliding apart all the time, she was dog-tired, but she did not say a word. She tried not to show me that she was struggling. I saw, of course, what was going on, but I pretended that I could not see anything and said nothing. This is the kind of person your mother was.' What kind of person is that then? Stoic, self-possessed obviously, not frightened by difficulties, the opposite of a wallflower no matter the high heels and those 'super-long lashes'. She was, you can say, someone who liked a *challenge* – that quintessential English word that, like the word 'privacy' has no equivalent in Russian – a young woman with a great capacity for happiness and joy. One day, Ira tells me and Billie, they bought tickets to the movies and then discovered that they were really hungry. So Mum and Ira counted what little money they had between them – a handful of coins, enough for one side dish of plain macaroni. They got the macaroni and divided it between two plastic bags. They watched the movie, pecked on macaroni and felt totally blissed out.

'Your mother,' says Dad, 'always had a unique combination of intelligence, beauty and a sense of humour. There was nothing ordinary about her. I could not believe those stories she told me in passing about what she did with Ira . . . I was so taken by them when I met her. I have never come across anyone like her . . . not before and not since.'

Until now, before this conversation with Ira in her kitchen, I had not really considered just how much my mother's move to Kharkov must have hurt both Mum and Ira, how different their lives could have been if they had stayed in the same city as grown-up women with families. And here is another thing I have never considered: how difficult it must have been for Ira, becoming a single mother in a country where being alone – with a kid but without a man – always spelt trouble. Ira separated from her husband when their son was still little. She has not spoken to him again (she had her reasons), nor has she ever remarried. Financially, it must have been hell to survive on one income, but much more debilitating was the way that Soviet society treated single mothers then. Most people simply could not allow the possibility that a single mother could prefer to remain on her own. I have often wondered what it would have been like for me to have raised Billie on my own in Ukraine. Not long ago a former classmate of mine from Kharkov, whom I considered fairly emancipated, seemed devastated to discover that, like her, I was on my own with kids. 'I am sorry to hear that your life too has not worked out,' she wrote to me (and I thought it had worked out pretty well, so far at least!). In Australia, no one has pitied me for my 'terrible misfortunes' (not that I know of, or care, anyway), and I have not been forced to compromise either personally or professionally because of my 'diminished' status. 'Optimism is simply a lack of information,' Faina Ranevskaya once quipped. I think in Ira's case her optimism was some kind of innate, almost biological resistance to the trappings of victimhood – a trait she shares with my mother and my auntie, and, I suspect, many other women of that 'war' generation.

Ira was a war child like my mum; her mother too was pregnant with her when the war began but, unlike my grandmother Faina, who was in her first trimester, Ira's mum was about to give birth. She was pushed onto a train to be evacuated, taken off it when her labour started and put back on another train with a newborn in her arms. There was a cloth that she used as an improvised nappy, drying it in one of the train windows as the train moved through the country. With constant bombardments, Ira's mother quickly lost all her breastmilk and the baby was fed some alarming mixture just to keep her going. Ira didn't have her first bath until she was a month old, after they finally arrived safely at the place of their evacuation (not surprisingly, she loved that soothing bath so much that she fell asleep straight after). 'And the children of today,' says Ira in a voice bristling with irony and energy, 'a generation of weaklings.'

The three of us walk together around Kiev, Ira consistently outstriding the two generations of weaklings trailing behind her. When we get to my mum's building on Mezhigorskaya Street in Podol, one of the city's oldest neighbourhoods, once inhabited by tradesmen and craftsmen, I barely recognise it. I whip out my mobile phone and call my mother in Melbourne just to confirm the precise address. Even Ira is unsure after all this time. Mum gives me the correct number and I hear strain in her voice. I try to hang up as quickly as possible – I understand that I have no right to drag her back here, to her Kiev life, even on the phone. She has made her choice and reached some kind of difficult peace with that choice and I have no right to disturb that peace.

When we finally identify her family's old home, the block seems so unremarkable and strangely small that my eyes simply slide off it. It is a shadow of the building I remember visiting in my childhood – that one looked important and you could not miss it if you tried. It was the place to which first my grandfather and then the rest of the family returned after Kiev was liberated in 1943 and where they remained more than forty years. They came back to find the city in a terrible state. Khrezhatik, the famous heart of town once lined with blooming chestnut trees, was obliterated by bombs. It had been blown up by the NKVD in the first days of the occupation, but German propaganda blamed the city's Jews. Victor Nekrasov, who saw Khrezhatik straight after the liberation, remembered 'mountains of smashed bricks covered by snow with twisted iron beams sticking out of them and narrow paths beaten through snowdrifts. That's it.'

The building in Mezhigorskaya Street is also the location of my mother's first memory: *She is not even three. In front of her is a white tiled Dutch stove that reaches to the ceiling. The stove is keeping the room warm. Malaria is making her shake with fever. She is going up and down on the precariously perched, high-legged fold-out bed. From all that shaking, the blanket she is covered with falls down on the floor. She cannot reach it, cannot pick it up and cover herself. She is waiting for someone to cover her up again, but no one comes. In her mouth is a bitter taste of quinine.* There are twenty apartments in the building. When mum was growing up, she would have gone inside every single one. Life was communal then, especially for kids. Every apartment was occupied by several families. My family was lucky to have only nine in their flat, all relatives too – Mum, her sister Lina, their parents and my grandfather's mother and sister, with her husband and their two boys. Our family was the first in their building to get a television set; after that a constant procession of neighbours entered the flat. And as on the inside, so on the outside, where communal living continued in the *dvor* – a yard space between apartment blocks, where parents knew their children could play safely and where kids spent most of their lives, especially before starting school. 'Any season,' Mum says, 'any free time was spent in them.'

We walk along Frunze Street (my mum and Ira's favourite street) to their old place of work. But the institute is no longer there: it must have been demolished not that long ago. I can see that Ira is stunned. The two of them loved that place – their entire collective was young, fun and creative, and they all got on spectacularly well. No office or lab has ever been like that again. Ira had wanted us to take a picture of the institute for Mum – the thought itself seemed innately pleasurable to her, maybe because she imagined the pleasure Mum would derive from looking at a photograph of this unlikely palace of fun where they had had such a ball together.

In the absence of buildings, all we have is stories and people. Ira organises lunch with two other women from the institute, Elya and another Sveta – a mini-reunion to 'make benefit' of their glorious Australian guests. This social occasion at Elya's place in Kurenyovka, near Babi Yar, is a chance for them all to catch up; they have stayed in touch, but do not get to see each other as often as they would like. Elya was always the impeccable hostess in the group, and she feeds us magnificent savoury and sweet cakes and, together with the other Sveta, asks question after question, trying to imagine Mum's life in Australia. I tell them as much as I can – about the blue skies and the ocean; about my mum's flower garden, which she reinvents every few months changing everything but the roses' unquestioned dominance; about health care; the Australian political system (strangely enough, the Ukrainian press has missed Kevin Rudd's apotheosis); and the size of utility bills as compared with an average monthly pension. I tell them that Mum is the same – still funny and irreverent – and I cannot help noticing their relief. They ask whether she drives, if and how she colours her hair, what her guilty pleasures are (once in a while she goes to a casino with one particular friend). I tell them that every working day my mum and auntie come to look after Miguel and that I have had the same level of support with Billie. I add that many of my girlfriends believe that I am the one who has hit the jackpot, and that if they had had Mum and Lina in their corners they could have done literally anything in this life (I know it!).

Elya and Sveta wonder what it was like for Mum to go from being an electrical engineer to a supervisor in a day-care centre for the elderly. I tell them that the assessment of overseas qualifications is a royal mess in Australia and that Mum could not get her engineering qualifications recognised, so she never worked another day as an engineer after we left Ukraine. I also tell them that when my mum recently retired (primarily in order to help me with Miguel), the whole day-care centre went wild, her bosses, colleagues and the elderly people she had looked after literally begging her to stay. In a place that could so easily have felt like a quick and dreary stopover on the way to the aged care home, Mum was for years one of the chief anti-depressants. I tell them how good my mum's English is and how – what better proof is there – she incessantly reads for pleasure in both English and Russian, without distinguishing between the two, and how when I write my English-language books it is Mum I invariably imagine as my first reader. I know that Australia will remain a phantom for Elya and Sveta, but perhaps their old, much-loved friend with an improbable second life in Australia will be less so.

We call Melbourne on Skype, the webcam is playing up but the connection is clear. We crowd around Elya's husband's computer shouting something in the direction of the screen. Jokes, interruptions, laughter, Skype disconnecting unexpectedly, but for a moment the whole ridiculous, loud, disorganised bunch of us all itching to say something to Mum feels absolutely right. Back in Australia a few weeks later, I try to recreate this afternoon for my mum – everything from the fillings in Elya's cakes to the trajectories of our conversation. I cannot stop wondering how this story makes Mum feel, but I can't bring myself to ask. I remember how strange it felt when my sister, who happened to be in Ukraine at the time, went to my class's graduation in Kharkov in 1991. Most generously, she took several of my friends out for a celebratory lunch and sent me pictures of them all sitting around the long table – looking so normal and so unrecognisable at once. During that lunch my sister represented me, stood for me, but also stood for the finality of my absence. Years later my friends told me that this was one of the saddest lunches of their lives. I know, of course I know, that you cannot go anywhere by proxy, let alone go back. But all I can do is tell Mum what I saw and felt. After all, I met Ira, Elya and the other Sveta because Mum trusted me with her friends and with her past. So I tell her everything I can about her city and her 'girls', as Billie listens on, tirelessly correcting me. I am a vessel in the middle so I try to let it all flow – from Melbourne to Kiev and all the way back.

13

BABI YAR

IF THERE IS A sacred site for my family anywhere in the world then it would have to be Babi Yar, a ravine on the outskirts of Kiev inextricably linked to the fate of the Jews in World War II. Romany people, Ukrainians and Soviet POWs were also shot in their thousands here, their bodies were also burnt by the German Army and formed part of the heavy, oily smoke that rose over the ravine and hovered in the air, but Babi Yar is first and foremost the site of the largest single massacre during the Holocaust. At least thirty-three thousand Jewish men, women and children were murdered there over two days in September 1941. A twelve-year-old boy living a stone's throw from the ravine later described the sounds of 'calm, measured shooting as if during a practice', sounds which finally dispelled any glimmer of hope, any illusion that those residents of the city who had obediently assembled in response to an edict from its German invaders were to be merely deported.

The first in half a handful of distinguished writers to speak about the fate of Soviet Jews during the war, Vasily Grossman came upon the story of Babi Yar as a war correspondent embedded, you might say, with the Red Army as it liberated Ukraine. Grossman was Jewish; his mother, Ekaterina, was one of the thirty thousand Jews of Berdichev massacred in northern Ukraine in the same month that was marked forever by the events at Babi Yar. Grossman's article 'Ukraine without Jews', which appeared in 1943, is a revelation. An obituary of his people (our people), it is unlike the great mass of Soviet war reporting, which converted all Jewish men, women and children into undifferentiated peaceful Soviet civilians brutally murdered by Fascists. Devastated by what he saw, Grossman refused to remove ethnicity from the equation. 'There are no Jews left in Ukraine,' he wrote. 'All is silence. Everything is still. A whole people has been brutally murdered.'

Grossman's war reporting went beyond the Holocaust – for instance, his remarkable reportage was used extensively in Anthony Beevor's *Stalingrad*, and Beevor subsequently edited and annotated the English-language translation of Grossman's wartime notebooks. Yet it is Grossman's writings concerning the fate of Eastern European Jewry that have proved most enduring. His article from 1944 on Treblinka, the first extensive account of a German concentration camp in any language, was used as testimony in the Nuremberg Trials. After the war, this kind of writing would become altogether unacceptable to the Soviet regime, as any specific references to the Holocaust were eradicated. In front of German machine-gun fire, inside the concentration camps of Eastern Europe, all Soviet victims were said to be created equal.

And so the *Black Book*, a collection of testimonies and historical materials about the fate of Soviet Jews that Grossman compiled with another writer, war reporter and Jew, Ilya Ehrenbuch, was not allowed to go to print. Decades later in 1961, in the middle of Khrushchev's thaw, all copies of Grossman's major work, *Life and Fate*, were confiscated by the KGB. In desperation, Grossman wrote directly to Khrushchev asking him to undo this banning of a book to which the writer had 'given his life'. Grossman wanted a response and he got one, not from the Soviet leader himself but from Mikhail Suslov, a member of the Presidium of the Supreme Soviet responsible for matters of ideology. *Life and Fate* could not be published *for at least two hundred years*, he was told. It finally came out under Gorbachev in the late 1980s, when the Holocaust ceased to be taboo; the *Black Book* followed in 1991. By that time Grossman had been dead for quarter of a century.

Four years after the 'imprisonment' of *Life and Fate*, and two decades after Grossman's groundbreaking reporting on the fate of Soviet Jews during the war, Anatoly Kuznetsov took a manuscript of his documentary novel *Babi Yar* to the editorial office of the magazine *Yunost*, that blessed child of liberalisation which my parents devoured cover to cover. The writer had been the twelve-year-old boy who heard the shots ring out at Babi Yar. Before the war the 'huge, you can even say magnificent, ravine – deep and wide like a mountain canyon' was the place of his childhood games. After his city's liberation, adolescent Anatoly went straight to the site to see for himself what was left there, to try to glean what had happened. From that day he began collecting stories and testimonies, everything he could find, about the ravine. In a sense, he had been writing *Babi Yar* since he was fourteen.

In 1965 when the novel was finished, Khrushchev was no longer at the helm but the thaw was still lingering, fresh in people's minds. At the offices of *Yunost*, Kuznetsov's manuscript was returned to him almost immediately, and he was advised in the strongest possible terms not to show it to anyone until he removed all the anti-Soviet passages, anything, in fact, that strayed from an attack on the barbarity of Hitler's Fascism. Kuznetsov edited the text, but whatever he culled from it was evidently not enough. When he realised that his work was being totally disfigured by censorship, he tried to stop its publication. Told bluntly that it was too late, the writer flew into a rage, grabbed the manuscript from the editor's desk and ran out into the street, tearing the pages on the way and stuffing them in rubbish bins. Of course, the magazine had other copies of the manuscript, and Kuznetsov's outburst did nothing to stop the novel, or what was left of it, from appearing in print. When *Babi Yar* finally came out in *Yunost* in a 'journal version' (a particularly cruel euphemism in this case), its author could not recognise his own text.

In front of me now is a copy of another version published in London in 1970, in which all the excised excerpts (a veritable sea of them) are reproduced in italics, and additions made by the author free of self-censorship appear in square brackets. Kuznetsov wanted his readers to understand how Soviet censorship operated, and his formatting techniques proved devastatingly effective. This edition of the novel was possible only because of Kuznetsov's defection to the West. The Soviet invasion of Czechoslovakia in 1968 was the last straw; afterwards, he secured permission to travel to London by claiming that he was writing his next book about Lenin and needed to research the time the future leader of the Soviet state spent in London in 1902. As a writer Kuznetsov said that he needed to feel the atmosphere of the place, to sit in the same library in the British Museum where the Great Leader selflessly slaved away planning the world revolution, and to visit the grave of Karl Marx at Highgate Cemetery. 'During the first four days,' *The Times* said in August 1969, after the writer's defection became a celebrated fait accompli, 'Kuznetsov behaved like a model Communist. On the fifth evening, during a tourist's stroll through Soho's lurid strip joints, Kuznetsov said that he wanted to find a prostitute. Andjapazidze [the secret agent who was assigned to him in the traditional guise of an interpreter] discreetly left his companion to his own fun.' That window of opportunity was enough for the writer to escape, a 35-mm film containing the uncensored manuscript of *Babi Yar* in his possession.

The novel is a work of burning dedication written by a man who comes close to losing himself entirely to his mission. Among many things, records faithfully, with not a word changed, the story told by the only survivor of the massacre that Kuznetsov could find – a young woman called Dina Pronicheva, an actor-puppeteer from Kiev Puppet Theatre. For decades after the war, faced with vicious State anti-Semitism no longer disguised or kept in check, Dina Pronicheva had to hide both the fact of her survival *and* her Jewish identity. Kuznetsov described how it took an enormous effort to convince her to tell how she managed to survive. 'She did not believe her story could be published, or that anyone was interested in it.' But eventually she told it to Kuznetsov 'in the same building on Vorovsky Street from which she left for Babi Yar, in the same dilapidated room'. The telling took several days, during which time Pronicheva suffered several bouts of angina or heart pain.

Even today, after Babi Yar has been recognised universally as a site of a singular human catastrophe, written about endlessly, commemorated, memorialised, her story is impossible to read without breaking down. How was it to read it then – in a country where a survivor like her, a walking miracle, had to swallow her tongue; where it took over twenty-five years, a scandal and another tragedy for so much as a stone to be erected on the site of Babi Yar? The whole book is, in fact, unbearable – how could a deeply truthful book that came out of a wound the size of that ravine be any other way?

Billie, of course, knows about Babi Yar. She has not read Kuznetsov's book or Grossman's reportage, but she knows what happened and what this site means to her family and to Ukrainian and non-Ukrainian Jews wherever they are in the world. Ira took us to the site of the ravine in Kurenyovka, now a large park with several monuments. When I was my daughter's age, my parents told me what had happened here. I had never heard about Kuznetsov's account (its publication, even in a heavily censored form, was deemed a mistake; no reprints were allowed and the book version was removed from the libraries). But I knew by heart Yevtushenko's famous poem *Babi Yar*, written after he visited the site with Kuznetsov in the early 1960s. (Whatever I think of the man who wrote it, that poem is unquestionably brave and powerful.) It starts with a lament over the absence of a monument on the site and ends with Yevtushenko declaring that he is a Jew to all anti-Semites and that that is why he is a true Russian. I remember being astounded by these words; they seemed to me in my adolescence to have the power of Emile Zola's '*J'accuse*', carrying within themselves not just the Russian poet's personal identification with Jewish people but a public accusation not qualified by disclaimers and delivered at the same volume as the other poems Yevtushenko declaimed during those famous stadium poetry readings.

Of course I have told Billie plenty of stories about growing up Jewish, about the infamous 'fifth line' in Soviet passports, in which people's ethnicity had to be recorded. (This mandatory line, I am pleased to discover, was abandoned in the late 1990s.) Some very good, very sane people did all kinds of elaborate things so as not to have the word 'Jew' in their children's birth certificates: fictitious marriages, fictitious divorces, bribes – anything to spare their children the fate of an identified Jew. My parents did no such thing. In all of our documents we were Jews and Jews only. I told my daughter these stories in part because I wanted her not to take for granted the world – her world – in which Holocaust deniers were vilified and the imperative 'We shall not forget' did not belong merely to a handful of people worn out by constant confrontation with a society that wanted them to shut up once and for all. But not taking for granted was not simply about counting blessings. Everything in my childhood, adolescence and grown-up life taught me that this world Billie inhabited, however natural it may have seemed to her, was intensely fragile. To protect it there were things, important things, we had to do. Finally, we were at Babi Yar. I had thought about this moment for a long time. Perhaps this was some kind of homecoming, maybe even more than taking Billie to Kharkov? No one from our family lay in the ravine's soil, but the dead under our feet were our dead. The least we owed them was a visit.

Writer Daniel Mendelsohn, a Jewish New Yorker of striking literary brilliance, has written about the deep reluctance he felt during his visit to Auschwitz in his memoir *The Lost*: 'The gigantic, one-word symbol, the gross generalisation, the shorthand, for what happened to Europe's Jews – although what happened at Auschwitz did not, in fact, happen to millions of Jews from places like Bolechow, Jews who were lined up and shot at the edges of open pits.' Bolechow is the place, once in Poland, now in Ukraine, where the Mendelsohn family (or its survivors) come from. But the same could be written about the Jews of Kiev or the Jews of Berdichev, where Vasily Grossman's mother was killed. Could Babi Yar, I wondered, be a similar kind of 'gross generalisation' for those East European Jews killed instantly by bullets (or buried alive in pits) instead of being murdered gradually in concentration camps? Could Babi Yar's 'vastness, the scope, the size' become 'an impediment to, rather than vehicle for, illumination'? More than anything else Daniel Mendelsohn wanted to rescue his relatives 'from generalities, symbols, abbreviations', and this is precisely what I wanted for Billie too, for whom the fate of European Jewry, while deeply affecting, could not have been more than a vast and heartbreaking generality.

We walked along the ravine for a while. I tried not to look at Billie's face. Ira, a small figure in the distance, waited patiently for us. It occurred to me then that despite its scale and iconic place in the history of Soviet Jewry, Babi Yar was in some important ways profoundly different from Auschwitz. Its entire history after the war worked to counter any possibility of the site becoming a hollowed-out symbol, a museum of the dead. This thought, which came to me as an unformed hunch, was confirmed loud and clear in Australia almost a year after our visit, when the BBC reported that 'Jewish groups have condemned a decision by the city of Kiev to allow a hotel to be built at the site of a Nazi massacre during World War II . . . Local authorities have approved plans to build dozens of hotels for the 2012 European Football Championship. One will be near a monument to victims of the Babi Yar massacre.' I imagined the outcry there would have been if such a proposal was made in respect to Auschwitz. For a moment I could not understand how this plan for Babi Yar could have been entertained in the first place, let alone approved by the local authorities. Then I remembered.

Like Anatoly Kuznetsov, the writer Victor Nekrasov was not Jewish, and lost no member of his family at Babi Yar. Just like Kuznetsov, Nekrasov considered the murder of Kiev's Jewish community to be a central reference point in his life – it was Jewish tragedy, his personal tragedy, Kiev's tragedy, Ukrainian tragedy and universal tragedy all at once. Nekrasov was devastated by the neglect of the site after the war, writing about its fate with bitter irony in his *Notes of a Gawker* published when he was in exile in Paris. In the first years after the war, he wrote with unmistakable irony, the country 'faced tasks more important than Babi Yar', and it was ignored for the most part, except by 'some suspicious characters who crawled along the ravine's bottom in search of either diamonds or golden dental crowns'. Then it became 'simply a rubbish heap. A small lop-sided post with the laconic inscription "It is forbidden to pile rubbish here, fine – three hundred roubles" did not in the least prevent local residents from getting rid of no longer useful old beds, tin cans, and other rubbish.'

In 1959 Nekrasov was the first to raise publicly the question of Babi Yar's neglect. He was writing in response to plans by the local authorities to build a stadium on the site. Who could have possibly thought of playing soccer on the site of such trag-edy? he asked. Nekrasov was not allowed to mention the word 'Jew' in the article, which had to be replaced with innocuous 'Kiev residents', but he still managed to fool censorship and the editorial board, and to do it in style – the article was published on the day of Yom Kippur, the Jewish Day of Atonement. It is almost impossible to believe that fifty years exactly separate the 'sports proposals' of 1959 and 2009.

At the time of Nekrasov's article, Babi Yar was being filled, in a massive logistical operation. The area was blocked by a dam and masses of pulp – a mixture of water and mud – from a nearby brick factory were pumped into the ravine through special pipes. The idea was that the sand contained in the mud would settle and accumulate and the water would drain through gutters and flow out through the dam. Then the good-for-nothing ravine could once and for all be wiped from the surface of the earth. Both Nekrasov and Kuznetsov watched the filling of Babi Yar in shock. 'I used to go there,' wrote Kuznetsov, 'and look in astonishment at the lake of mud devouring ash, human bones, rocky screes of gravestones. The water in it was rotten, green, still, and night and day you heard the sounds of pipes pumping the pulp. This lasted for several years. The dam was added to, it grew, and by 1961 it became the height of a six-storey building.'

On 13 March 1961 the dam collapsed. 'At 8.45 in the morning a terrifying roar was heard, a great billow of liquid mud around ten metres high rolled out from the mouth of Babi Yar. Surviving witnesses, observing from a distance, insist that this wave flew out of the ravine like an express train, so no one could escape it.' There were thousands of victims – most of them in the adjacent and lower-located Kurenyovka neighbourhood. (In official reports the number was slightly over a hundred.) Those who lived at ground level were killed instantly – the rescuers would later find their bodies thrown up to the ceilings. The rest could only hope to survive by escaping to the roofs of their buildings and waiting to be airlifted to safety. This is what happened to my mum's four-year-old second cousin, Vadik (the son of her cousin Arkady). My auntie Lina's friend from university was not so lucky; she perished in the slide (together with my auntie's invaluable maths notes).

The catastrophic mudslide, however, did not convince authorities to change their attitude to the site, although among the people of Kiev the idea of the curse or the revenge of Babi Yar became understandably widespread. Of course what happened at Babi Yar was, in the words of the Holocaust historian Ilya Altman, part of the official policy to 'systemically thwart any efforts to preserve sites of Holocaust memory'. In a number of places across the Soviet Union, Altman notes, six-pointed stars of David were turned into Soviet five-pointed stars. In Babi Yar, Nekrasov tells us, people used to come to a site overgrown with weeds and shrubs, weep and spread flowers. There was little point in bringing wreaths, as there was nowhere to put them, nothing to lean them against. 'But no, one day in 1966, a crowd of many thousands of people gathered here [Twenty-five years so to speak, an anniversary!] and several people, including one member of the Communist Party addressed the crowd with speeches that were not checked by anyone and were not approved anywhere. I was that member of the Communist Party.'

Nekrasov's speech was improvised, a spontaneous reaction to people weeping all around him, to the shame and anger he felt over the profound, vicious disrespect shown to the dead and the living. Other non-Jewish Ukrainians spoke too. All said the same simple thing – Babi Yar was a common tragedy of the Ukrainian and Jewish people. Two weeks after the gathering, a grey stone of polished granite appeared on the site with a carefully vetted inscription. Authorities must have been outraged by the unauthorised, unlawful gathering, but they also understood they had to do something to control the situation. 'A monument will be erected on this site,' said the stone. Yet again there was no mention of Jews, only of peaceful Soviet citizens, victims of the Fascist occupation. (The official monument erected ten years later in 1976 followed the precedent, again invoking the theme of slain Soviet citizens.)

For his part, Nekrasov was to pay dearly for his involvement in 'a mass Zionist gathering' at Babi Yar. (The first 'official' ceremony at the site did not take place until 1991.) He was reprimanded, warned and threatened. Even Stalin's Prize, the highest literary accolade in the land, which Nekrasov had received after the war for his good, honest, talented book on the Battle of Stalingrad, could no longer protect him. The writer's refusal to leave Babi Yar alone sealed his fate. In 1974 he was pushed out of the country, spending the last thirteen years of his life in Paris. Anatoly Kuznetsov, who found himself in the West five years before Nekrasov, died in London from a heart attack in 1979, aged not yet fifty, only a few months after the birth of his daughter. His son from his first marriage, Alexey Kuznetsov, a young boy at the time of his father's defection, had virtually no contact with his father before his death – any association with those who defected to the West had the most serious of repercussions. As a grown man, no longer living in the country where his father was persona non grata, Alexey translated *Babi Yar* into Ukrainian but, as it turned out, no one was particularly interested in publishing his translation. The son had to wait till 2008 for his father's book to come out in Ukrainian in Kiev.

As Billie and I walked through Babi Yar, the site seemed vast and peaceful. There were no people around us, only birds, green grass, leaves and gentle wind. The area is now a memorial park with several monuments scattered around the place, disconnected from each other. Birch trees, three hundred of them, stand in the Alley of the Righteous. The vast ravine is now just a hollow in the ground; it may seem large at first, but it is a small, shallow fraction of the original pit. Yet its presence at the site is vital, providing as it does a moment in which the ground is taken from under your feet. 'It is so beautiful here,' Billie said dreamily.

'How can you say this?' I raised my voice and then began to shout, no longer caring if I was breaking some unspoken code of behaviour. 'What's wrong with you? This is a terrible, ugly place. How on earth can you call it beautiful?'

'Saying that it is beautiful is a good thing, Mum. What would you like to see here instead? Death?'

By the time we walked back to Ira, we were barely speaking to each other. 'What's wrong?' she asked. I told her what happened, expecting Ira to nail Billie with a disapproving look. Let Billie have it. I no longer wanted to protect her from anyone. 'Billie is right,' Ira replied. 'It is beautiful here. What is it that you want?' I felt devastated, first by Billie's response to the site, which seemed to me to signify her refusal of engagement, then by Ira – honest, decent, stoic Ira – siding with Billie. For a while I wanted both of them to vanish so I could be left all alone. I wanted the world to stop. I did not want anything to be normal, beautiful or peaceful. It was at that moment I remembered a story my mother once told me, a story which, with time and rather unexpectedly, became deeply important to me. It happened more than fifty years ago, when my mum was just fourteen, and concerned the death of a much-loved uncle, Mitya.

The dead man had been handsome and universally liked, with a young family of his own. A tank commander who had come out of the war alive, in the postwar years he became a highly sought after professional. It was some mundane condition, such as appendicitis, that carried him off at the age of forty-two. After the funeral, his mother came home and, to the complete astonishment of the girl who was my mum, proceeded to wash and cut the vegetables for a salad. Instead of wailing and beating her head against the wall, the older woman calmly washed an assortment of cucumbers and tomatoes, one by one. The salad vegetables looked very fresh, straight out of the soil – the same soil in which her son was now ensconced forever. My mum, who was distraught at Uncle Mitya's death, was shocked to see how her grandmother simply carried on in industrious fashion trying (or so Mum imagined) to fill the gap left by her son's death with a ridiculous mountain of cut-up vegetables.

The girl, who couldn't stand her grandmother at the time anyway, thought this behaviour one more proof that something was terribly wrong with her senior relative, who had somehow managed to march with a peeler in her right hand through devastating tragedy. By the time my mum told me this story, she was no longer disgusted with her grandmother, not by a long stretch. But I felt ill to my stomach. Just like the girl all those years before, I wanted Mitya's mother to grieve so that walls would shake and little birds would fall from the sky crying, so nothing around her would ever be the same. And if she had to cut the bloody vegetables, she could at the very least cut off a finger or something.

It took me a while to see what Mum had also realised – that at that moment of acute, unbearable loss, chopping salad was not a manifestation of some kind of shameful repression, or an inability to mourn, or an attempt to take refuge in some kind of 'pretend' normality. All my great-grandmother was doing – unconsciously, unwittingly – was trying to take care of her broken heart. Staying plugged in, letting the rhythms of ordinary, everyday life wash through her and around her. It was about the basic human need for connectedness, for being needed, useful, a part of things.

American journalist Philip Gourevitch, who was in Rwanda in the aftermath of the 1994 genocide, writes in *We Wish to Inform You That Tomorrow We Will Be Killed with Our Families* how he learned that in itself survival was meaningless until one found 'a reason to survive again, a reason to look to tomorrow. The so-called survival instinct is often described as an animal urge to preserve oneself. But once the threat of bodily anni-hilation is relieved, the soul still requires preservation, and a wounded soul becomes the source of its own affliction; it can-not nurse itself directly.' This is because, he says, the needy soul needs to be needed. 'As I came to know survivors,' Gourevitch continues:

> I found that, when it comes to soul preservation, the urge to look after others is often greater than the urge to look after oneself. All across the ghostly countryside, survivors sought each other out, assembling surrogate families and squatting together in abandoned shacks, in schoolyard shanties and burned out shops, hoping for safety and comfort in hastily assembled households.

Soul preservation requires this reaching out, taking care of things and people. Not for some lofty moral reason, not because it is the right thing to do, but because often it is just about the only thing that works, the only thing that makes sense. I wanted Babi Yar to be frozen in the moment of catastrophe. I wanted my great-grandmother to reject rituals of everyday life surely rendered meaningless by her loss. But why? What was the alternative? In the face of loss, the idea of life going on may seem like an ultimate insult or a self-serving fiction, but this is all we have in the end. Green grass comes back. Birds return, caressed by gentle wind. Women put on make-up and heels again. Billie was right. Babi Yar is beautiful *and* all those other things.

Before Billie and I got on the plane to Europe, a dear friend, a non-Jewish Ukrainian my age, who lives in Sydney but travels to Kiev at least once a year, rang me up to say she was worried about someone with *my* face going to Ukraine all alone, worse still with a prepubescent girl. She wanted to introduce me to some people, but she was worried about their reaction to me (must be that face again). She said the usual maternal things about not walking down unlit streets and the kind of care I needed to take while getting rides in other people's cars. My friend is married to a Jewish guy, with a son half-Ukrainian and half-Jewish (the boy is both gorgeous and talented, oh those products of mixed marriages), so she is acutely sensitive to the traditional anti-Semitism of her country. (Her late and much-loved grandmother, a true bastion of tolerance, said about the choice of her husband, 'So what he is a Jew, at least they are good family people.') Now, she believed unequivocally that anti-Semitism was going from strength to strength in post-Soviet Ukraine, despite whatever 'good news stories' I may have gleaned from the media. And there was some 'feel-good' stuff out there – independent Ukraine's first president, Leonid Kravchuk, officially apologising for the persecution of Jews in his country; the incumbent, Viktor Yushenko, describing Babi Yar on its sixty-fifth anniversary as 'the tragedy of Ukraine with the shot Jewish heart'; Ukraine becoming the only country of the former Soviet Union where it was compulsory for the Holocaust to be included in history textbooks and State exams. Clearly, anti-Semitism was no longer practised by the State, but I had no illusions that it could be magically expunged from people's thoughts and fears, especially when the economy was going badly and there was no stability. (I thought of the little ditty from my childhood – 'If there is no water in your tap, kikes have drunk it all.') Policy is powerless in the face of ingrained prejudice; all we have going for us is time.

So I did not come to Ukraine on the lookout for feel-good stories, nor did I want to find proof that 'Ukrainians were the worst' – a much-repeated refrain after the war and certainly the one still heard today. I wanted none of that. In truth, I just wanted to walk the streets of this country which was once my home, and for no one to care how I looked. I wanted to go inside a synagogue in Kiev's centre, a synagogue no longer masquerading as a puppet theatre, with my back straight, Billie by my side and no need to look over my shoulder (which is exactly what happened). I wanted to see men and boys walking freely in the streets with their *kipas* on. I wanted small, ordinary things – to me they were miraculous in themselves – not the total and absolute death of anti-Semitism.

We meet Svetlana Kandeeva at McDonald's near the girls-only Jewish school where she works. There is no other place for us to have a conversation, as the school is a long train ride from the city's centre and, besides, we can only see each other after hours, after Svetlana has finished her teaching and all the other meetings scheduled for the day. This is our first face-to-face meeting. I have found Svetlana through two organisations she is involved with, the Ukrainian Centre for the Holocaust Studies and the Centre for Jewish Education of Ukraine. At McDonald's, we buy Billie a sundae as a bribe and talk about things that at first sound utterly improbable to me – seminars about Jewish persecution for teachers at non-Jewish schools, projects that present Jewish and Ukrainian histories as inextricably linked, youth summer camps for kids of all ethnic backgrounds entitled 'Sources of Tolerance'. She tells me of a new discipline, *Ukrainojudaica*, created by the late Professor Marten Feller. Svetlana travels across Ukraine, but also to most of the other parts of the former Soviet Union, conducting workshops and seminars. 'If you manage to get to the teachers,' she says, 'then you have the kids.'

It takes me a while to understand that Svetlana is in fact neither Jewish nor Ukrainian. She is actually Russian, born in Siberia. 'I was once introduced at an international conference, "Here is a strange Russian who lives in Ukraine, teaches in a religious Jewish lyceum and gives lectures to Tadzhiks in Uzbekistan and to Armenians in Tbilisi."'

It is completely dark when Svetlana shows me and Billie the girls' school where she works, one of four private Jewish schools of its kind in Kiev. To reach it, we walk through *dvory*, our path illuminated by the lights in people's windows. For at least ten minutes, if not more, we bang on the school's door. 'Baba Nadya, Baba Nadya, open up,' Svetlana shouts. When Baba Nadya finally appears, herself like a classical representation of an old Ukrainian woman wrapped up in layer after layer of clothing, she is apologetic. 'Sorry, was in the toilet, didn't hear you knock,' she says to Svetlana and lets us come in. We enter a school in which the walls are plastered with Hebrew and Ukrainian posters, side by side – I never thought I would see these two languages alongside each other, especially in a Ukrainian school of all places.

I tell Svetlana of my friend in Sydney who is worried sick for me in Kiev, but Svetlana will have none of that. She is a teacher, a doer, a spreader of tolerance and, even though she never says it out loud, it strikes me that she is sick of people complaining that there is no cure to Ukrainian anti-Semitism. There is never a cure if you do not want to look for it. 'People see what they want to see,' she says. 'It is the same with everything. I remember a conversation at an airport in Kazakhstan about the Kremlin. For the person I was speaking to, the Kremlin meant Stalin. But for me it means Aristotle Fioravanti [the fifteenth-century Italian architect of the Kremlin]. For me, Shostakovich is a musical genius. For another, a collaborator. Each one sees what they want to see.'

Svetlana is full of stories of non-Jews in Ukrainian provinces identifying mass graves and erecting stones or monuments, gathering documents and testimonies, creating memory books. (No, it doesn't undo what happened to Jewish people there, but what possible good can come from us not acknowledging that this is happening too?) 'Do you think that the knowledge and the legacy of your neighbours being exterminated in front of your eyes has simply evaporated from the mass consciousness?' she asks me. Many people who saved Jews never told anyone about what they did. People capable of risking their lives for

others do not tend to publicise their good deeds. Svetlana is a
diehard optimist and refuses to be cynical. I suspect that the
only way to stave off cynicism when it comes to something as
complex, unsettling and endlessly disheartening as the relationship between Ukrainians and Jews is to do things. Of course, it
would be a mistake to view people like Svetlana as representative of anyone but themselves, but the fact of their existence
and the work that they manage to do is in itself a sign that
things have changed, that not everything in Ukraine is permanently, inexorably 'the same'.

September 2009 in Melbourne, another anniversary of Babi
Yar. The media is full of reports about the hotel proposal. The
proposal is followed by condemnation from the international
Jewish community and, eventually, the mayor's withdrawal of
planning approval. (One of my dear friends sends me a link
to the story with 'Sorry to do this to you, but I thought you
should know' in the subject line.) As I read about the proposal,
I come across another, much less reported story – a new monument has just been unveiled to commemorate the victims of
Babi Yar. The newspapers report that it was funded by a busi-
nessman who chooses to remain anonymous but who funded
the publication of Alexey Kuznetsov's Ukrainian translation of
Babi Yar a year earlier. I search for a photo of the monument,
and there it is – a boy cast in bronze reads a sign on the wall
of a building: *All kikes of the city of Kiev and vicinity must appear
by 8.00 a.m. on Monday, September 29 1941* etc., etc. I cannot quite believe my eyes. I read everything I can find about

the monument; I watch podcasts of Ukrainian news just to make sure and, yes, I did get it right the first time. This is a monument both to Anatoly Kuznetsov, who so bravely wrote the story of Babi Yar, and to the young Kievan boy Tolya, Kuznetsov's fictional alter ego. The monument depicts Tolya/Anatoly at the moment when he first read the edict and realised that Kiev's Jews were to be separated from the rest of the population, their fate yet unknown. As Kuznetsov told it, 'I re-read it twice and for some reason my skin went clammy and cold . . . It was somehow too cruel, words written with cold hatred. The day was cold and windy, the street was virtually empty. I could not go home so, shaken up, not quite knowing why, I wandered off to the market.'

14

78 CHERNYSHEVSKY STREET

BILLIE AND I START at the bottom of Chernyshevsky Street. First we walk towards the building (the very essence of Soviet nondescript) that right through my childhood, up to the day my family left, I knew as *my best friend Sasha's house*. All these years later, even though Sasha has not lived here for a long time, my eyes can still pick it out in an instant from its almost identical neighbours.

We walk slowly, counting down the buildings, shuffling our feet through fallen autumn leaves, following the route I used to take every day after school – the home stretch, from Sasha's place at number 96 to mine at number 78, on the corner with Garshin Street. We stop opposite the empty academic bookstore, which wears a 'Leasing Now' sign. Sasha's mother used to work here when we were kids. (How did you think we got to read all those books rarer than hen's teeth in the first place? *Jane Eyre, Hamlet,* Freud's *The Interpretation of Dreams* – all from here.) This is where Billie and I wait, not for Sasha, but for Natasha, another childhood friend.

Here she is running towards us – tall, svelte and blonde in a skirt and girlie heels, with a magnificent bunch of red roses in her hands. It has been twenty-five years. 'Happy birthday, love,' she says and hugs me. Yesterday Natasha got on a bus from the town of Dneprodzerzhinsk and travelled for six hours just to meet us. Doubly remarkable as we have not seen each other since we were nine. At the end of Year 2, her family moved away and, all of a sudden, Natasha was no longer in my class, no longer a friend I played with after school. For a while we maintained our connection through letters – she has saved all of mine and unexpectedly brings them along – but soon enough this correspondence died down altogether, in the way that children's correspondence does.

Natasha, until she left Kharkov, was Huckleberry Finn to my Tom Sawyer. With her by my side, galvanised by her adventurousness and purposeful courting of danger, I got cut, bruised and, often, almost caught, learning the hard way in those few hours between school and supper the wrath of strange men and women in our neighbourhood. Together we dug the soil of our local park, fossicking for human skulls. (With the Soviet planners' usual regard for the past, this park had been plonked straight on top of a cemetery; students of the Kharkov Arts Academy used its relics for their anatomical drawing classes.) Or else, we studied closely the faces of wanted criminals in the glass display outside the local police station. When we had committed their features to memory, we scoured the streets, hoping to become the indispensable instruments of justice. Perhaps we sensed then that, as Jvanetsky wrote, the police did not protect the nation under dictatorship, they guarded that nation, 'especially in places of incarceration'.

Sometimes we turned our recklessness on each other. When Natasha and I fought, we fought hard. Once our debate over Stalin's culpability for crimes against his people degenerated into a brawl. (This would have been just pre-Gorbachev, 1983 or thereabouts.) 'He knew nothing, you idiot,' Natasha shouted, sounding outraged, as if Stalin was her friend or little brother accused most unfairly of someone else's misdemeanours. 'Yes, he did – it's all his fault,' I shouted back. Both of us were drawing on adult conversations overheard in our respective kitchens, of course. We made up quickly too. We never got to lock horns as adolescents, I reflect now. We skipped that whole period when fighting with friends can produce the deepest of cuts.

The three of us – Billie, Natasha and I – walk together to 78 Chernyshevsky Street. Our balcony has been enclosed with ugly unpainted cladding and sliding glass windows. A fat, middle-aged woman in a massive bra is on the balcony, hanging out her washing. There goes the idea of a nice family keeping the *genius loci* of our apartment alive. That bra – its size, its make and ostentatious display – in combination with the woman's face, and the way she seems angry with the wet grey socks and tracksuit pants that evidently require from her too much bending and stretching, is like a death sentence to my fantasies of homecoming. Women like that do not let women like me into their apartments. Despite being neither *that* old nor really *that* huge, such women simply cannot be imagined as young and light. They smell of cabbage and sweat, sit in their flats with their legs wide apart, as if in the middle of a collective farm, and for 'cultural leisure' start fights with other neighbours on the stairwell.

When we left in 1989, in the days before private property was once again allowed, most people did not own their apartments. They 'borrowed' them from the State, which wanted them back in perfect condition (not so much Nanny State then, as Evil Stepmother State). Nineteen years later the doors of 78 Chernyshevsky Street no longer open to the uninitiated; the security entrance takes care of people like me who have no business lurking around other people's homes. Laughing, because it is, after all, rather funny to come from the other side of the world only to be stopped dead in our tracks by an intercom, we wonder what it would take for this door to open. What about buzzing our old apartment, or just any apartment really, and saying, 'Excuse me, could you let us in? We used to live here two decades ago!' Or, perhaps, 'Mail, open up!' Or offering no justification or excuse, but instead appealing to the basic goodness of people, or (better still) their indifference: 'COULD YOU PLEASE LET US IN?'

'If I only knew the phone number of the woman who used to live in the apartment above us,' I say to Billie and Natasha. 'Rimma Evlampevna was her name, if I knew her number she would have definitely let us in. I don't even know if she is alive, though, so I guess that's a dumb idea.'

As I say these words and move away from the building, seriously considering whether fifteen minutes of banging my head on the tightly shut door is enough to concede defeat, I see Rimma Evlampevna walking towards us. Our middle-aged neighbour with her impeccable high hairdo (so intricate I always thought of it as simultaneously spectacular and spooky) is now an old woman; her hair lies limp, no longer twisted and raised in salute to her superior grooming prowess. I stand frozen, trying not to breathe, not sure how much work will be required before Rimma Evlampevna recognises the young Masha Tumarkina who used to live below her with her nice parents and an older sister. Is twenty years an eternity for neighbourly bonds? Rimma Evlampevna heads straight towards me, not looking the least bit surprised.

'Hello, Inna,' she says, recognising my breed instantly, but thinking me my sister.

'Rimma Evlampevna, it's Masha.'

'Oh, Mashenka, good morning.'

Rimma Evlampevna speaks so calmly, as if it is entirely in the nature of things that your neighbours from many decades ago, the nice ones who stuffed everything up by leaving 'forever' (the first out of the building, in fact), will one day casually greet you at your building's door. I am grateful for the serenity of her welcome (and it is serenity, not senility – Rimma Evlampevna's mind, as we have plenty of opportunities to verify, is intact), grateful for the modesty and tranquillity of her hug. Rimma Evlampevna takes Natasha's lush, magnificent roses from my hands, assuming the flowers are for her. I am utterly unprepared for this development, and as I watch myself surrendering my birthday bouquet – I can hardly wrestle it from this dignified matron, or can I? – the sense of entitlement that my former neighbour still possesses strikes me as wonderful. In her mind the flowers are intended for her and, of course, they are nothing short of spectacular.

'Shall we go in, girls?' Rimma Evlampevna opens the door. Here we are, inside, and instantly I feel as if I am looking at an X-ray of my internal organs. For the past two decades I have internalised these stairs and walls decades overdue for major works, these letterboxes that look like long-forgotten bird-houses perched between the ground and the first floor and now, all of a sudden, these things appear outside me, reassembled as material objects, three-dimensional as anything.

We walk up the stairs (I am last in the procession, an old habit) past the door of the apartment that belongs to the woman and her bra. 'This is the one,' I say to Billie. She nods and we keep walking. On the next floor the apartment Rimma Evlampevna used to share with her husband Nikolai Pavlov-ich – who she still calls by his full name with the patronymic, even now almost five years after his death – is just the way I remember. Most of its furniture is from that golden era when Nikolai Pavlovich was dean of some prestigious institute and Rimma Evlampevna a senior lecturer there. (Kharkov, being a major research centre, had an incredible number of such estab-lishments. I remember my father calculating that from our place you could easily walk to seven of them.) In the 1980s, when we lived below them, Nikolai Pavlovich and Rimma Evlampevna were a power couple, able, I assume, to entertain in style. Now the once status-proud, dust-free furniture, and the assorted china on display in glass cabinets look pitiful and lost. Rimma Evlampevna points out the family in their photo frames, introducing both the living and the deceased by their full handles – so and so is a Dean; her brother is a Professor; the husband is a Leading Engineer. 'So glad you are in academia and not in business,' she says, having established what it is that

I do now that I am all grown-up. I see Natasha's face go just a tiny bit red – she is in business, not in academia, God bless her.

Natasha and I leave Billie with Rimma Evlampevna as a deposit and run to the shop around the corner, where we go halves buying cheese, sausage, a lemon, a loaf of bread and a semi-stale jam roll. Rimma Evlampevna tries to stop us (any self-respecting hostess from this latitude would), 'Don't go anywhere. I have enough for us all in the fridge.' 'It's my birthday,' I shout, already at the door, 'and I am the birthday girl, so you cannot stop me, Rimma Evlampevna. You cannot offend me like that.' The old birthday trick.

To enter that shop again, not as a child dispatched by my parents with a handful of kopeks for the most basic of provisions, but as a discerning consumer in a rush somewhere (a cashed-up one too compared with the pensioners crowded next to the counter), someone who just wants to buy things quickly and be out of the store – this feels unexpectedly gratifying. It is good to be grown-up. I do not think I was ever particularly good at being a minor. When some of my friends reminisce nostalgically about their carefree childhoods with not a worry in the world, I can never quite join in. Perhaps because I have always craved self-determination more than I feared responsibility. I always wanted to call the shots.

By the time Natasha and I run back into the apartment, the table is fully set. In the middle is a bottle of Cahors wine in my honour, as well as fruit preserve served in little china vasettes. *You can take the woman out of high society, but you cannot take high society out of the woman.* Compared with other pensioners, Rimma Evlampevna is doing very well, for she receives a scholar's pension, far higher than the pension paid to mere mortals. Her capital however is frozen, and she is scared about what might happen now that the global financial crisis is taking hold. (In front of my eyes the exchange rates go through the roof and euros, American dollars and other foreign currencies disappear altogether from the city's banks.) All alone in her three-room apartment, prime real estate now, Rimma Evlampevna seems deeply sad and lost. 'Something in me got broken after Nikolai Pavlovich's death. Terrible thoughts come into my head,' she says. Being an ethnic Russian, she feels ill at ease in the independent Ukraine. The Ukrainisation of every aspect of life in the past two decades – media, government, education and social services – has disconcerted her and made her feel out of place, but she is too old now to move to Russia.

Even for people who do not care for politics, the massive tension between Russia and Ukraine is impossible to ignore: television programs from Russia are no longer shown on Ukrainian channels, while homegrown corruption and continuing disputes with Russia over the supply of its natural gas for Ukrainian consumption means that heating is by no means a certain proposition in the autumn and winter months. It is minus-two degrees outside now, but half of Kharkov's central heating, including in the home of a dear family friend where we are staying, has not been turned on by the authorities. We all go quiet listening to Rimma Evlampevna's woes. Then, using my discretionary powers as a birthday girl, I completely change the topic.

'Rimma Evlampevna, how did you manage to get your hair looking like that?'

'I went to the hairdresser's every week, would never miss an appointment.'

'It was some spectacular hair, I must say.'

Billie and Natasha laugh, but I can see that Natasha gets it – she can instantly recognise how hard old age is on women like Rimma Evlampevna, especially when they find themselves on their own on the margins of their families, their community and their city. Rimma Evlampevna apologises for the state of her apartment. 'Oh,' I say, 'please don't ever apologise. You know how my mum used to be – she kept our apartment so beautifully clean – and still every night I would have to wait for a minute after turning the lights on in the toilet so that cockroaches could scatter away.'

'Oh, Mashenka,' she says, 'there are no more cockroaches in Ukraine, all gone!' And I thought cockroaches and rats could survive even a nuclear holocaust.

Stuck in its time warp, her place is as close as Billie is going to get to imagining her mother's childhood home. The layout is much the same as ours was and, as we discover when Rimma Evlampevna takes us downstairs to introduce us, the woman in the bra has rearranged and reconstructed our old apartment within an inch of its life. The bathroom and toilet now share a single space, while my parents' former bedroom, once lined with floor-to-ceiling bookshelves, has been demoted to a storeroom. We learn that the occupant, who is now wearing a loose top (you should see the relief on Billie's face), is called Tatyana, and she lives there with her husband, a former policeman. 'Thank God he quit the police force. He is an investigator and a lawyer now. When he was still with the police, half of his mates from the local police station used to hang out here all the time, drinking and some such, in this tiny kitchen – can you imagine?' *Yes, I can. My parents managed to get most of their friends*

273

inside that kitchen, and they had a lot of friends, none of them police-men. What's the point of actually saying anything? Tatyana asks no questions about where we come from, how long ago we lived in this apartment, what brings us back, nothing – as if her curiosity cannot stretch even for a moment beyond her own concerns.

'Look at what this bitch has done to my ceiling. She has flooded us all. I will get to her yet. She will be begging for mercy.' I can see Rimma Evlampevna squirming silently as she listens to Tatyana going off. She cannot afford an enemy like that, not in her building. Natasha looks at me. Both of us can see Rimma Evlampevna shrinking – *this is what the world has come to; this building never used to be like this; we had some decent, well-brought-up people here*. She is visibly embarrassed. Embar-rassed, and also deeply sad. I remember when I was discussing anti-Semitism with Svetlana Kandeeva, the teacher I met in Kiev, that she told me how sad many Ukrainians and Russians felt about their Jewish neighbours leaving the country. At the time I wondered if this was wishful thinking on the part of a natural-born optimist. But now, standing next to Rimma Evlampevna, watching her face, I can see at least for a moment precisely what Svetlana was trying to tell me.

We stay for five unbearable minutes, then take our leave. Rimma Evlampevna hugs us and tells me to send her best wishes to my parents and, of course, to my sister, Inna. I feel strangely calm, almost still inside, as the three of us walk out of number 78 and head towards the other places that made up our world – our *dvory*, our bakery, our library, our shop with toffee lollies sold by weight and, of course, my old school. 'Mum, I am not going in,' says Billie. 'I do not feel comfortable being at a working school in the middle of the day on the other side of the world.'

Sasha doesn't want to see me. My Sasha. In fact, she has not wanted to speak to me for years. This is not the first of our dry spells. We lost touch once before, a few years after my family left the country on the day she turned sixteen. Some sweet sixteen she had, counting down the last day on earth with her best friend and then spending the evening at the train station seeing us off. Before we left, I gave her a bouquet of flowers that I had been saving up to buy for almost a year. What a bunch of flowers! They were long, almost her height, and had to go into a floor vase. (I cannot quite recall how her mother happened to own such an exotic object.) I wanted Sasha to have something of me that was big and tall and would last a long time. If I could have given her a hundred of these flowers, if I could have surrounded her by a forest of them, I would have. I was desperate to leave something behind to protect her from my absence.

For the first few years we wrote countless letters and spoke on the phone a few times when we could afford to. Then it all stopped in a way that the most intense of long-distance friendships sometimes do, suddenly grinding to a halt, and it is hard to figure out exactly why – someone moved again, someone hit upon hard times, someone began to wonder what was the point of it all. Sasha and I reconnected a decade or so later, post-internet, but not before I called every single household listed under the same surname as hers in Kharkov's online directory. My telephone marathon turned up no traces of Sasha (not surprising, as by now she had a different surname), but when I hung up after the last call – talk about embodied memory – the six digits of our mutual friend's old home number suddenly lined up in front of my eyes in perfect sequence. I called the number straight away, without stopping to think about what it might mean to speak to that friend, Tanya, after all these years. Her sister-in-law answered, and soon Tanya and I were crying together on the phone.

We had all been in the same class at school, Sasha, Tanya and me. Tanya was athletic, smart, popular, well adjusted and not Jewish. In other words, she could have had a rollicking good time at school if only she had not chosen to stick by her difficult Jewish friend (me), the one with a propensity to fall out of step with 'the collective' and a habit of picking fights with teachers and peers alike in the name of 'justice'. I realise now that Tanya's sturdy loyalty was even more remarkable given the fact that she did not come from a Jew-friendly household. Sasha and I were always an item, but Tanya was close to both of us, and in my absence Sasha and Tanya grew closer still.

Once Tanya had put me back in touch with Sasha, it seemed like everything was all right. But after our first long conversations, so easy and joyful, so lacking in strain that I declared to all those sceptics around me that *real friendships do not die, they simply hibernate*, Sasha no longer wanted any part of it. In fact, as she made abundantly clear, she wanted me to stop calling altogether. 'There is nothing connecting us in the present,' she said, or something perhaps less palatable still (my memory has been all too gentle with me on this point). 'This *friendship till death do us apart* business is nothing but hot air.' It was, she said, a dangerous illusion that we could sustain our friendship based

on the past. The past was all good and well, but it was no sub-
stitute for a shared present. I disagreed but, of course, she had a
point. I wondered what was behind my dogged insistence that
no mountain was too high and no ocean too deep for our friendship.
It was never my style to force myself on anyone, but with Sasha
I was fighting not to let go.

'OK,' I said. 'I can hear you, but what if you actually don't
mean it; what if you are simply in a crap mood? How about I
hang up now and call you in a month? If you still feel the same,
I promise to stop calling.'

She still felt the same in a month.

That was in 2003 if I remember correctly. And now, at the
end of 2008, Sasha is still refusing to make contact. But Tanya,
gorgeous and slim (and this after two kids), is genuinely excited
about seeing me. She loves me still, although she too, once the
surface is scratched, feels hurt and abandoned. She too, deep
down, cannot quite forgive me my disappearance and the fact
that I still get to call the shots all these years later, just like when
I left. These days, after borders have been opened up, people
who leave can decide when and for how long they pop back
into the lives of those who stayed. Tanya tells me about some
of our classmates who have emigrated to various countries in
the West and who have everything worked out when they
come back to Kharkov for a visit: a tight schedule of dirt-cheap
dentists and gynaecologists, merchandise to stack up on, quick
suntan at some Black Sea resort and, in the middle of their full
'cultural' program, they catch up with their former friends in
two-hour blocks.

'How much time have you got for me?' Tanya asks when
Billie and I meet her at the train station near Kharkov State

University, where she works as a lecturer. I don't understand the question at first, but then I get it – Tanya expects me to have allocated a certain number of contact hours to her before I move on to someone or something else. I instantly scrap most of the plans in my head. I would rather see only a very few people on this visit, and see them properly so they never feel part of my touring schedule, slotted back-to-back. We spend the evening with Tanya's family – her son, Nikita, who is eleven, unexpectedly bonds with Billie and wants her to teach him English. As Tanya and I sit in the kitchen talking, I hear Billie's voice repeatedly enunciating the word 'diary' in the distance. Tanya and the kids come to see us the following night, partially on Nikita's insistence.

Nineteen years have passed, so Tanya and I have no time to waste on chatter. 'Did you ever think that I would become a maths lecturer at uni?' she asks. 'You know, maths dries you up terribly. Do you think I should start all over again? But what should I do? Who did you think I was going to be?' I always loved this about Tanya – the absence of a defensive posture, the utter lack of preciousness with friends.

Tanya is not the least bit surprised by who I have become. This is what she always thought: with me it had to be something to do with words.

'What the hell,' says Tanya, perplexed, after trying unsuccessfully to connect me with Sasha. She doesn't know why Sasha is kicking and screaming. She thinks it is a pose. Surely after twenty years we all have nothing to lose and at least something to gain from being in the same room together. She gives it one last go. 'OK,' Tanya says, 'Sasha said to give you her mobile number, but don't get carried away. She makes no promises.' I am angry, of course, at Sasha for making it so hard, for her giving up on us – after all, how many real friends do we have in a lifetime? But I don't think that Sasha's deep hesitation is a pose. I take it to mean something quite basic – *If you in your smug self-delusion want to believe that friendships are forever and expect us to bend over backwards on your lightning-fast visit to make you feel that everything is OK, that nothing has been broken, that nothing has been torn, you can go and fuck yourself.* That, I cannot argue with. But it is one thing to stay away from her when I am in Melbourne, Australia. To be in Kharkov and not do my best to see her, that feels entirely different, like a form of betrayal.

I know that it is impossible ever to insist on friendship, to drag the other party back in, but nevertheless I refuse to accept a sunset clause, to concede the inevitablity of becoming strangers to friends just because I can no longer see them regularly. To concede as much would mean all my pre-emigration friendships were doomed. 'Sasha, this is Masha, please give me an hour of your time, that's all I ask' – this is my text message, a message in a bottle to you, Sasha. The reply comes surprisingly quickly – 'OK, meet me at 10.30 am tomorrow. Sasha.' I lie awake that night. Three blankets are not enough to keep Billie warm; we are hugging each other so tightly as if trying to squeeze any remaining air out between us. I wait for my daughter to fall asleep so I can disappear into my thoughts. I am not vain enough to suppose that in an hour I can convince Sasha to change her mind. This is not what it is about. I don't want to persuade her, just to see her.

I grew up surrounded not only by my parents' friends but by my sister's, and almost all of them I liked. I liked them not just as people but for the quality of these friendships themselves – they seemed exciting and spontaneous, yet also surprisingly stable, glued together by a sense of deeply shared loyalty. Inna was a student at the Kharkov Arts Academy and, although she was hardworking and even brilliant, her bohemian ways were no doubt conducive to relationships that seemed to grow organically because the soil was right and fertile. In her room, she scribbled the phone numbers of friends and acquaintances on the wallpaper, and gradually they took over the walls. My sister had a gift for friendship. One day she would see outside her window a bunch of university students sent to dig a trench in our street – the next day some of these students would be on our balcony drinking coffee and, inevitably, one or two of them would become a proper friend. They were invariably generous and accepting of me, and from the time I was twelve I wanted to grow up with friends like that. As strangely contradictory as it may sound coming from someone who has chosen the unsociable, solitary role of writer, this became my sustaining image of the grown-up me, surrounded by friends, not just one or two but by a gang, a flock, a school of friends, just like my gregarious sister. Watching my parents and Inna at the centre of their respective circles, I understood that that was how people survived in our world, by creating their own well-balanced micro-climates.

To this day, I am sustained in some essential way by the belief that there are friendships that do not need to be lubricated and reconfirmed at every turn, that are strong enough to absorb long hiatuses as easily as daily talk. Such friendships are essentially time-proof, distance-proof. I do not naively think there will be no friction, no shocks, but I trust that our differences can be bridged. (It was just like that with Marina in St

Petersburg; with Katya Margolis, the granddaughter of Marina Gustavovna; and with Tanya in Kharkov.) But why should Sasha feel the same as I do about long-distance friendship? I am wrong to expect her to. Perhaps what I am not allowing for is that, though we both lost something when my family emigrated, there was more at stake for her. After all, I was her best friend jumping out, if not out of my own accord, on a particularly sharp curve – her sixteenth birthday, a stage of life when no one can afford to have their closest friend disappear. My timing was terrible in other ways too. No matter how many memoirs and essays are written about the post-Soviet experience of the early 1990s, I can never read my way into even the most approximate understanding of how it felt to live through those times of unravelling. Yet for my generation that era of political change, economic dissolution and mass emigration coincided with the start of our adult lives. The end of 1989 and 1990 witnessed more goodbyes than all the postwar years combined, and the exodus ruptured not only bonds of blood and friendship but something larger, the very social fabric itself. Today, the class I went through school with divides almost equally between those who left and those who stayed. I wonder, ruefully, if my friendship with Sasha is inevitable collateral damage.

Thinking about our generation before we came away on this trip, I remembered a girl my age by the name of Nika Turbina. In 1984, when I was ten, Nika seemed to be everywhere, declaiming the poems she had been composing since the age of four to packed stadiums and concert halls across the Soviet Union. She was on television too, all the time or so it seemed, with her eyes half-closed, reciting as if possessed, addressing all of us in a manner moving in its intensity yet also unnervingly theatrical. I watched her countless times, on the black-and-white television set in our lounge room that also served as my bedroom.

Nika's debut collection, *First Draft*, was a resounding success, translated into twelve languages. The book's foreword was written by Yevgeniy Yevtushenko (Yevtushenko again!), who, for a while at least, became Nika's most famous and persistent champion. 'Uncle Zhenya' she called him. For years the adoring and adorable Uncle Zhenya toured Nika around as if she was a rare cultural treasure (a Fabergé egg perhaps, although that would have been politically incorrect) or, in Nika's words, a bear cub. Their crammed itinerary included a trip to Italy, where at the age of eleven Nika received the Golden Lion of Venice Award, awarded previously to only one other Russian poetess, Anna Akhmatova (in her sixties at the time of her own award). Uncle Zhenya and Nika even made it to Boston and New York, where *The New York Times* described her as 'already a star at age twelve'. In other words, Nika Turbina was rapidly turned into a cultural commodity, and this is in a nation where commodification of culture was seen as one of the deadly sins of the West. But her gift, nonetheless, was unmistakable, compelling many to speculate that someone – a dead genius, a god, a muse – was writing through her. A child could not have written these lines, people said.

Here was a girl of my own age who had everything I could ask for – an authentic talent, the attention of the world, beauty even. Most importantly, she had the opportunity to live her life as a poet. After coming to Australia I forgot to ask what happened to Nika Turbina, until Billie and I were getting ready to go on this trip. Then I Googled Turbina, convinced that she had become some world-renowned performance artist with her own blog and a flat in Venice, still beautiful, still a freak. Instead, Google told me that Nika was dead. Killed in 2002 in a fall from a fifth-storey balcony. No one was sure if she jumped, fell or was pushed off by someone who had had enough of her. It was an ugly, messy death, made uglier by the fact that only three people came to her funeral. This was the girl whose name was known to millions. In my generation, the one most likely to succeed. And now drugs, alcohol, failed university studies, failed relationships, psychosis, had culminated in an idiotic, humiliating death. In my study in Melbourne, I watched on YouTube our little poetess *sans* frontiers, our baby-faced National Treasure as a young woman, and felt out of my mind with grief.

And so, the night before my meeting with Sasha, my thoughts return to Nika and what happened to her. Could there be any doubt that I left too early, when all the events that would make up the bulk of my generation's shared experience and identity were yet to take place? I left before tanks rolled into Moscow in 1991, and before Gorbachev was put under house arrest in a failed coup. I left before Yeltsin, then Putin, became president; before Russia and Ukraine became separate countries; before an old teacher of ours, one of the most respected and the best, was spotted by her former students rummaging through piles of garbage, looking for food. I left before the opening of the KGB archives, before the word 'Gulag' appeared in textbooks, before the Russian version of *Wheel of Fortune*, before shoot-outs in the streets. I left before Soviet troops were pulled out of the 'brotherly nations' of Eastern Europe, before the mass renaming of cities and streets, before you could go into a shop and openly purchase the books of Brodsky, Pasternak and Nabokov. I left before the death of rock musician Viktor Tsoi, which produced one of the most powerful outbursts of public grief in a nation too accustomed to secretly mourning its beloved dead. I left before the start of the Chechen Wars, with their resulting explosions and hostage dramas; before the devaluation of the rouble; before real, unmistakable poverty and hunger. I left too early, I missed the whole point. I was not there when my generation was cornered by history.

Is Sasha right then?

In the morning I leave Billie in bed. She is pleased to just lie around most of the day, covered by a trillion blankets, her battered copy of Isobelle Carmody in her hands.

I recognise Sasha straight away. I always thought her the most beautiful girl in our class (a Jewish beauty with symmetrical features, a dream!). She is still beautiful, but she is clearly worn-out. And she has this Robert de Niro thing – has she always had it and I simply never noticed? – when she laughs, she looks like she may be crying.

I tell myself an hour is plenty. Besides, I have a lot to do today, not the least of which is a trip to the outer suburbs to find Liya Izrailyevna, the de facto wife of my grandmother's brother, who used to live upstairs from us opposite Rimma Evlampevna and was a beloved companion of my childhood.

I meet Sasha on the street corner, not in a café, which suits both of us. We can just walk alongside each other, exchanging a sentence or two from time to time. 'Do you remember how you got hit on the head here?' Sasha asks me as we walk through a big park in the city centre. When Sasha and I were fourteen (or rather she was fifteen, being a year older) we sat on a bench in this park, reading an old Soviet encyclopedia of philosophy published before Stalin's death – a rarity, which her mum had managed to acquire somewhere. We laughed, because the encyclopedia entries were ridiculous in their dogged insistence on portraying Stalin and his inner circle as the leading philosophers and scientists of their time (as if who they really were was somehow not enough). And then I remember being surrounded by a large group of young men with shaved heads, taunting us and calling us kikes before we somehow managed to push through them and run away. At the time this felt like a very precarious, touch-and-go moment for both of us. When I would retell this story years later, I would always mention how there were enough of these young men to encircle us, and how no one in the lively, busy park intervened to help.

'No,' says Sasha, 'there were only three guys who hassled us, but one of them hit you over the head.'

'How is it that I have tripled the numbers and managed to forget a blow to my head?'

'Go figure,' says Sasha.

An hour passes by, then two, then three. We have a cup of tea in a café just to get warm and keep walking. It is as if both of us are trying to understand what it feels like simply to be in each other's presence after nineteen years apart. Without much discussion about it, Sasha comes with me to see Liya Izrailyevna. 'Where is this place?' she asks after we catch a train to the very last stop on the line and then get in and out of two crammed minibuses. 'You need to really try hard to find a bigger shithole.'

The instructions Liya Izrailyevna gave my mum are not much help. The routes of minibuses have changed, and every set of directions we get from drivers, passengers, people on the street and in the shops negates the previous lot. I cannot remember the last time I was so confused and lost. I look at Sasha, who does not seem to be the least bit irritated by our misadventure. She seems to accept entirely that this is how things happen – you go somewhere, the directions are wrong, people give you contradictory advice, buses take you in the opposite direction. I stop completely, wondering if it would be best to call the whole thing off. And then I notice Sasha starting to walk.

'Where are you going?' I ask, catching up with her.

'Let's stop asking people where to go and just go.'

'But go where? Why walk there and not here? We don't even know if this place is in walking distance. What's the point of just going?' (I am not the daughter of a scientist for nothing.)

'Let's just go, Masha,' says Sasha.

Did we get to the place where Liya Izrailyevna lives? Yes, we did. I cannot explain how and if there was any method at all to Sasha's madness. All I can say is that I followed Sasha, who did not know where she was going, and we reached the place where we needed to be. Almost on time too.

And the spell – the black spell between us – was broken, which I cannot explain either. Maybe we realised that we simply needed each other just as we did all those years ago. There were no cathartic moments (except perhaps seeing Liya Izrailyevna's building materialise in front of our eyes, seemingly out of nowhere). I don't think either of us cried. We did not have a conversation about what happened to 'us' and why it all went terribly wrong.

I wondered what Sasha saw that made her forgive me for leaving her, that made her accept that I have not become a different species. Some kind of vision she had about my safe, privileged, easy life in the West – perhaps me walking in white pants near palm trees with a margarita in my manicured paw – evaporated during the hours we spent walking together. Perhaps she simply saw how much like her I was – tough, deeply unsure of myself, cocky, tired, fragile. That the lines on my face were not covered by some super-restorative facial crème, that I wore jeans just like her and no jewellery, that I had to count my banknotes carefully every time I bought a small gift or a souvenir. And as we slowly started talking – about men, money, dreams, crossroads – perhaps she understood that my life was easily as messy as hers, that I didn't ride into her world on a white horse.

God only knows what we imagine about our friends when we do not see them for decades. Perhaps more than anything we fear them looking at us; we anticipate and fear their concealed appraisal of us: *Is this what has become of you? Who could have guessed? And I thought . . .* This becomes especially daunting if the spectre of migration is involved. But Sasha and I did not appraise each other. It just did not happen. Something else took over – a kind of gentleness, a gratitude for something, a silence that did not need to be chased away. Whatever happened in those two decades was not enough to turn us into strangers. Maybe this is all both of us needed to know. Maybe this was enough. We finally said goodbye at nine or ten that night, just in time for Sasha to catch the very last bus home.

We speak on the phone once a month or so these days. The phone, of course, is hard. It was much easier when we were simply next to each other. But it does not matter, because I know that the cynical, tense and suspicious undertones are gone. We are not on our guard, we are not second-guessing each other. Sasha will come to Australia, it is just a matter of time. Secretly I am working on a plan to help her immigrate here, since she has no family left in Ukraine. I have floated the idea and she has not rejected it out of hand. Is the secret plan just for Sasha's benefit, or is it for mine as well? The cynics would say that I am doing this entirely for me, domesticating my past or healing some private wound of my own. I cannot demolish such accusations, all I can say is that I honestly do not believe that is my motive. I remember Dina Rubina's words about running her hand across her chest and feeling the stitch holding the two parts of her together. Finally, after all this time, I am fine with my stitch, it no longer feels like it is concealing an injury or a disfigurement. It is simply a distinguishing mark. I have not 'embraced' my stitch, rest assured, but twenty years have gone and it has simply become part of my skin. The past may be a foreign country, who am I to argue this point, but Sasha, Marina, young Katya, Petya, Natasha, Tanya do not live in that country. I have been there, so I know.

EPILOGUE

AT KHARKOV INTERNATIONAL AIRPORT – the size of someone's ostentatious villa – we wait for the plane that will take us to Vienna. We are used to shiny, vast, frenetic, alpha-spaces – pleasantly cool no matter what the temperature is outside, bright no matter the time – but in Kharkov the airport looks more like a monk's cave: dark, silent and medieval. At the check-in our suitcase is pushed through what looks like an opening in the wall; I see a pair of hands grabbing it from the other side. For a moment I fear that it is gone for good. Our tiny plane is like a poor, emaciated cousin to all the big, beefy Boeings out there, so small it seems fragile and painfully unsure of itself.

Yet again I cannot wait to leave, and yet again I feel overcome by regret. We should not be going now. It is too soon. I, for one, am not ready. But this time the equation is pretty basic. Miguel is waiting for us in Australia. He has turned one and a half today, and we haven't seen him for almost six weeks. And so in the airport lounges of Kharkov, Vienna and Bangkok, Billie and I pore over his blurry photos on my mobile, noticing that on most of them he waves his hand. ('A distinctly presidential wave,' says Billie.) We piece together the last sighting of Miguel before we left – our little boy with a bruised eye and scratched nose, feeling something, clinging desperately to his mother, the three of us singing 'Twinkle, Twinkle, Little Star' with an abandon more befitting a rousing gospel number.

'Next time we will come with Miguel,' says Billie. 'We will wait till he is three or four, and we will all come together. We will show him St Petersburg, we will take him to Kharkov. Let's make it a family tradition.' Whether it is a passing moment of magnanimity now that we are on our way home, or she really means it, I cannot tell. I am simply grateful for these words, for the fact that Billie can imagine the three of us coming back together.

'Insofar as we retain the capacity for attachment,' writes Eva Hoffman, 'the energy of desire that draws us toward the world and makes us want to live within it, we're always returning.' But returning not only to that first place that we have known and loved and which is the source of our 'original heat and hunger for the forms of the world', but returning also to other places in our lives and, perhaps, in the lives of our parents as well.

In Melbourne several months later, Billie writes about Kharkov, about how it felt to actually see the places in all those stories her mother, Nanna and great-aunt had for years told her.

She writes about coming to our *dvor*, the place she was perhaps most curious to see, since the stories she had heard about it made it sound positively enchanted. What Billie says catches me by surprise — only why on earth should I be surprised? There is something in her words so emblematic of the experience of second-generation homecoming, of the kind of travelling required to go from family stories to actual places that are never, not even remotely, the way you imagined them to be.

Dear Diary,

'Dvor' is a kind of communal garden for apartments in one block. I have heard many stories from Mum and Nanna about 'dvor', where the old and young coexisted in their separate corners of the same world — games of hide-and-seek and snow chucking, nannies with prams, old women eating sunflower seeds and drunken fathers smoking on the children's playground. You had your friends and half the population of your school living next door to you and everyone would be in shouting distance from each other, so instead of organising meetings with your friends you could have a spontaneous wish to see them and all it took was to shout their name loud enough and they would be beside you. The idea of having something that resembled a park as your shared backyard was so appealing, the joy of going nowhere to be surrounded by friends, where transport was as simple as your own two feet and the range of your communications depended on the size of your lungs.

But unlike Dorothy who found Oz so much more colourful, bright and appealing than home, there was no magical yellow brick road and no Emerald City awaiting me. Dear Diary, instead of happy children playing on the bright yellow playgrounds, I found, well . . . to tell you the truth, a rubbish tip.

I would have never used the word 'garden'. I could not possibly, because it would have gentrified the whole experience, made it sound like some kind of a New Age local community veggie garden slash adventure playground. After all, we are talking here about dirty, rectangular blobs of space between adjoining apartment buildings with benches, rubbish bins, some trees and occasionally some playground equipment thrown in. There were some beautiful *dvory* steeped in history and literary allusions, most notably in central Moscow and St Petersburg, but not where we lived. Yet *dvor* was our default location growing up. It was, and Billie got this absolutely right, both the place and the time of my childhood.

I had no idea how Billie would see it – that, first and foremost, she would be taken aback by the smell. Rotting rubbish, human and animal urine, the odours decrepit buildings tend to ooze. She was also scared of the stray dogs, which often ran around in tight, growling packs. Those dogs, I must say, have grown significantly more vicious in the two decades since we left. Perhaps they are simply hungrier now. But that is not the point. I was wondering if it is possible to imagine how a space that looks so barren and decaying could be a source of such joy, of such complex cultural exchanges, of so much friendship and daily, mind-boggling accommodation. If, for a moment, Billie could see what I see, she would see, not some kind of nostalgic, euphoric, rose-coloured vision of a 'communal garden', but a place, which was just the way it was meant to be. We are born into spaces and we grow up in them. We are blessed not to know any better. As children we do not smell three weeks' worth of rubbish that makes adults gag. We play with the puddles in which grown-ups step, cursing bad roads and general disorder and decay. We fit whatever size is given to us. And the dirt is much more fun to play with than sand. We are not deprived. We are not to be pitied. We are on top of the world.

I do not know if my daughter could see any of it even for a moment and, if she did, could this glimpse of her mother's undiminished life cure her of condescension, of the quick emotions of a tourist, be they shock or awe, of the eagerness with which we let ourselves be fooled by places? Since our return to Australia, Billie has written several more things in her diary. Her post-trip voice is markedly different from the one that ascends from most pages of her diary as a guttural lament and a Baroque fugue at once. It is not simply that Billie can be more lucid or reflective now that she is no longer caught up in the emotions of the trip and, perhaps even more importantly, no longer infuriatingly dependent on her mother, it is just that she is already a different Billie. I keep forgetting how it all goes in this age-bracket, that I'll be lucky simply to be able to keep up.

Dear Diary,

After a journey like this I think you are expected to have a certain reaction to it all. I think you are meant to change your outlook on the world and go, 'Oh, I am so lucky, blu di-blu di-blah!' I have had an image of what a perfect person in my situation would feel and believe after coming back from Russia and Ukraine. There is something in me that makes me think that I should start blessing every crumb of food that I had. But that's not what it's like for me.

'But this is all the "poor, desperate, Third-World Russia and Ukraine" kind of stuff – what about everything else?' I ask Billie.

'Yes, the people were amazing and the architecture and culture were beautiful, but the way people live, I'm sorry, Mum, I just could not get over it. Not the city centres, but – how should I put it? – in the outer suburbs. I wish we went there when I was older. I am a different person now; I would have gotten so much more out of this trip.'

'But imagine how infuriating you would have found me these days!' I am half-teasing Billie, half-stating the fearful fact.

'Yes, that's true, but you are still the only person I would want to travel with.'

Before we left Australia I debated with myself how best to prepare Billie for what lay ahead of us. Should I avoid giving her a pep talk, or try to scare the living daylights out of her? Re-reading those pre-departure thoughts, I am surprised by how off the mark I was. How could I have been so blind to the possibility that it was our own relationship that would prove the most contentious part of the trip, our relationship *and*, of course, Billie's 'beginner' Russian? If only she could speak for herself, if only she could communicate with others as an equal. As to the things that worried me – the woes, mishaps and mini-crises – none of them really mattered in the end, not even the God-awful toilets. (On the last leg of our flight home, Bangkok to Melbourne, she entertained herself by joyfully compiling a list of the worst toilets we had experienced.) In fact, Billie counts our detour to Belarus as one of her fondest memories of the trip: *Everything was so terrible at first and then it all turned around, and we were eating ice-cream and a comical dinner of pickles, sausage and biscuits and feeling so warm and at home. I just felt so purely happy and comfortable with myself and everything around. I have absolutely no idea why, but remembering this moment makes me smile every time.*

Remembering this moment makes me smile too. This was a moment that could have so easily come from my child-hood – the best-laid plans decimated, an unexpected detour to some hellhole, hours of waiting, and in the middle of this the best, the purest kind of happiness. What was *good for the book* turned out also to be *good* for my daughter and me.

I think rather ruefully about the timing of our trip, just as Billie was preparing to go to high school. Did I get it really wrong? (My daughter, for one, thinks so.) But when exactly is that mythical 'right time' when children are perfectly recep-tive to the stories their parents have been dying to tell them? I was desperate for Billie to feel attached, entangled, viscerally connected to her family's history. And do you know what? I think she actually does. Not the way I would have wanted her to, of course – she did not rush home from the airport and straight into the Russian language school; she did not hang maps of Europe on her bedroom wall (right next to the poster of Audrey Hepburn that dominates it now); nor did she tor-ture her grandparents and beloved great-aunt with questions: 'And then what happened? And then?' But I do think she saw something deep and important – that the spider veins of our family history spread well beyond the world familiar to her. That the act of going anywhere beyond the boundaries of that familiar world asked of us at a bare minimum that we unlearn many of the connections between people, places, history and fate we thought self-evident (cutting a branch while sitting on it if need be).

'If where people lived was a reflection of who they were inside,' Billie wrote in the diary, 'only murderers and villains should have lived in Kharkov.' Only in Kharkov and all the other places we went, people she met were magnificent in their generosity and loyalty: 'These people who had barely anything compared to what I knew in Australia and we came into their houses and they gave us absolutely everything they had. They were so open and completely un-self-centred, and that experience was amazing.' So analyse that, Billie Tumarkin.

I open Billie's diary straight onto the last entry written almost a year after the trip:

> *Dear Diary,*
>
> *Throughout the trip things with Mum would go up and down. Sometimes we'd be best friends, and other times I would just start screaming at her for no given reason. I felt so frustrated, and everything was so foreign and there was nothing that I knew besides Mum. And it's pretty much impossible especially for me, to remain on good terms with someone 24/7 for over a month. I don't think that in the long run it actually affected our relationship. If I hadn't have gone on this trip with Mum, I would have still at this same period of time gotten frustrated and angry with her. And the location of this in the end really did not matter.*
>
> *This trip was like four seasons in one day. I felt absolutely every single emotion on the spectrum but, even though it was really hard, I'd go back and do it again and again and again.*

Could it be that we actually never find out what is really happening between us and our kids if we stay home? I saw something of myself on this trip that I was not prepared to recognise before, what a bizarre and dangerous hybrid I was – a libertine parent who gave Billie all kinds of petty freedoms and privileges, *and* an autocrat intent on mercilessly scrutinising her inner life. I saw how desperately I was hanging on to her, while on the surface making all the right 'loosening the leash' moves. I saw – I couldn't miss it if I tried – that Billie was like an iceberg that needed to break off the big mamma iceshelf to survive. And that there was not much I could do but watch myself receding in the distance. I recognise now that the real reason we went away together on our trip was so that we could come back and start learning how to live apart. Adolescence is just like all the other parents warn you it will be – at least a seven on the Richter scale. And now we are where you would expect us to be, being blown around and around. One day in a few years, the tempest will stop, I know. My mum got through it with my sister and me, and I will too.

My mum is holding Miguel in her arms when Billie and I first walk back into the house. None of us knows how Miguel is going to react to our reappearance after such an insanely long absence: Will he recognise us? Will he reject us or treat us with suspicion or unease? A few minutes later Miguel is on the floor at his own request and my overjoyed mum is hugging my overjoyed daughter. I sit in the armchair and wait. Miguel looks at me and his sister for a while, trying to make sure we do not catch him stare. He says nothing but circles around me slowly and deliberately, like a Sufi whirling ritual, sometimes quickly glancing in my direction and sometimes looking as far away from me as he can. Bit by bit my little boy comes closer, still insistent on maintaining the distance between us, until his body finally touches my leg. He stops. In the corner of my eye I can see my mum and my daughter grow perfectly still. I keep my hands to myself and my sobs in my chest: Miguel had no choice in our leaving, but our return will have to be on his terms. And then my son does a BASE-jump, sudden and fearless, and lands in my lap. His body locks into mine, and for a while we hold each other in that bare embrace not embellished by words or tears. Then Billie joins us. 'Gruppen Hug!' she proclaims (it's a tradition, a bastardised, family-friendly version of the German word '*Gruppensex*'). 'Come on, Nanna! Get in here!' My mum puts her arms around us, and in that moment they seem to me just long enough to embrace us all.

ACKNOWLEDGEMENTS

AT TIMES I FELT so alone writing this book, but now that it is all over I realise just how much support I have had all along. All those gentle giants on whose shoulders I have stood – how could I forget you?

My publisher Meredith Curnow has guided the book's creation gently and respectfully from start to finish. Nurtured by her patience, intellect and faith in the project, I have felt safe, understood and truly supported. My agent and friend Clare Forster was my brilliant emissary and the book's most astute and insightful reader. My editor and friend Sybil Nolan has worked day and night to turn a thick maze of impressions, voices, disjointed narratives and impenetrable historical material into an actual book. Yet again – this is our third time together – with

Sybil by my side what seemed like a mission impossible meta-morphosed into a manuscript proper.

Random House's senior editor Brandon VanOver brought his talent, humour and humility to the manuscript: gifted hands, I think they call it in surgeons. Thank you to Random House's Nikki Christer and to writer Elliot Perlman for their support and for believing that this dangerously vague idea could one day turn into a good book.

I must take my virtual hat off to the book's first readers – Monica Dux, Sarah O'Donnell and Jessica Little, and to my friend Inna for laughing with me at least once a day and for not letting me dry up.

My dear auntie, Mum and Dad – where would I be without your daily, life-giving support? In some kind of metaphorical gutter no doubt. Thank you. And Miguel, thank you for enduring our separation and for taking us back.

I would like to thank my colleagues and management at the Institute for Social Research at Swinburne University where I have been a Post-Doctoral Fellow for the past two and a bit years and where my creative projects have found a great deal of intellectual and logistical support. And to Chris Healy from the University of Melbourne, thank you for all your support in my attempts to be both a writer and an academic.

In writing this book, I have received financial assistance from Australia Council for the Arts and Arts Victoria. Without the generous support from these two organisations, and with two kids and no savings, it could have taken me many years (instead of a year) to finish this manuscript. Thank you.

And finally (did I give you a fright?), my darling Billie, thank you for truly coming along with me, rather than simply playing along (big difference!), for defending your integrity and autonomy, for speaking in your own voice, for saying 'Well, that's the truth, put it in' in response to some of the book's least flattering passages. I did put it in Billie, it is all there. Scary, I know.

NOTES

Many times in the text it has not been possible to attribute sources by name or to quote them at any great length. All of these key sources are acknowledged in full below.

Throughout this book, I have generally relied on my own translations of works originally published in Russian. Any imperfections or infelicities in them are my own responsibility. In fact, most of the Russian sources below are not available in English translation. I reproduce their titles in Russian alongside their English translations so those readers who speak Russian can find them for themselves if so inclined.

Prologue

p. 3 **Dubravka Ugrešić, a Croatian-born writer I admire greatly**: Ugrešić is one of the most interesting chroniclers of post-Communism, particularly her novel *The Ministry of Pain* and her book of essays *Thank You for Not Reading*. Her reflections on the literary market in the wake of Communism's collapse come from the essay 'The Souvenirs of Communism: Home as Marketplace or Deletion of the Past', *The Hedgehog Review*, Fall 2005.

Chapter 1: 1989

p. 12 **'In our day Europeans have been hurled out of their biographies'**: Epigraph taken from Osip Mandelstam's essay 'Badger Hole', written in 1922 on the first anniversary of Russian poet Alexander Blok's death.

p. 17 **Václav Havel once described people living under the Communist system**: From Havel's 1978 essay 'The Power of the Powerless', available freely (and in English) on the web.

p. 20 **All is clear by now. By the time there is a government that can satisfy us**: To my knowledge, Jvanetsky's monologues have not been translated. From his sketch 'No Need to be Afraid' ('Бояться не надо') written in the 1990s. Many of Jvanetsky's texts are available in Russian on his website – www.jvanetsky.ru.

p. 26 The Greek-born French novelist Vassilis Alexakis: Alexakis's reflections come from his book *Paris–Athens*. It has not been translated into English; those of us who speak neither Greek nor French have to content ourselves with an extract from the book translated in English posted on the website of the online magazine *Words Without Borders*. The extract was initially written in French and then translated by the author into Greek. So what we have now, rather fittingly, is an English translation of the authored Greek translation of the French original.

p. 27 'Like everybody,' writes Eva Hoffman: Eva Hoffman, *Lost in Translation: A Life in a New Language*, Penguin, 1989. In her memoir, Hoffman, who left Poland in 1959 and became an acclaimed American writer and academic, has some deeply important things to say about what it means to truly inhabit another language.

Chapter 2: Vienna–Moscow

p. 34 The great tragic history of the emasculation of men: For historical material on creative ways of overcoming shortages of cosmetics and women's clothes, I'm indebted to the interviews conducted by cultural historian Kseniya Gusarova in ' "I was never that interested in cosmetics": Soviet experience of the "artificial beauty" ' ("Я никогда не увлекалась косметикой": советский опыт "искусственной" красоты'), *Neprikosnovenniy Zapas 4*, 2007.

p. 35 In her utterly unsentimental memoirs, Nadezhda Mandelstam: Two volumes of Nadezhda Mandelstam's memoirs have been translated into English by Max Hayward as *Hope Against Hope* and *Hope Abandoned*. (Nadezhda is 'hope' in Russian, hence the brilliant titles.) Hayward has done an admirable job, yet I have felt the need to personally translate the passages from Mandelstam's memoirs used in this book, maybe because by doing so I felt I could communicate more directly and more intimately with my readers.

p. 36 Wherever you live, clothes are never just about clothes: I have come across the thrilling hybrid that is Nicholay Uskov while watching *Gordonquixote (Гордонкихот)* – an 'ideas' talk-show presented by journalist Alexander Gordon on Russia's Channel One. The program dedicated to Uskov and *glamur* was aired on 20 February 2009.

p. 38 A contemporary Russian writer Tatyana Tolstaya: This is from a much-quoted article written by Tolstaya in the late 1990s for a short-lived quality newspaper, *Russian Telegraph*, closed down by the Russian financial crisis (default) of 1998.

p. 41 **Yes, the queues**: Vladimir Sorokin's 'Farewell to the Queue' is available in English translation on the Words Without Borders site.

p. 42 **My family left before the 1990s**: I have drawn here on philosopher Natalya Zarubina's essay 'About mythology of money in Russian culture: from the modern to the post-modern' ('О мифологии денег в российской культуре: от модерна к постмодерну'), published by the Russian-language *Sociological Research* in my discussion of all the things I no longer know about money. Victor Pelevin's quote comes from his mega-seller *Generation 'P'*.

p. 43 **This refashioning and unleashing of Money as a force of nature**: Susan Richards's first book on the region, *Epics of Everyday Life: Encounters in a Changing Russia*, was published in 1991 by Viking. Her second book, *Lost and Found in Russia: Encounters in a Deep Heartland* (I.B. Tauris) took sixteen years to live and write. It is, in other words, not a quick journalistic job, but a deep and long-burning exploration of what has happened to the people and the country since the collapse of the Soviet Union.

p. 45 **One of the benefits of straddling two worlds**: Ariel Dorfman, 'The Nomads of Language', *The American Scholar*, January 2002. This essay can be found under the title 'The Wandering Bigamists of Language' in Ariel Dorfman's collection of essays *Other Septembers, Many Americas: Selected Provocations, 1980-2004*, Seven Stories Press, 2004.

p. 45 **It suddenly dawns on me that I am practising my favourite game**: This image is borrowed from Dina Rubina's essay with an untranslatable title 'And Not Here You Couldn't Not Walk, or How Klara and I Went to Russia' ('"А не здесь вы не можете не ходить?" или Как мы с Кларой ездили в Россию'). It is available on Rubina's official website. Rubina immigrated to Israel in 1990, but she is one of the most widely read and brilliant Russian-language writers working today. Several of her books, including the novel *Here Comes the Messiah*, have been translated into English.

Chapter 3: The space inside

p. 49 **I have never previously visited Petya and Natasha's apartment**: Brodsky's words are taken from the essay 'A Room and a Half', dedicated to the memory of his parents. It can be found in *Less Than One: Selected Essays*, Joseph Brodsky, Farrar, Straus and Giroux, 1986.

p. 50 **The Hungarian historian István Rév**: These quotes are taken from Rév's brilliant book *Retroactive Justice: Prehistory of Post-Communism*,

Stanford University Press, 2005. A very interesting English-language reflection on the making of Zhirinovsky and on the meaning of everyday life and everyday spaces can be found in Svetlana Boym's 'From the Russian Soul to Post-Communist Nostalgia', *Representations* 49, Winter 1995. Boym is definitely worth looking up, particularly her books *Common Places: Mythologies of Everyday Life in Russia*, Harvard University Press, 1994, and *The Future of Nostalgia*, Basic Books, 2001. For their part, Lev Rubinstein's ideas come from the essay 'Communal Pulp Fiction', taken from his book *Music Played at Home*, Moscow, 2000. The essay is reproduced and translated in English on the very remarkable bilingual website Communal Living in Russia: A virtual museum of Soviet everyday life. The website, designed as a virtual ethnographic museum, has a wealth of literary, pictorial and documentary materials on communal living and spaces: www.kommunalka.spb.ru/.

p. 52   **'Long before collective farms and Gulag camps'**: I am indebted here to Russian anthropologist Ilya Utehin's argument that the defining feature of communal apartments was 'the transparency of space'. Utehin is one of the people behind the virtual museum Communal Living in Russia.

p. 59   **To 'imagine what [Boris] Grebenshikov means**: Music journalist Artemy Troitsky had a book on the history of Soviet rock music translated in English in the late 1980s: *Back in the USSR: The True Story of Rock in Russia*, Faber and Faber, 1988.

p. 60   **As I was growing up, we called him by his initials**: Kirill Kobrin is a cultural historian, essayist and journalist. (Last time I looked he was working for Radio Liberty, among other things.) The observation about his peers communicating in quotes from Aquarium is taken from a chapter entitled '"Words" and "things" of the late Soviet childhood' ('"Слова" и "вещи" позднесоветского детства') in Kobrin's third book of essays *Descriptions and Discussions* (*Описания и рассуждения*), Moscow 2000.

Chapter 4: Enemies of the People

p. 67   **Marina Gustavovna sits at the kitchen table**: Satirist Mikhail Zadornov's observations about the triumph of Soviet ingenuity come from his book *I Have Never Thought* (*Я никогда не думал*), Moscow, 2006. 'What can the aforementioned French woman do with a pair of stockings? Just wear them – and that's it! That doesn't take much brainpower. And our woman? . . .'

p. 69   **His name may have been largely forgotten for most of the twentieth century**: I have drawn here on the work of Tatyana Shedrina, the most prominent and dedicated scholar of Shpet's legacy in Russia and Marina Gustavovna's best friend ('My best friend is thirty,' Marina Gustavovna tells me). See G.G. Shpet, reconstructed, compiled and annotated by T.G. Shedrina, *Essay on the Development of Russian Philosophy. Volume 2,* (*Очерк развития русской философии". Том 2. Материалы*) and T.G. Shedrina, *'I Write as an Echo of Another': Essays on the intellectual biography of Gustav Shpet,* (*"Я пишу как эхо другого . . ." Очерки интеллектуальной биографии Густава Шпета*), Moscow, 2004. I have also used **M.K. Polivanov, N.V. Serebrennikov, M.G. Shtorkh (eds),** *Shpet in Siberia: Exile and Death,* (*Шпет в Сибири: ссылка и гибель*), Tomsk, 1995. M.G. Shtorkh is, in fact, Marina Gustavovna herself. Shpet can now be read in English. See his *Appearance and Sense: Phenomenology as the Fundamental Science and Its Problems,* translated **by Thomas Nemeth,** Kluwer Academic Publishers, 1991.

p. 70   **As an unambiguously non-Marxist philosopher**: See here Lesley Chamberlain's *Lenin's Private War: The Voyage of the Philosophy Steamer and the Exile of the Intelligentsia,* St Martin's Press, 2007.

p. 74   **In 1937, the year of the Great Purge**: Memorial, an international historical and human rights society, and perhaps the most important organisation now committed to the task of preserving the historical memory of Stalinism, says about this year: 'Nineteen thirty-seven was massive-scale repression engulfing all regions and all layers of society without exception, from the leadership of the country to peasants and workers infinitely removed from politics.' The year's extraordinary brutality signified 'the revival in the twentieth century of the norms of the medieval Inquisition with all its traditional features of people being tried in their absence (in the vast majority of cases), quasi-judicial procedure, the lack of defence and the effective merging within one department of the roles of the investigator, prosecutor, judge and executioner'. An English translation of the document detailing Memorial's assessment of 1937 can be found on the organisation's website, www.memorial.krsk.ru/eng/Dokument/Other/1937.htm.

p. 76   **As Marina Gustavovna tells me the story of her father**: Mandelstam's words are from *Hope Abandoned* (*Вторая Книга*).

p. 78   **In one of his most influential works, *Don Quixote on Russian Soil***: The book (*Дон Кихот на Русской почве*) was published in New York in 1982. The translation is mine.

p. 80   **The scene that Aikhenvald paints was replicated**: Irina Sherbakova's quote comes from the English translation of a pamphlet she prepared for the Russian National History Research Competition for High School Students: 'Man in History: Russia in the Twentieth Century'. Sherbakova is the national coordinator of the competition. Please note 'man' here stands most definitely for a human being.

p. 84 I write for a different reason: Brodsky's words are from the essay 'In a Room and a Half' mentioned earlier.

Chapter 5: Moscow Metro

p. 87 Our train departs; the last we see of the woman: In my all-too-brief description of disability in Russia I have drawn on Anton Borisov's Russian-language essay 'Private Thoughts About One State Issue' ('Частные мысли на одну государственную тему'). The essay was published in the special issue 'Excluded from Society' ('Исключенные из общества') of the Russian edition of the international journal *Index on Censorship*. Severely disabled from birth, Borisov was abandoned by his family while in his early twenties. He currently lives in the United States.

p. 90 In 2004, a nineteen-year-old student was travelling on the Metro: Galdetsky's story was covered quite extensively in the English-language media. I have used the coverage provided by *Novaya Gazeta*.

p. 93 When we fight, Billie and I are like two cocks: Clifford Geertz, 'Deep Play: Notes on the Balinese Cockfight', *The Interpretation of Cultures: Selected Essays*, London, 1975.

Chapter 6: *Glubinka*

p. 102 Venichka is not the stock Russian alcoholic: Michael Epstein, 'Charms of Entropy and New Sentimentality: The Myth of Venedikt Erofeev', in Mikhail Epstein, Alexander Genis, Slobodanka Vladiv-Glover, *Russian Postmodernism: New Perspectives on Post-Soviet Culture*, Berghahn Books, 1999.

p. 108 Evgeniy Grishkovets, a much-loved contemporary playwright: The passages are taken from Grishkovets's play *How I Ate a Dog* (*Как я съел собаку*), which premiered in Moscow in 1999.

Chapter 7: Mothers and daughters

p. 121 Sheila Munro recalls her mother: Sheila Munro, *Lives of Mothers & Daughters: Growing Up with Alice Munro*, Toronto, 2002.

p. 131 In a famous short story, writer Boris Akunin: Boris Akunin, *Fairytales for Idiots* (*Сказки для Идиотов*), Moscow, 2000.

p. 134 Mishki's slogan is 'Thank you Mr Putin for our stable future': Lev Rubinstein, 'About Teddies and People' ('О мишках и людях'), www.grani.ru, 6 December 2007. As to Dmitry Bykov, his article is rather entertainingly titled 'Theology of Late Putinism: Putin as the Main Russian Sacred Object, or the Cult of Substance' ('Теология позднего путинизма. Путин как главная российская святыня, или Культ субстанции'), 25 October 2007. Published on the APN (Agency of Political News) website: www.apn.ru.

Chapter 8: St Petersburg

p. 139 Although I fell head over heels for St Petersburg: Vladimir Toporov, *Petersburg Text of Russian Literature* (Владимир Николаевич Топоров, *Петербургский текст русской литературы*), St Petersburg, 2003.

p. 140 Toporov died in 2005, but it is safe to say: Elena Schwarz's poem is entitled 'Black Easter' ('Чёрная Пасха'); Part 2 'Where Are We?' ('Где мы?'), 1974.

p. 140 It is summer holidays, and I am fourteen: The Shevchuk /DDT lyrics are from the song 'Leningrad' off their 1990 album *Thaw* (*Оттепель*).

p. 141 Yes, it's true I am jealous: I have come across Brodsky's response to his city as a child in Solomon Volkov's *Conversations with Joseph Brodsky* (*Диалоги с Иосифом Бродским*). The book has been translated in English by Marian Schwartz and published by The Free Press in 1998.

p. 144 All these years later, I still suspect that I am a St Petersburg person: These two lines of Mandelstam are from the same poem, 'Leningrad', written in December 1930.

p. 149 For many decades, the official Soviet rhetoric of equality and emancipation: On the role of Soviet women in WWII, see Belarusian oral historian Svetlana Aleksievich's *War's Unwomanly Face* (*У войны не женское лицо*), Moscow 2008. Aleksievich has used oral testimonies and eyewitness accounts to create twentieth-century history books of unparalleled power. Several of Aleksievich's books have been translated in English, including her book on the legacy of Afghan war: *Zinky Boys: Soviet Voices from a Forgotten War* (translated by Julia and Robin Whitby, Chatto & Windus, 1992) and the legacy of the Chernobyl nuclear reactor explosion: *Voices from Chernobyl: Chronicle of the Future* (translated by Keith Gessen, Dalkey Archive Press, 2005).

p. 149 Though the Constitution guaranteed Soviet women equal rights: I have drawn here on Natalya Ivanova's brief essay, 'P.S.', *Znamya*, no. 6, 2005 and Rozalia Cherepanova, '"What Do I Need Irons For?" Happiness for Female Intelligentsia' ('"Зачем мне утюги?" Интеллигентное женское счастье'), *Neprikosnovenniy Zapas* 3, 2009.

p. 151 Billie's birthday present from Marina and family: Mariinski Theatre went back to its original name in 1992. Its artistic director is Valery Gergiev who, according to *The New Yorker* 'carries on his shoulders a disproportionately large part of the music world' and whose ambition is only to make his share more disproportionate still by turning Mariinski into the greatest opera and ballet theatre in the world.

p. 152 *Carmen*, everyone knows, is based on Mérimée's 1845 novella: Mérimée, in fact, translated *The Gypsies* into French, alongside other works in Pushkin's oeuvre.

p. 153 The femme fatale was, of course, the antithesis of the Soviet woman as comrade: Kollontai's writings have been translated in English: *Selected Writings of Alexandra Kollontai*, translated and annotated by Alix Holt, Allison and Busby, 1977.

p. 154 Despite multiple refutations, the rumours of Lenin's long-standing affair: See, for instance, **Michael Pearson's** *Inessa: Lenin's Mistress*, Duckworth, 2001. For my brief discussion of Lilya Brik, I have drawn on an essay by Irina Chaykovskaya, 'Partial Eyewitness' ('Пристрастный свидетель'), *Neva*, no. 8, 2004.

p. 156 The parallels between the persecution of Jews and gypsies: N. Demeter, N. Bessonov, V. Kutenkov, 'The History of Gypsies – New Perspective' (*История цыган - новый взгляд*), Russian Academy of Science, 2000.

Chapter 9: Leningrad

p. 166 In the 1970s Daniil Granin and Ales Adamovich: *The Book of Blockade* (*Блокадная книга*) was translated in English by Hilda Perham, Moscow, 1983. Its Russian text is available on the web.

p. 167 After everything they had heard, exhausted and made ill: Daniil Granin, 'The History of the Creation of the *Book of Blockade*' ('История создания Блокадной книги'), *Druzhba Narodov*, no. 11, 2002.

p. 168 'Leningradka' is the word for a female resident of Leningrad: The play was created and staged by St Petersburg's puppet theatre Karlsson Haus (Карлсон Хаус): www.karlssonhaus.ru.

p. 173 The rest of the Soviet nation was not to learn about Leningrad's plight: I have drawn here on Daniil Granin, 'The History of the Creation of the Book of Blockade' (mentioned above).

p. 176 Even though Misha, Marina and I were born almost three decades after the end of the war: The key sources cited below are Svetlana Aleksievich's *War's Unwomanly Face* (fully cited above); Lev Gudkov's

'The "Memory" of the War and Russian Mass Identity', ('"Память" о войне и массовая идентичность россиян'), *Neprikosnovenny Zapas*, nos. 2-3, 2005; Aleksey Levinson's 'War, Wars, about War' ('Война, войны, войне . . .'), *Neprikosnovenny Zapas*, nos. 2-3, 2005.

p. 177 Russian journalist Aleksandr Minkin: From an interview of Aleksandr Minkin and historian Victor Suvorov with a Radio Freedom journalist on 21 May 2009. (*"Наша история – это взорванный по пьянке атомный реактор". Виктор Суворов и Александр Минкин размышляют, кого назначат фальсификаторами*). The full transcript is available on the Radio Freedom website.

Chapter 10: A train platform somewhere

p. 178 'Under dictatorship everyone is scared': From Jvanetsky's monologue 'Back to the Future', ('Назад в будущее').

p. 179 Chudakova, who at one point was a member of President Yeltsin's Advisory Committee: Marietta Chudakova, 'Was There August or Is It Still to Come?' ('Был Август или только еще будет?'), *Znamya*, no. 8, 2006.

p. 181 A few years after the events of 1991: Dmitriev's words are from 'Russia 1991-2001. Victories and Defeats' ('Россия 1991-2001. Победы и поражения'), *Znamya*, no 8, 2001.

p. 183 Back to Mikhail Jvanetsky: This comes from Jvanetsky's monologue 'To Emmanuel Moiseevich Jvanetsky from Son', ('Эммануилу Моисеевичу Жванецкому от сына').

p. 188 A milky-white statue of Lenin is in front of us: Aleksandr Feduta, 'Collective Propagandist and Agitator: Selected Excerpts from the Textbooks of the State Ideology of the Republic Belarus', ('Коллективный политинформатор и агитатор. Избранные места из учебников по государственной идеологии Республики Беларусь'), *Neprikosnovenniy Zapas*, no. 3, 2006.

Chapter 11: 1941

p. 194 Historian Jehanne Gheith tells a story about Mikhail Afanasievich: Jehanne M. Gheith, '"I Never Talked": Enforced Silence, Non-narrative Memory, and the Gulag', *Mortality*, vol. 12, no. 2, May 2007.

p. 195 As a historian I have come to see that a great deal of our memories: Ruth Wajnryb, *The Silence: How Tragedy Shapes Talk*, Allen & Unwin, 2001.

p. 197 In my field when historians talk about social memory: Irina Sherbakova, 'Over Memory's Map' ('Над картой памяти'), *Neprikosnovenny*

Zapas, nos. 2-3, 2005. Edward S. Casey, *Remembering: A Phenomenological Study*, Indiana University Press, 2000.

p. 206 **When the war came, a sizeable minority of ethnic Ukrainians**: Vladislav Grinevich, 'Cracked Memory: The Second World War in the Historical Consciousness of Ukrainian Society' ('Расколотая память: Вторая мировая война в историческом сознании украинского общества'), *Neprikosnovenny Zapas*, nos. 2-3, 2005.

p. 206 **In Nazi propaganda campaigns, the invading German Army**: Rudolf Boretsky's memoir is entitled *Swings (Качели)*, Moscow, 2005.

p. 207 **From Dubovyazovka Tamara, Faina and the kids**: Evgenia Frolova, 'Lychkovo, 1941' ('Лычково, 1941 год'), *Neva*, no. 8, 2007.

p. 208 **Samarkand is an ancient and famed city**: For Anna Akhmatova in Uzbekistan, I have used an essay by Svetlana Somova, 'Anna Akhmatova in Tashkent' in two parts: ' "I was given the name – Anna" ' and 'A shadow on a clay wall' ('Анна Ахматова в Ташкенте': ' "Мне дали имя - Анна" ' и 'Тень на глиняной стене'), available at http://www.akhmatova.org/articles/somova.htm.

p. 209 **My grandmother and great aunt arrived in Samarkand**: Dina Rubina, *On the Sunny Side of the Street (На солнечной стороне улицы)*, Moscow, 2006.

p. 217 **In my mind Zoya Kosmodemyanskaya served as a trigger**: For the revisions to Kosmodemyanskaya's mythology, see A. Zhovtis, 'Some Corrections to the Canonical Version' ('Уточнения к канонической версии'), *Argumenty i Fakty*, no. 38, September 1991. 'Zoya Kosmodemyanskaya: Heroine or Symbol' ('Зоя Космодемьянская: Героиня или символ?'), *Argymenty i Fakty*, no. 43, November 1991.

p. 218 **Svetlana Aleksievich writes that women remember**: From *War's Unwomanly Face*, cited earlier.

Chapter 12 Kiev

p. 229 **Of course, that time in Kiev, the time of my mother's late teens**: Ilya Milshtein, 'Children of the 20th Congress' ('Дитя XX съезда'), *Zarubezhnye Zapiski*, no. 6, 2006. William Taubman, *Khrushchev: The Man and His Era*, W.W. Norton, 2003.

p. 232 **While the late 1950s and early 1960s was undoubtedly one of the best times**: I am indebted here to the musings of writer Aleksandr Ageev, 'They Were Lucky' ('Им повезло'), *Znamya*, no. 11, 2007.

p. 235 **I remember reading writer Zoe Heller's description**: In Joanna Goldsworthy's (ed.) *Mothers by Daughters*, Virago, 1995.

p. 238 When we finally identify her family's old home: I have found the description of Kreshatik after the war in Viktor Nekrasov's *Notes of a Gawker* (*Записки зеваки*), ImWerdenVerlag, München, 2009. I have drawn on this book in my discussion of Nekrasov's ideas about his city, in particular in chapter 13 which deals with his response to Babi Yar.

Chapter 13: Babi Yar

p. 243 If there is a sacred site for my family anywhere in the world: I have drawn here on Anatoly Kuznetsov's *Babi Yar: A Documentary Novel* (*Бабий Яр. Роман-документ*), Kiev, 2008. In English: *Babi Yar: A Document in the Form of a Novel*, translated by David Floyd, Jonathan Cape, 1970.

p. 244 His war reporting went beyond the Holocaust: See Vassily Grossman's *A Writer at War: Vassily Grossman with the Red Army, 1941–1945*, compiled and translated by Anthony Beevor and Luba Vinogradova, Pantheon, 2006.

p. 248 Billie, of course, knows about Babi Yar: I learned about Zola's famous open letter to the French President from the most treasured book of my pre-migration adolescence, Aleksandra Brushtein's autobiographical trilogy *The Road Disappears into the Distance*. In all the books I went though growing up (whatever I could get my hands on really) there was no other character with whom I identified more than Sashenka – Brushtein's fictional rendition of herself as a young girl. A daughter of a much-admired doctor in the pre-revolutionary Russian Empire, Sashenka is a deep, compassionate and brave young woman – just the kind I have always wanted to be. She is also obviously and importantly Jewish. Throughout the three parts of the book, her quest essentially is to figure out just one thing: what it means to be a decent person. She doesn't have any ready-made answers, which in itself is remarkable; she just keeps searching page after page. I bought a copy of the book in St Petersburg with Marina by my side – I wanted to have it on my bookshelf, whether Billie would let me read it to her or not. Already in Australia, I Googled *The Road Disappears into the Distance* and discovered many people like me (women mainly) who consider Brushtein's trilogy to be the best, most important book of their childhood. I, for one, read and re-read it an untold number of times, coming back in particular to the section dedicated to the Dreyfus Affair, which was taking place in France at the same time as the book's narrative. Brunstein gives us Sashenka completely consumed by the story of the French writer's public defense of captain Alfred Dreyfus (another assimilated Jew), wrongfully convicted on fabricated espionage charges. As Sashenka is devastated, enraged and inspired, so am I. Every single time. I leafed through the book back in Australia and saw what I could not have seen before – how Dreyfus's Jewishness is sidelined and his affair reconfigured as a confrontation between France's progressive and reactionary forces (the only way Brushtein could have written this part of the book). There is no mention of Zola's accusing the French establishment of anti-Semitism, of his timeless words: 'It is a crime to poison the minds of the meek and the humble, to stoke the passions of reactionism and intolerance, by appealing to that odious anti-Semitism that, unchecked, will destroy the freedom-loving France of Human Rights.' But at the time I was growing up – what the book could and did say was a true gift. In the book Dreyfus is a Jew and, unquestionably, a hero – an embodiment of dignity and courage, as is his Jewish wife. What is more, he is publicly defended by a famous and deeply respected non-Jew – one of the most influential people of his time. The famous non-Jew puts himself on the line to fight for the wrongfully accused Jew. Are you kidding me?

p. 250 Writer Daniel Mendelsohn, a Jewish New Yorker of striking literary brilliance: Daniel Mendelsohn, *The Lost: A Search for Six of the Six Million*, HarperCollins, 2007.

p. 251 Like Anatoly Kuznetsov, the writer Victor Nekrasov was not Jewish: I am drawing here on Nekrasov's *Notes of a Gawker*, cited above.

p. 254 For his part, Nekrasov was to pay dearly for his involvement: Kuznetsov's son has written movingly about re-discovering his father already as an adult: Anatoly Kuznetskov, 'Mama, I am alive-and-well! All is fine' ('Мама, я жив-здоров! Все хорошо'), *Znamya*, no. 5, 2001.

p. 257 It took me a while to see what Mum had also realised: Philip Gourevitch, *We Wish to Inform You That Tomorrow We Will Be Killed with Our Families: Stories from Rwanda,* Farrar, Straus and Giroux, 1998.

Epilogue

p. 290 'Insofar as we retain the capacity for attachment', writes Eva Hoffman: Eva Hoffman, *Life in Translation*, cited above.

ABOUT THE AUTHOR

MARIA TUMARKIN HAS PUBLISHED two books, *Traumascapes* (2005) and *Courage* (2007). She lives in Melbourne with her two children and is currently working as a Research Fellow at the Institute for Social Research, Swinburne, on the international Social Memory and Historical Justice project.